"That Fiend in Hell"

"That Fiend in Hell"

Soapy Smith in Legend

CATHERINE HOLDER SPUDE

UNIVERSITY OF OKLAHOMA PRESS : NORMAN

Also by Catherine Holder Spude
(co-ed. with Robin O. Mills, Karl Gurke, and Roderick Sprague) *Eldorado!: The Archaeology of Gold Mining in the Far North* (Lincoln, Neb., 2011)

Publication of this book is made possible through the generosity of Edith Kinney Gaylord.

Library of Congress Cataloging-in-Publication Data
Spude, Catherine Holder.
"That fiend in hell": Soapy Smith in legend / Catherine Holder Spude.
    p.   cm.
Includes bibliographical references and index.
ISBN 978-0-8061-4280-7 (hardcover : alk. paper)
1. Smith, Jefferson Randolph, 1860–1898. 2. Skagway (Alaska)—Biography.
3. Swindlers and swindling—Alaska—Skagway—Biography. 4. Skagway (Alaska)—
History—19th century. I. Title. II. Title: Soapy Smith in legend.
F914.S7S676 2012
979.8'02–dc23
[B]
                                                                2012013827

The paper in this book meets the guidelines for permanence and durability of the Committee on Production Guidelines for Book Longevity of the Council on Library Resources, Inc. ∞

1 2 3 4 5 6 7 8 9 10

To Susan Tanner Schimling
and Renee Rowan
Descendents of real heroes

Contents

Illustrations

A number of the illustrations in this book are sketches taken from newspapers and magazine articles. In the early days of photography, print media were not well adapted to reproducing photographs, so the editors made lithographic or line drawing versions from photographs for their publications. It was not until about a decade after Jefferson Randolph Smith was killed that quality photographs began to appear in newspapers and popular magazines. Unfortunately, most of these newspapers are only available as microfilm copies today, the effect of which can be seen in the sketches reproduced here.

Maps

Figures

Acknowledgments

No one researches and writes a book in solitude, therefore, I'd like to thank a few bookmaking conspirators for taking time out of their busy schedules to read my manuscript.

My former colleagues at the National Park Service have been very helpful in helping me collect data for this book. Primary among them was Karl Gurcke, historian at Klondike Gold Rush National Historical Park, a good friend and constant source of information. In addition to reading and commenting on a draft of the manuscript, he loaned me the park's microfilm of the Skagway townsite files, for which I am grateful. We have shared countless conversations about Skagway and I know few people more knowledgeable about the town's history and photographic record.

Another Skagway historian, Frank Norris, agreed to read the manuscript on very short notice. He was especially helpful in correcting facts dealing with park history, tourism, and early twentieth-century history in the port city, not to mention helping me with my grammar and sentence structure. We've been friends and colleagues a long time. I am very grateful to him.

My good e-mail buddy, historian Rogan Faith, sent me a copy of the 1941 article in the *Fairbanks Daily News Miner* in which Matthew Sundeen said he had seen Jesse Murphy kill Soapy Smith. This event set me on a trail that eventually led me to the Sam Steele letter mentioned in a debate in Jeff Brady's 1998 *Skagway News*. It was not until another year that a lengthy correspondence with Soapy Smith's great-grandson, Jeff Smith, would confirm much of the research Rogan had set me on with his article from the *Fairbanks Daily News Miner*. I am grateful to both Rogers and Jeff Brady for sending me what they knew about Murphy because of my interest in Si Tanner.

I also acknowledge the contribution made by my husband, Robert Spude, who had interviewed George Rapuzzi in the late 1970s and revisited his old notes. He, likewise, confirmed the story of another killer of Soapy, as he heard it from Mr. Rapuzzi. Both Bob and I had long known about the doubts expressed by Martin Itjen.

Any historian who works with popular historical materials related to the Klondike gold rush owes a debt of gratitude to Pierre Berton, who blazed the path. The pathfinder inevitably wanders off in odd directions from time to time, and those of us who follow may find a truer course. We have time to dawdle over details or discover sidetracks he overlooked. Berton admits in his autobiography, *Starting Out*, that he sometimes enhanced the truth to make a better story. My analysis of his rendition of the Soapy Smith legend reveals that he appropriated other people's words as his own without giving them credit. Nonetheless, he did so for the ease of the reader, not to make himself look good. From my viewpoint, Pierre Berton set the standard for the legend of Soapy Smith, and no one in the North has so excelled at it.

I am very grateful to historians Gary Roberts, Bill Hunt, and Bob Spude, who read early drafts of the manuscript and gave me direction for further reading, reorganizing, and revising. I am particularly indebted to Paul Hutton for taking time out of his busy schedule to recommend a reading list on the American frontier myth. I thank architect Bob Lyons also for reading the draft and giving me his comments.

Renee Rowan is the great-granddaughter of James Mark Rowan, the deputy marshal who was killed by bartender Ed Fay on January 31, 1898. Her e-mail inquiry about her ancestor spurred me to do the research into the court records that I had been putting off, and launched me on the final phases of writing this book. Thank you, Renee.

Susan Tanner Schimling is the great-granddaughter of J. M. "Si" Tanner and a good friend. The family history she had shared with me aided my understanding of the events of the winter and spring of 1898, and what happened in the thirty years that followed. I have enjoyed many fruitful letters and e-mails with Susan and her mother, Lynn Melody Tanner. Her corrections to my manuscript improved it greatly. As Susan knows, this book is a prelude to a biography of my real hero, Si Tanner.

Maxine Harriet Selmer is a lifelong citizen of Skagway and the great-granddaughter of Harriet Pullen, Skagway's first historian. Maxine kindly read a draft of my manuscript. I am pleased that she was able to set me straight on a number of facts, not to mention typos.

Steve Hites, owner of the Skagway Street Car Company, is the spiritual descendent of Martin Itjen, having heard Martin's stories from George Rapuzzi and Nova Warner. He's passed them on to each of his street car "conductors" each summer (and there have been some one hundred of these costumed storytellers over the last quarter of a century). Steve also acted in a number of the original Days of '98 shows back in the 1970s, when they were first revived, sometimes playing Soapy himself. I could not ask for more authentic accounts of those times. His first-person recollections are an invaluable addition to my work.

The editorial staff at the University of Oklahoma Press has been a joy to work with, from Chuck Rankin, who enthusiastically embraced this project, to Connie Arnold and Julie Rushing, who helped manage maps and illustrations, to Emily Jerman, who coordinated the editing. I am especially grateful for the splendid job that Jay Fultz did in copyediting. They and the anonymous reviewers have done so very much to make this book free of errors.

The staffs of the many libraries and archives listed in the endnotes, bibliography, and photograph credits went out of their way to help a pesky researcher with one more Soapy request. I am grateful to the Alaska State Archives; Alaska State Library; Alaska State Museum of History; Anchorage Museum of History and Art; City of Skagway Museum; Clallam County (Washington) Historical Society; Colorado Historical Society; George and Edna Rapuzzi Foundation; Glenbow Museum in Calgary, Alberta; Klondike Gold Rush National Historical Park; Library of Congress; Royal British Columbia Archives; Seward Community Library at the University of Alaska; Fairbanks Rasmuson Library; University of Washington's Zimmerman Library; and Yukon Archives. I am particularly grateful to the staff of the New Mexico State Library, which assisted me with a great deal of interlibrary loan requests for material on Alaska history.

And then there is my husband, Bob Spude, who, as the first research historian at Klondike Gold Rush National Historical Park in the late 1970s, spent many long hours talking to George Rapuzzi and other old-timers about people like Harriet Pullen and Martin Itjen and their influence on the community. I wasn't able to interview George myself, but I've talked often to the man who did, and that counts for something. I also relied heavily on the rough maps Bob Spude made of the locations of businesses in 1898 newspaper advertisements and the 1899 business directory. Using the spring and summer photographs and his sketch maps, I was able to put together the 1898 map shown on facing page. For those contributions, for your repetitive reading of the manuscript, and for all of your support, thank you, sweetheart.

Despite all the help from these individuals, none of them should be held responsible for my interpretations or mistakes.

Map Key

1. Bishop Rowe Hospital (12th and Alaska Street)
2. Pullman Gallery (Judkins and Peiser), 13th and Main
3. The Cottage Brothel
4. Clancy's Music Hall
5. Future site of the U.S. Court House (1901)
6. Future site of the Pullen House Hotel (1902)
7. Peoples' Theater (Theater Royale)
8. H. A. Bauer and Co.
9. Jeff Smith's Parlor
10. The Mondamin Hotel
11. The Red Onion Saloon
12. The Board of Trade Saloon
13. The Pack Train Saloon
14. The Kelly Block (Dr. Moore)
15. Bernard Moore House
16. The Union Church
17. A&NTT Co. Mill Bunkhouse
18. J. M. Tanner's Express and Storage
19. J. G. Price's Attorney's Office
20. City Hall
21. William Moore Hotel
22. Manila Saloon
23. Burkhard Hotel
24. Kalem's Grocery
25. Klondike Trading Company (Sylvester Hall)
26. Clayson's Hardware
27. Case and Draper Photographers
28. H. C. Barley, photographer
29. E. A. Hegg, photographer
30. Mascot Saloon
31. Headquarters for WP&YR
32. Place where Soapy Smith was killed

Map of Skagway, Alaska, in July 1898. Map by author.

Introduction

"When the legend becomes fact, print the legend."

John Ford, director, *The Man Who Shot Liberty Valance*

What is myth? An invention? Hardly. In a way, myth tells the truth about what a group of people believe about themselves more effectively than the individual facts of history. The Montana writer William Kittredge articulated the function of mythology in a culture when he wrote, "A mythology can be understood as a story that contains a set of implicit instructions from a society to its members, telling them what is valuable and how to conduct themselves if they are to preserve the things they value."[1] He took his cue from Joseph Campbell, who taught that "myths are clues to the spiritual potentialities of the human life," and that a society's myths are "stories about the wisdom of life."[2]

Within the last four decades, a number of writers have explored the mythology of the American frontier. They argue that Americans, due to their particular history of breaking from authoritarian rule and "conquering a wilderness" inhabited by non-Europeans, tend to populate their narrative histories with elements of a common myth. This myth includes such themes as the coming of age, perpetual self-improvement, taming the wilderness, falling from grace, transcending chaos, Christian conversion, and community redemption. In an almost uniquely American approach to these classic themes, success comes not so much through group cooperation but through individual achievement, and regeneration comes through violence. Americans proved that when they won their war of independence from England.[3]

1

A legend gives voice to a particular aspect of mythology. In the words of folklorist Timothy R. Tangherlini:

> Legend, typically, is a short episodic, traditional, highly
> ecotypified historicized narrative performed in a
> conversational mode, reflecting on a psychological level
> a symbolic representation of folk belief and collective
> experiences and serving as a reaffirmation of commonly held
> values of the group to whose tradition it belongs.[4]

Familiar legends include those of Beowulf, King Arthur and the Round Table, Odysseus, Robin Hood, Romulus and Remus, and William Tell. Legends of the American West could include the tales of Billy the Kid, Jesse James, Wild Bill Hickok, and Wyatt Earp. Such folklore has evolved about these characters that dissecting the histories from the inventions has become almost impossible.

The importance of legend in any society, including such a complex one as modern Western Euro-American society, is its reinforcement of myth and cultural ideology. The corpus of legends and folklore, grounded in historical events and transmitted into mythology, in the words of Richard Slotkin, "dramatize a society's moral consciousness."[5] One of America's most enduring myths is that, as a nation, it has managed to free itself from authoritarian rule and class hierarchy in its revolution from Great Britain and civilized itself by overcoming the American wilderness. Periodically, however, Americans redeem this ideology "by playing through a scenario of separation, temporary regression to more primitive or 'natural' state, and *regeneration through violence.*"[6] American mythology, as revealed through its folklore and legend, is rife with examples of history explained through the metaphorical tales of community redemption.

The legend of Soapy Smith is one such tale of regeneration through violence and of community redemption that reinforces the myth of the American frontier. As it has come down to us since 1898, the legend is easily retold, and readily reflects other American mythic themes noted above, but the morality play of regeneration through violence and redemption through sacrifice will be emphasized here.

On January 31 that year, in Skagway, Alaska, laborer Andy McGrath became drunk and disorderly in People's Theater. The threatened bartender, Ed Fay, killed McGrath and, unintentionally, U.S. Deputy Marshal James M. Rowan. Skagway's citizens rose up against the bartender, who had taken refuge among the gambling and "sporting" element, led by Jefferson Randolph "Soapy" Smith. According to the legend, Smith calmed the lynch mob and saved Fay's life. From that day on, Smith was recognized as a leader of Skagway.

In mid-March, a public safety "Committee of 101" met and threatened to evict all of the gamblers, bunco men, and other members of the sporting fraternity in Skagway. Soapy led a group of men, the "Committee of 317," in repelling the attempt. That uprising marked the beginning of the reign of the "uncrowned King of Skagway," who worked from his headquarters, Jeff Smith's Parlor, at 317 Holly Street.

As the Klondike gold rush reached its peak in the spring of 1898, Soapy and his bunco men conned and robbed the stampeders going through Skagway. He ameliorated his unlawful activity with a long series of charitable works. Smith was instrumental in having the first church in Skagway built; he was generous to widows, orphans, and dogs. A renowned con man, robber, and head of a band of thieves, he was so feared that Skagway businessmen and vigilantes did not dare to curb his predations on travelers to the Klondike. So popular did Smith become that he was able to assemble a crowd of two thousand for a Memorial Day parade. He led Skagway's Fourth of July parade and sat on the podium with the governor of Alaska.

On July 8, 1898, a miner named J. D. Stewart, returning from the gold fields, was robbed of his poke in Jeff Smith's Parlor. Finding no satisfaction with the U.S. deputy marshal who was in Smith's pay, this miner turned to the vigilantes who had first tried to lynch Fay. Delegations of citizens approached Smith about returning the gold, but he refused, supporting the men who were loyal to him. Mass meetings were called, but Smith's men disrupted them.

That evening, in a final confrontation, Smith and the head of the vigilantes, Frank Reid, met face to face at the entrance to the Juneau Wharf. There, a number of shots were fired. Both men fell to the ground, Smith instantly dead, and Reid dying.

Citizens rallied around the remaining vigilantes. The rest of Smith's gang was rounded up and deported or arrested. The town had been saved. Klondike-bound travelers—and, more importantly, returning gold-toting miners—could now pass through Skagway in safety.[7] The Legend of Soapy Smith was born.

––––––––

So soon a legend? But Smith was a historical figure who died only a little more than a century ago. Stacks of books, articles, and archives document his existence. How could anyone dress up the story of the death of Soapy Smith as legend?

Anyone who has tried to study such "legendary" figures as Wyatt Earp, Doc Holliday, or General George Armstrong Custer can tell you how hard it is to cull the facts from the way participants and observers wanted the narrative to be told, often from the very day events happened. Ask Casey Tefertiller, author of *Wyatt Earp, The Life Behind the Legend*; Robert Utley, *Billy the Kid: A Short and Violent Life*; or Frederick Nolan, *The Billy the Kid Reader*.[8] So powerful is the narrative power of legend that those relating the story are rarely aware of the part they play in perpetuating myth.

It appears that the events of August 1897 through July 1898 have been manipulated by journalists and novelists to the point that they have obscured history in the larger cause of creating legend and building on American frontier myth.

––––––––

The legend of Soapy Smith is fully developed in Pierre Berton's seminal work, *Klondike Fever*, which was published in the United States in 1958, revised in 1975, and is still in print.[9] As a classic and highly readable telling of the Klondike gold rush, it is the first place most readers encounter the rascally scoundrel. In the 1990s, I began researching the primary documents related to Skagway's 1907 mayor, Chris Shea, who published one of the first stand-alone versions of the Smith story, and Josias M. "Si" Tanner (Skagway mayor from 1909 to 1912), who was instrumental in rounding up Smith's gang in the days after the con man's death. It was then that I began to understand the local political and historical contexts of the early days of Skagway. As I became more familiar with the primary sources, I began to identify contradictions in the various versions of the Smith story. These were not minor alternatives, simple variations that might occur because different people observed the event from different vantage points. I found major gaps and deliberate miss-tellings, sometimes lies meant to obscure a truth to which no one would admit. What truths were being withheld? And why?[10]

As I began to ferret out previously obscured portions of the Soapy Smith story—such as evidence that Frank Reid was not the only one who put a bullet into Soapy Smith—it became obvious that those who wanted to protect Reid's honor and authority were so intent on doing so that they were willing to raise Smith to the status of an uncrowned criminal king, someone worthy of elevating Reid to the standing of a hero. The community needed to make Smith seem worse than he was, so that by killing him it could root out the negative images of the town held by its competitors. Scapegoating Soapy and his gang purged Skagway of its bad reputation.

What a thought.

Soapy Smith was not historical so much as legendary. Just who was he, anyhow?

Born Jefferson Randolph Smith in Coweta County, Georgia, in 1860, he and his family moved to Round Rock, Texas, in 1876. Not staying in one place very long, the young man soon picked up and moved around the Middle West, where he earned a living as a bunco and "sure-thing" man, learning to bilk gullible people from their hard-earned dollars with card tricks and sleight of hand. By 1879, he had found his way to Denver, Colorado, where he picked up the trick of wrapping a cake of soap in a five-dollar bill, covering that with plain paper, mixing it with a number of other plain-wrapped cakes, and selling them off for a dollar apiece. Gullible customers were duped into buying an overpriced bar of soap, which was replaced after a Smith confederate in the audience bought the one wrapped in the five-dollar bill. It was in Denver that he earned the nickname "Soapy."[11]

In the years that followed, Smith set up his soap-selling, pea and walnut shell, and three-card monte games in Denver, Leadville, and Creede, Colorado. Every place he went, he earned a reputation for petty con games and graft—ameliorated by an indubitable charm. In each of these mining camps today, the modern tourist will find odes and tributes to a legend created by a mixture of his roguish charm and Robin Hood-like deeds.[12]

In the late 1880s and early 1890s, he opened the Tivoli Saloon in Denver, where he built a reputation for bribing police and aiding corrupt city officials in buying votes at election time. His foray into city politics, helped by his euphonious nickname, earned him a brief notoriety in the Colorado newspapers where he was associated with more famous, corrupt officials for whom he worked. After the 1894 city election, a reform-minded city hall closed down the saloons and gambling halls, and Smith was forced to leave Denver for more lucrative fields.[13]

During the Denver years, Soapy met and married Mary Noonan, a performer at a dance hall. In order to protect her and his rapidly growing family from his dangerous profession, Smith moved her to St. Louis, where she raised their three children. Smith sent her money and visited her and the children frequently, but did not call St. Louis home.[14]

Smith's way of life did not change in Skagway, Alaska. In Colorado, as much as in Skagway, his legend is due as much to the fact that he died a violent death as to his personal charm. I do not believe that it owes anything to personal distinction or to any idea that Jefferson Randolph Smith was a cut above any other criminal of his stamp who lived during the late nineteenth century. Through his considerable charm, he managed to garner a bit more self-serving press than the usual con man, giving journalists somewhat more material with which to work.

————

The *Oxford English Dictionary* defines the word legend as "a traditional story popularly regarded as historical but which is not authenticated." Its second definition is "an extremely famous or notorious person." While the word is used both ways in this book, it most often should be ascribed the meaning given it by folklorist Timothy R. Tangherlini earlier.[15] As a symbolic narrative based on a historical event, the Soapy Smith tale tells us more about the values of the people of Skagway at the turn of the century than it does about the individuals in the story.

By the time the first full-length biography of Smith had been written in 1935, nearly four decades after the culminating events it portrays, much of the story had become legend, and the journalists assembling his tale did not attempt to authenticate it, verify the facts, list their sources, or question the assumptions about the premises of the story—nor had any of their predecessors. In fact, the first account to include a bibliography was not written until 1944,[16] and that one was not a detailed rendering of the story. Not until the chapter in Pierre Berton's 1958 *Klondike Fever*, written sixty years after the death of Soapy Smith, did anyone make a partial effort to list some of the sources for the telling of the legend, most of which had been filtered through secondary sources. The same deficiency applies to the second major biography of Smith, written by Frank G. Robertson and Beth Kay Harris in 1962. Their bibliography included twelve books, none of them primary sources, eight magazine articles, only three of which might be considered primary sources, and nine newspapers, only one in Alaska. *The Skaguay News* is archived in very spotty and parsimonious issues, and cannot convey to the researcher the true conditions of Skagway during the winter of 1897–98. Most of what Robertson and Harris really had to work with was unauthenticated, or legend.[17]

In my effort to verify details of the Smith legend in Alaska, I discovered that it had been told and retold in print about a hundred times (see appendix A). Within these pages the reader will find not a new version of the tale, but an exposé. The primary sources and accounts by direct witnesses have been separated from the secondary sources and so indicated in appendix A. Other primary historical documents (lands files, court records, deed records, lot claim records, military files, diaries, letters, and photographs) are noted in the endnotes.

Every secondary author came to tell his or her version with certain biases, and not all accounts can be accepted on equal footing. The second part of this book evaluates the authority of individual eyewitnesses, journalists, and storytellers. Formed by economic and political pressures at the time of their writing, many of which could not be known to modern readers, these biases were not always readily apparent. As time went on, minor squabbles, deliberate inside jokes, and political sarcasm became lost to history, but the bigger morality play, the larger legend, remained. The character and identity of the individual witnesses became lost. Researching the lives and histories of the major contributors to the legend helps the reader understand how the perception of basic premises changed through time.

Only three professional historians have attempted to examine the Smith story within some context other than that of an adventure. The chief historian of the National Park Service, Ed Bearss, examined the Smith story in the context of the larger tale of the Klondike gold rush. Relying heavily on Pierre Berton's book, which had just been republished, Bearss gloried in the Smith legend as told by Berton and did not question it. Instead, he accepted it as a given, then categorized the events in such a way that the National Park Service could place them in the agency's interpretive framework.[18]

The next scholarly treatment of the Smith story appeared in William R. Hunt's discussion of frontier justice. His chapter on the killing of Soapy Smith places it in the context of vigilantism. Like Bearss's, his treatment is focused on a narrow subject, in this case using the Smith incident as an example of vigilante justice in Alaska.[19]

Finally, Smith is discussed in part in Jane Haigh's Ph.D. dissertation about the interconnection between con men and political corruption in Denver between 1889 and 1894. Haigh dispels the notion that Smith was influential in Denver politics, concluding that he was used by Denver politicians as a tool to buy votes. His infamy was due more to the pleasure Denver newspapermen took in making fun of him—and by extension the candidates that he supported—than any real influence he had in Denver politics.[20] This conclusion has bearing on the evaluation of Smith's overall legend.

––––––––

As much as possible, I read the accounts in the order they were written. In doing so, I discovered a repeated effort to reinforce a morality tale at the expense of a more complicated story of town formation, government-building, and the creation of law and order. This morality tale—the redemption of a lawless town, thereby making it safe for all travelers—was much to the liking of economic boosters who worked hard to banish a bad reputation instigated by rival port cities on the northwest coast. Willing to sacrifice their past image to a sans-Soapy one of law, orderliness, and public safety, Skagwayans did little to correct the perceptions of the months that preceded July 1898. They exaggerated the power held by one common criminal, and made their town a haven of propriety and public safety when they eradicated him and his gang from their streets.

———

Part 1 evaluates the following elements of the Soapy Smith legend against the primary historical literature: Skagway was lawless before July 1898; Smith prevented a hanging in February 1898; he became the uncrowned king of Skagway in March; he led a Memorial Day parade and the Fourth of July Parade; his loyal men conned a returning miner out of almost $3,000 in gold on July 8; he was killed by Frank Reid on the Juneau Wharf; and Skagway, in clearing out his gang, rid itself of crime forever.

Part 2 demonstrates how the legend was conceived and executed, and shows how it was to the advantage of the people of Skagway to perpetuate the legend as a morality play, casting history aside in the interest of propagating values through mythology. The final chapter interprets Smith the Legend in the context of a modern critique on American heroes, folklore, and mythology.

The Soapy Smith legend continues to play a basic role in the story of Skagway's history, just as the Earp Brothers play a role in the history of Dodge City, Kansas, and Tombstone, Arizona; Billy the Kid in Lincoln, New Mexico; Jesse James in numerous Kansas and Missouri communities; and Wild Bill Hickok in Deadwood, South Dakota. Understanding historic fact in the context of myth and legend enables Americans to appreciate their culture and their past in a richer and more meaningful way.

PART ONE

Authentication

CHAPTER ONE

Conceived
in Lawlessness

The town of Skagway was conceived in lawlessness and
nurtured in anarchy.

Pierre Berton, *Klondike Fever*

C ritical to Soapy Smith's legend is the premise that before July 8,
1898, Skagway was a town in which there was no law or order,
and where chaos ruled. An examination of this, most basic principle
requires going back to the beginning of Skagway's history.

Skagway was first used as a seasonal camp by local Tlingit peoples.
They referred to both the river and the bay it emptied into by the
word Shghaghwei, which means "wrinkled," or "rugged," and refers
to the appearance of the water when the wind blows. Later stories
applied the name Skugua to a beautiful woman whose husband
insulted her. She disappeared into the side of a mountain in retalia-
tion. When the cold wind blows, it is the icy breath of Skugua blowing
down from the mountains. Either way, the word refers to the ubiqui-
tous Skagway wind.[1] English speakers would debate whether to spell
the word Skaguay or Skagway until well into 1899, but the matter was
first decided by the United States Postal Service on November 11,
1897, when it designated the Skagway post office.[2]

––––––––

Adventurer William Moore and his son, Bernard (Ben), came to the
Skagway River Valley area in the fall of 1886 and settled in early 1887.
The elder Moore anticipated a gold rush to the interior and envi-
sioned building a trading post at the base of White Pass and improving a pack trail over the summit. As a Canadian citizen, William

Moore could not make a legal homestead claim; however, Bernard, who was naturalized in 1896, could, and did. In 1888, Bernard posted a location notice for a 160-acre homestead, which he revised in 1896 by posting a notice for a trading and manufacturing site. Shortly thereafter, the Moores sold an interest in their homestead to the British investors, the Alaska & Northwest Territory Trading Company (A&NTT Co.), with the support of the Close Brothers Company, a London firm incorporated in West Virginia. At Skagway, the A&NTT Co. began constructing a lumber mill, wharf, and trail over the White Pass into Yukon Territory. In May 1897, the company sent its first workers—most of whom had British accents—to Skagway Bay.[3]

As William Moore had foreseen, on July 11, 1897, the steamer *Portland* landed in Seattle with more than a ton of gold on board, all taken from tributaries of the Klondike River in Yukon Territory. Three days behind her, the *Excelsior* sailed into San Francisco boasting equal amounts of gold. On July 21, 1897, the S.S. *Queen* steamed into Skagway harbor bearing two hundred passengers wanting to cross the Chilkoot and White Passes and head to the Klondike regions.[4] Within a week, several more ships from West Coast cities landed at Moore's Wharf, filled with passengers. Among them was a civil engineer from Oregon named Frank Reid.

Reid was born in Peoria, Illinois, in 1844. He and his brother, Dick, became orphans before reaching manhood and put themselves through college by laboring in the orchards and riverboats along the Mississippi River. They both got their degrees in engineering in 1873, at which time they headed off for the Dakotas, where they worked as surveyors. By the 1880s they had found their way to the Willamette Valley in Oregon, where Dick married and settled down. Frank came and went with various jobs, but always found his way back to his brother's home and family.[5]

Reid came to Skagway on July 28, 1897, on one of the first steamers arriving in Skagway Bay, traveling with a Mr. Hilts, who wished to open a saloon. The first tasks he undertook for Hilts were to purchase flour and bacon and to tend bar while Hilts returned to Juneau to gather more supplies for his enterprise. By August 5, a committee of about a hundred townspeople came to Reid, knowing he was a surveyor, and asked him to begin laying out a townsite. He began his survey at the southeast corner of the town's largest store, Burkhard's Hotel and outfitters. This corner he called Lot 1 of Block 1. The hundred or so citizens who asked for the survey called this beginning point the corner of Broadway and McKinney Street, after Dave McKinney of their group. It later became known as Broadway and Fifth.[6]

In his haste to plat Skagway, Reid brushed aside the Moore claim. A protesting Bernard Moore was allowed to fence off five acres around his cabin and pasture, which the citizens' "committee" asked Reid to survey and eliminate from the street grid. The A&NTT Co. was also allotted room for its lumber mill and access to the Moore wharf. To complicate matters, Bernard's father, Captain Moore (who had no rights to the claim), had initially given leases to the first businesses putting up tents on the Moore homestead. He was up on the White Pass working on the trail construction when the decision to stake a townsite was made. He returned to Bernard's claim aware of its questionable validity, but no contemporary sources mention him trying to stop the citizens' committee—just the opposite. He had a financial interest in the trail, the sawmill, and the wharf, and made good money collecting docking fees. In early July, he had placed an advertisement in a Juneau newspaper urging people to use his pack trail over the White Pass.[7]

Captain Moore, who occupied a bunkhouse on one of the surveyed lots at the northwest corner of State and Fifth, was told he could stake that lot. No one seemed to pay any attention to Bernard Moore's claim to his 160-acre homestead, which included five buildings at what would become the northeast corner of Fifth and State. These prime lots would later become occupied by early arrivals such as attorney J. G. Price, steamboat captain J. M. Tanner, and by a structure that would become the city hall. Newly arriving townspeople ignored the larger homestead boundaries because of the mistaken impression that both Moores were Canadian and therefore could not homestead under United States law. Apparently no one believed Bernard when he said he was a naturalized American citizen.[8]

On September 16, 1897, almost a month after the first stampeders arrived in Skagway Bay, Moore filed an application for the patent for 160 acres of land as a trading and manufacturing site under Alaska's homesteading laws, land that constituted about a quarter

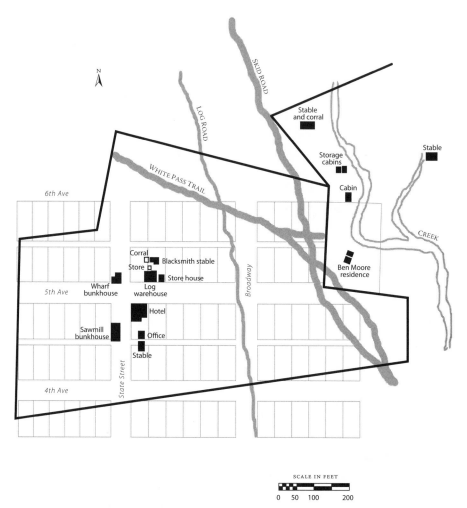

Map of Moore's improvements by late 1897, as presented in *J. G. Price, et al. v. Bernard Moore* in 1898. Map by author, from R. Garside 1898 and 1914 Sanborn maps.

of the booming city of Skagway. It amounted to everything south of Eleventh Avenue, including all of the downtown businesses, which by that time numbered around five hundred. A total of 196 lots had been filed with U.S. Commissioner John U. Smith, for which he had collected fees of five dollars each, and each owner considered his

Map of the 160-acre Moore claim superimposed on the townsite of Skagway, September 15, 1897. Map by author.

claim legitimate. In addition, the U.S. Customs Office had exempted twenty-four lots from location, taking two entire blocks for its exclusive use.[9] Moore's partners at the A&NNT Co., especially the British representative of the Close Brothers, E. E. Billinghurst, tried to consolidate their claim by building a bunkhouse in the center of Fifth Avenue at the corner of State, not on any of the city lots (see maps 2 and 3). This bunkhouse has long been confused with that used by William Moore, but it was a later building built for the employees of the mill. It occupied the middle of the street for over a year, and was not moved until fall of 1898.[10]

Billinghurst pushed the Moores to fight for the questionable 160-acre homestead claim of Ben Moore. The filing of this claim—by lawyers paid for by the British company—stopped the location of town lots for over a month. Unsure how to proceed with allowing people to settle in Skagway, about a hundred merchants, in democratic fashion, held a meeting on October 9, 1897, to talk it out and come up with a solution.

They elected M. Klinkonstein, J. Allan Hornsby, and Frank Clayson, as a committee, which, in turn, hired attorney John G. Price to prepare a lawsuit to protect their interests in the townsite.[11]

This citizens' committee was first referred to as the Committee of One Hundred and One in an article by *The Skaguay News* dated December 31, 1897. As early as the 1880s, citizens' committees in mining towns of the West had styled themselves "The Committee of [Blank] Hundred and One," depending on the size of their group, when forming to dispense justice in the absence of formal law and order (see Roger McGrath's 1984 discussion of vigilantes in Nevada as an example).[12] Skagway's Committee of One Hundred and One was formed to protect the property rights of the merchants from the filing of a homestead claim by Bernard Moore—not to oust Soapy Smith, as the legend would later tell it.

Besides Klinkonstein, Hornsby, and Clayson, members of the citizens' committee included David J. McKinney, who chaired the meeting and for whom one of the main streets in town had been named; Thomas Ward, who would be important in negotiating the capture of bartender Ed Fay in February 1898, and in the capture of members of Smith's gang in July 1898; and David Samson. These last three men supervised the election of the committee of three men who eventually elected attorney J. G. Price to represent them in the lawsuit against Moore and the A&NTT Co.[13] Membership would be fluid during the coming months, and would consist of whoever was currently active in city politics. Other members would include J. F. A. Strong, later to become editor of the *Skaguay News* (and eventually governor of Alaska); Captain J. M. Tanner, who lightered goods from ship to shore (and would one day be appointed a U.S. marshal); attorney Sam Lovell; and H. C. Bradley, C. B. Beeson, Henry Shea, and W. L. Berbee. Other players included William F. Saportas (a correspondent for an eastern newspaper), W. J. Rose, J. G. Goslett, Jacob Bloom, H. J. Foster, George E. Coes, Thomas M. Stephans, and Charles Sperry. These latter merchants, along with J. M. Tanner, would break ranks with Price in December 1897 and enlist the services of Emery Valentine of the Skaguay Wharf Improvement Company to bring another suit against Moore and the A&NTT Co.[14] Importantly, too, the name of the group would change through time. Sometimes the members referred to themselves as the Citizens' Committee; sometimes as the Committee of One Hundred and One. At times, the newspapers would refer to a Merchants' Committee. It was all the same thing, a group of concerned businessmen who had originally become concerned about title to their lots.

On October 15, the day after the Committee of One Hundred and One formed for the purposes of hiring J. G. Price to bring a lawsuit against Bernard Moore and the A&NTT Co., the U.S. commissioner once again began recording lot claims in Skagway. He evidently found the decision to sue Moore to be a satisfactory legal way to allow people to continue developing the Skagway townsite, deciding that the courts would be the final arbitrators on whether the individual claimants or Moore could hold title.[15]

In addition to processing the lawsuit, the Committee of One Hundred and One met again on December 4, 1897, to elect a city council. This council was charged with "originat[ing] measures for the material and moral welfare of the town; arrang[ing] for police and fire protection; look[ing] after the sanitary condition of the town and in short . . . discharg[ing] every duty falling upon the shoulders of a city council of any incorporated city or town." Council members promptly appointed committees to take up each of those matters.[16]

In 1897, Alaska was not a formal territory of the United States. It would not become one until 1912 with the passage of the Alaska Second Organic Act on August 24, that year. Before that time, it was a military district, governed by the U.S. Army and the federal courts. With no elected officials, the code of laws pertained only to the criminal code, trade, and land claims; there was no provision for the incorporation of new cities and towns. With the sudden onslaught of thousands of American citizens into the district beginning in 1897, Congress slowly responded with the creation of a Civil Code. By 1899, it created a code of laws for Alaska that allowed cities to incorporate and form and enforce their own ordinances. Skagway became Alaska's first city to incorporate in July 1900 because it already had a functioning city government, one that had been organized since December 1897.[17]

The city council elected that December promptly selected a police force, which they called the Safety Committee. It should be noted that "Safety Committees," or "Committees of Public Safety," were common titles of militias during the American Revolution, being terms reserved for military or police organizations with no official authority. To the members of such groups, the title denoted public service, whereas "vigilante" had a negative connotation that the moral citizens of Skagway could not condone.[18]

Just as the primary purpose of the Committee of One Hundred and One and the city council was to protect land owner rights, so the police force, or Safety Committee, was largely responsible for enforcing the rights of land claims. For the most part, the estimated seven thousand to eight thousand citizens[19] of this northern port on the edge of the Alaskan wilderness relied on a handful of federal officials charged with enforcing customs law. These officials included the U.S. commissioner, John U. Smith (no relation to Jefferson Randolph Smith). He was stationed in Dyea, at the beginning of the Chilkoot Trail, four miles from Skagway by boat up the Lynn Canal, a perilous stretch of rough water when the seas were high, as they often could be in the winter. No trails or road connected Skagway and Dyea in the winter of 1897–98. A single U.S. marshal, John H. Shoup, served all of Alaska from his courthouse and jail in Sitka, then the capital of

Alaska. He assigned one U.S. deputy marshal to Dyea and Skagway, whose name was D. H. McInness.[20] With only one authorized federal law enforcement officer between tidewater and the Canadian border, it is quite likely that Deputy Marshal McInness would frequently call upon the services of the volunteer city police—the Skagway Safety Committee—when occasion needed.

———

Between the time it had published its first issue on October 15, 1897, and its final issue of 1897 on December 31, the *Skaguay News* placed advertisements for 136 businesses, including twenty outfitters, nineteen hotels, fifteen restaurants, and twelve saloons. This count occurs in only half of the twelve issues the newspaper produced during that time period (the only ones that survive), probably a very good sample of the more permanent merchants that had come to town. A round-up of the businessmen selling liquor without a license in December of that year indicated that there were actually eighteen saloons, not twelve. Obviously, a third of them did not advertise in the newspaper.[21]

The 130 Businesses that advertised in the *Skaguay News* between October 15 and December 31, 1897

20 Outfitters and General Merchandise	3 Storage Companies
19 Hotels	3 Coal or Wood Suppliers
15 Restaurants	3 Builders, Architects and Contractors
12 Saloons	and Painters
8 Tobacco Stores	2 Stationeries
5 Shipping /Packing Companies	2 Games and Recreation
5 Real Estate Dealers	2 Barbershops and Baths
5 Meat Markets	1 Photographer
4 Groceries	1 Newspaper
4 Clothiers, Tailors and Dressmakers	1 Music Instrument Dealer
4 Blacksmiths	1 Laundry Cleaner
4 Bakeries	1 Hay / Feed / Grain
4 Attorneys	1 Hardware / Stoves
3 Doctors and 1 Dentist	1 Furniture Store

On December 31, 1897, the *Skaguay News* boasted:

> There is no more orderly town in the world than Skaguay. . . .
> There has been a nominal supervision exercised over the town
> by the Committee of One Hundred and One, a body of men
> elected by the people during the first great influx into this place.
> It was a sort of committee of safety or vigilance committee, but
> this has fallen into a state of innocuous desuetude, for the very
> good reason that there has been nothing for it to do. Law and
> order prevail.[22]

In a district administered by military law and federal courts, the
people of Skagway had gone about starting to resolve their biggest
contention in the fall of 1897 through legal mechanisms and the
American tradition of representative democracy. They had formed
committees; they had, in the absence of constituted authority, elected
a city council, provided committees to look into matters of civil concern, and gone about forming a relatively safe town in which people
could live. For a community of almost five thousand more or less
permanent citizens, little evidence outside of the Soapy Smith legend exists that Skagway was "conceived in lawlessness and nurtured
in anarchy."

———

Where was Soapy Smith in the fall of 1897? He sent a letter to his
wife, Mary, from Skagway on August 28, 1897, indicating that he
had arrived and would be sending her money. Seattle and Denver
newspaper reports indicate that he had left Alaska on September
14, less than a month later. A Denver article of September 23 states
that the people of Skagway ran him out of town. He travelled to St.
Louis to visit Mary, then to New York City and Washington, D.C.,
to get permission to start a franchise for a business on the Yukon
River at St. Michael. During these travels, he curried favor with old
acquaintances and people of some influence, particularly in Washington, D.C. Many of these contacts are well-documented by newspaper reports and letters published by Smith's great-grandson, Jeff
Smith.[23] In particular, an interview published in the *Washington Post*
establishes Smith's presence in that city at the beginning of Novem-

ber. The January 21, 1898, issue of the *Skaguay News* announced that "Jeff Smith arrived at Skaguay direct from Washington D. C." This indicates that he did not return to the North until early in that year after a four-month absence.

Why were Denver, Seattle, and Washington, D.C., newspapers interested in Soapy Smith in 1897? According to Jane Haigh, who wrote about the part con men played in political corruption in the Denver city elections of 1889 and 1892, Smith, besides appearing on the crime pages of the city newspapers for the petty con schemes he ran, was a member of a loosely defined "gang" that assisted city officials in obtaining votes fraudulently. Along with better-known and more powerful members such as Ed Chase and Bat Masterson, police officials, city officials, and local politicians gained high positions in part by using members of the saloon and gambling community to vote repeatedly at elections and intimidate rivals. In some Denver newspapers, the "gang" became synonymous with a Tammany Hall–like political style. Evoking Smith's name or his image in political cartoons served to spoof the political party that stooped to using such measures to gather votes. The Democratic *Rocky Mountain News* disparaged the Republicans as being associated with the "gang," whereas the *Denver Republican* referred to the *News* as supporting "Tammany Hall."[24]

When Denver City Hall closed down all of the saloons in 1894, including Smith's, he left the Queen City of the Plains and drifted somewhat aimlessly, no doubt sorry his reputation as a con man had been so widely published in the Denver newspapers. The Yukon gold rush, set in a territory with no vice laws and limited law enforcement, gave him and his gang new opportunities. His passing through Portland was noticed; his presence in Washington, D.C., was marked by an interview with a cousin on the staff of the *Washington Evening Star*. His occasional whereabouts were noted in Denver newspapers because of the current political reform climate in Denver. The *Denver Times*, which catered to the saloon world, boasted of Smith's interview in his cousin's newspaper; the *Rocky Mountain News* and the *Denver Republican* mentioned him in the years to come in much the way any community would that was thankful to have rid itself of a troublemaker.

Wholly calm and unperturbed, Soapy faced the angry,
threatened mob. . . . "Anyone who tries to put a rope around
Fay's neck will get a bullet in his own head!" he shouted. . . .
The crowd fell back, leaving Fay surrounded by Smith's squad,
which escorted him to jail. Fearing that unruly elements
might make a second attempt to lynch him, the authorities at
once sent the prisoner to Sitka. . . . At his trial, later, Fay was
acquitted on the ground of self-defense.

William Ross Collier and William Victor Westrate, *The
Reign of Soapy Smith*

The next major component of the Soapy Smith legend in Alaska is
that the con man moved into lawless Skagway, and found it much to
his liking. With no duly constituted law or authority, Smith quickly
insinuated himself into the sporting world of gamblers, saloon-keep-
ers, and music halls, where he assumed authority. When bartender
Ed Fay killed saloon-owner Jake Rice's customer Andrew McGrath
and acting U.S. Deputy Marshal James R. Rowan, the town citizens
became an uncontrollable lynch mob. The only man with the power
to control that mob was Soapy Smith, who, through his cool actions,
thwarted the lynch mob, saved the life of the bartender, and worked
with the U.S. commissioner to send him away to Sitka for trial.

Examination of first-hand reports, and court records, finds little
mention of Smith, and then only in an ancillary role. They tell the
story this way:

Andy McGrath liked to drink, he liked to gamble, and he liked
women of shallow morals. He found all three at the People's Theater
in Skagway, Alaska, on the afternoon of January 30, 1898. Typical of
the combined gambling hall, music hall, saloon, and brothel that was
called a "variety theater," Jake Rice's opera house offered all types of
entertainment for the men entering and leaving the Klondike gold
fields in the winter of 1897–98. Like so many other men that winter,
McGrath probably worked for the Brackett Wagon Road improving
the pack trail to the summit of White Pass. The job gave him enough
time to spend a Sunday afternoon and evening drinking, gambling,
and whoring at Jake Rice's gambling house.[25]

By well after midnight on January 31, McGrath had become royally drunk, and true to his reputation in both Skagway and Juneau, he was loud and obnoxious about it. He had found the lady of his choice, spent some time with her, and returned to the saloon for more gambling and drinking. When he became violently ill, as often happens to men who drink too much, he began to harangue Jake Rice, the owner of People's, for serving him poisoned liquor. About the same time, McGrath noticed that the $140 he had been carrying seemed to be missing, and it occurred to him that Rice's gamblers had been running a "sure thing" game, the sort of con that he, the mark, was guaranteed to lose. Convinced he had been robbed and poisoned, he loudly insulted the proprietor of the opera house, its attachés, and its patrons. A nod from Rice brought out his "heelers," what today would be called bouncers, who tried to evict the noisy drunk. But McGrath was reputed for being not only quarrelsome but also "violent and dangerous," as witnesses later testified at his killer's trial. Apparently he did not take kindly to being asked to leave a saloon where he had been "robbed" and "poisoned." Rice's heelers dealt him several severe blows on the head, one of which knocked him out cold.[26]

Brought to his senses a short time later, McGrath's temper had not improved. According to later trial testimony, he threatened to go out of the People's Theater, get a gun and a friend, "shoot the house full of holes," and kill all of those with whom he had been fighting.[27]

Jake Rice was an experienced barkeeper. Arriving in Skagway in the fall of 1897, he set up Rice's Place, the precursor of the People's Theater, at the corner of Trail and Sixth.[28] Rice knew the better part of valor. Without a doubt, the owner of the People's Theater decided a shift change would diffuse the drunken Andy McGrath's temper. He called for his bartender, John Edward Fay (referred to in most newspaper reports and court documents as Ed Fay), who had not previously been present, to take over his duties behind the bar, and he probably arranged for alternative "heelers" as well. After warning Fay of the trouble that had occurred shortly before, Rice left the premises. The bartender armed himself with a revolver and immediately took up a position with a commanding view of the entire room.[29]

Sometime during the early morning of January 31, McGrath left the saloon and encountered James Mark Rowan, who was substituting that day for U.S. Deputy Marshal D. H. McInness, off escorting prisoners south to Sitka. Rowan had come to Skagway in the very first days of the rush from Mt. Vernon, Washington, where he had served as a city marshal. He had located on one of Skagway's first city lots on August 6, 1897, just a day after surveyor Frank Reid had begun laying out the townsite. Rowan later helped build the Brackett Wagon Road from Skagway to White Pass City, and had become one of the city's most respected citizens.[30]

Not two hours earlier, Beryl Rowan, the acting deputy's wife, had given birth to their first child and now needed medical attention. As the young deputy made his way to Dr. Isaac H. Moore's office at 526 Broadway, a drunken, bloody-headed McGrath accosted him on the street.[31]

"Give me a gun!" the boisterous McGrath is reported to have demanded. Unwilling to comply, Rowan abandoned his original mission and sought to settle the difficulty by acting as a mediator. Understanding that McGrath believed he had been robbed and beaten in The People's Theater, the deputized marshal followed him to the saloon.[32]

Upon entering the bar, McGrath took off his coat, walked up to Ed Fay and punched him in the nose, making it quite clear he did not care who was in charge at the moment, he was going to find satisfaction. Next, he reached into his pants pocket. It was the last act he ever committed. Interpreting his gesture as an attempt to pull the promised gun, bartender Fay drew his revolver and fired into McGrath's left side, dropping the trouble maker into a chair and killing him almost instantly.[33]

Standing behind McGrath, James Rowan turned to pull his revolver from his hip pocket. Not realizing that the pioneer (Skagway) citizen had been made an officer of the law, and believing that the deputy was the friend that McGrath had threatened to go fetch, Fay pulled his trigger a second time. His bullet hit Rowan in the right side, piercing his stomach. The deputy reeled around and stumbled to the street, where the gunshots had attracted a crowd.

In an almost macabre series of events inside the saloon, another drunk named Jones, awakened by the shooting, drew his revolver, and began firing indiscriminately. He sent one bullet through both thighs of a third customer, leaving only grazed flesh.[34]

U.S. Deputy Marshal James Rowan was not so lucky. He lay in Dr. Isaac Moore's office for two hours, hemorrhaging internally, his dying thoughts on his young wife, now a mother about to raise a son without his father.[35]

With the death of one of their leading citizens, James Rowan, the businessmen of Skagway were outraged. The death of a drunken laborer who frequented saloons and often engaged in brawls was one thing; killing a man who helped found the town, helped build the road that got the people who paid the bills over the pass, and who helped maintain law and order was quite another. Bartender Ed Fay no sooner disappeared through the back door of the saloon than rumors began to circulate that Mrs. Rowan had died from the shock of hearing that her husband had been killed. Talk of a hanging began to circulate.[36]

Tom Ward, co-owner of H. A. Bauer and Company, a clothing store established in Skagway in the fall of 1897, approached saloon-owner Jake Rice on Monday afternoon, February 1, to lay out the facts for him. If Rice would turn Fay over to the Safety Committee, Ward would guarantee that he would receive a fair trial. If the townspeople had to ferret the man out for themselves, there was no telling what would happen. Most likely the bartender would be hung on the spot.[37]

Facing reality, Jake Rice saw reason. Within an hour Ed Fay was in the custody of the Skagway Safety Committee, which had been appointed by the Committee of One Hundred and One in December 1897 to act as a voluntary police force.[38] Consisting of ten men, this group proceeded to guard him at the Hotel Burkhard, one of the most substantial structures in town, located at the southwest corner of Fifth Avenue and Broadway.

According to documents filed by Commissioner John U. Smith and a Skagway newspaper report, once Fay was under the guard of J. M. Tanner and the Safety Committee at the Burkhard Hotel, the commissioner held a hearing at which Fay pleaded not guilty. John U. Smith appointed Major John F. A. Strong, then editor of the *Skaguay News,* as judge and twelve men as jury. His brief commissioner's log of February 1, 1898, states that the jury of twelve men sat to hear whether Edward Fay should be bound over to Sitka for trial and found enough evidence against him to hold him for the murders of Andrew McGrath and James M. Rowan.[39]

Harry Suydam, the city's assessor, and a member of the Safety Committee, remembered the trial somewhat differently and in considerably more detail three years later when he wrote for *Frank Leslie's Popular Monthly*. He reported that a large group of law-abiding citizens met in Skagway's nondenominational Union Church on Monday, January 31 (this building was located on the north side of Fifth Avenue between Main and State streets). They elected Major Strong to act as judge. It was this big citizens' meeting that appointed ten guards and a group of twelve jurors charged with hearing the case and bringing in a verdict by 3:00 p.m., Monday, the following afternoon. Suydam claims the jurors failed to agree, therefore a committee of a hundred—no doubt the Committee of One Hundred and One—took over, and charged the judge with sentencing the murderer. In essence, in Suydam's version of the story, the Committee of One Hundred and One established Fay's guilt; they simply wished for Strong to determine Fay's sentence.[40]

Major Strong asked that he be given until 9:00 a.m. on Tuesday, February 2, to consider the sentence. Suydam then introduced Commissioner Smith, incorrectly identifying him as a land commissioner, to the proceedings. While one of John U. Smith's duties was to register land claims, his principal job was to hear and process all legal records in his subdistrict. He had been holding at least a weekly, if not more frequent, court hearing criminal cases, assessing fines for people pleading guilty, establishing bail, and processing prisoners for transfer to Sitka, then the capital of the District of Alaska. According to Smith's records, he was summoned from Dyea to Skagway early on Monday, February 1, at which time the town's Safety Committee, or police force, already had Ed Fay under lock and key. Suydam, as a member of the Safety Committee and as the city assessor, had had his clashes with J. U. Smith in adjusting lot claims. Without a doubt, Suydam felt inimical towards the commissioner, and his prejudice showed in his 1901 depiction of the man.[41]

During this same time, the people of Skagway were preparing their legal case against William and Bernard Moore and their partners, who would eventually build the White Pass and Yukon Route railroad,[42] and who were threatening to take title to all of the recorded lots in their town. People like Harry Suydam and the Safety Committee—indeed all of the Committee of One Hundred and One—viewed the "land commissioner" ambiguously, as someone who represented a government that might not be on their side when the matter of the lands claims would be adjudicated later that spring. All of Suydam's dealings with Commissioner Smith to this point had probably been in the arena of land controversies. Suydam, the members of the Safety Committee, and John U. Smith all knew one another through their real estate squabbles.[43]

According to Suydam, Soapy Smith encountered J. U. Smith when the latter arrived in Skagway on the evening of Monday, February 1. In this account, Soapy Smith immediately complained that Fay was to be lynched. Of course, the commissioner, hearing only J. R. Smith's version of the story, and already disposed to view the Committee of One Hundred and One as a bunch of mavericks, saw a miscarriage of justice. He went immediately to Fay's place of captivity, deputized J. M. Tanner and the nine guards of the Safety Committee, ordered them to take the prisoner to a steamer, and shipped him off to Sitka. In Suydam's words, "Fay escaped."[44]

When the ten guards took Ed Fay into custody, the legend of Soapy Smith says that the con man intervened to "save" Ed Fay. A first-hand account states otherwise. Josias M. "Si" Tanner, a deputy sheriff from Harrison County, Iowa, and Pierce County, Washington, later recalled that on or around February 1, he was approached by a man who "fancied himself a leader of the sporting world. . . . That was the first time I spoke to Soapy," Tanner told Customs Commissioner Clarence L. Andrews. "[He] asked if I needed assistance, saying he had had considerable experience and had some good men who would help. I thanked him and assured him that I thought we could keep the prisoner safely."[45]

Although Suydam describes a committee of a hundred citizens pressuring J. F. A. Strong to pronounce sentence on Ed Fay, by the time Commissioner Smith arrived on the evening of February 1, he had not yet made his decision about Fay's guilt or his sentence. In reality, he probably asked for time for the commissioner to arrive from Dyea and for the crowd to cool down. His plan was then to send Fay to Sitka, for a trial, all according to law. Strong knew he had the reliable men of the Safety Committee guarding the prisoner, including such cool heads as J. M. Tanner, who would later prove how little he approved of lynchings and how effective he could be in preventing them.

Si Tanner had come to Skagway in late July 1897, claiming one of the first lots surveyed by Frank Reid on August 7, two days after the city surveyor began laying out the townsite. Owning a small steamship and lighter barges, he was known as "Captain" Tanner. He had been a founding member of the Committee of One Hundred and One, and knew most of the more permanent citizens by name and on sight. For Tanner not to have spoken with Soapy Smith before demonstrates how little known the con man was to the merchants and prominent businessmen of Skagway at the time.[46]

Having returned to Skagway on January 21, four months after being run out of town, Smith had been there only ten days. Tanner, now a member of Skagway's Safety Committee, previously concerned with enforcing the rules about lot locations, probably would have had little reason to come into contact with the con man. Reverend Robert M. Dickey, who built the first church in Skagway, stated that early in his Alaska career Smith made a habit of not practicing his con on town residents.[47] The professional gamblers of Skagway (such as Lee Guthrie and Frank Clancy) regarded a "confidence man" in a different league, much the way cattlemen contrasted themselves to sheepherders.[48] In the 1880s and early 1890s, Soapy had caused endless trouble for the Denver police, continually bilking naïve men out of their hard-earned money with card, pea and walnut, and other shill games. He did it by his charm and pretentions as a learned gentleman given over to generous donations to widows and worthy charities. When the rush to the Klondike started, Smith had decided that the anonymity of the boomtown would suit him and his gang of thugs just fine, and they all moved north. But for the most part, they confined their depredations to portable shill games set up on the White Pass Trail and did not mix with town politics.[49]

Smith has often been described as attractive, with an undeniable charisma. Modern civil rights protesters, who like rebels, might view his dark looks and full beard as mysterious and debonair. While some fans have praised his genteel demeanor, turn-of-the-century observers had other opinions. The *Seattle Post-Intelligencer* in 1898 spared him few positive words:

> He was 5 feet 6 inches tall and weighed 146 pounds. He was
> slouchy in appearance and made no pretensions as to dress.

> He wore a very stubborn, full black beard. His chest was
> covered with a thick mat of black hair. He had dark, expressive
> eyes, and his features when closely inspected gave one the
> impression that he knew a thing or two.[50]

In the language of the times, this description was not meant to be flattering, but down right disparaging.

The beard might not seem unusual to anyone today, but in 1898 it was seriously old-fashioned. Dandies had not worn full beards since Rutherford B. Hayes left the White House in 1881; by the turn of the twentieth century, the clean-shaven look was all the rage. At the most, a pencil-thin mustache graced a real man's face. Middle-aged men, such as J. M. Tanner, clung to their bushy mustaches, but very few allowed a full beard to grow. It only raised the question of a city man's suspicious character that he would grow a beard in 1898.

Perhaps the gang members who accompanied Smith north made him look good in comparison: "Reverend" John L. Bowers knew the "secret handshake of most fraternal lodges and used it to gain the confidence of strangers in saloons and on the trails. Frank "Blue Jay" Brown had a felony arrest record from Colorado, including attempted murder and larceny. Braggart and bully "Big Ed" Burns served a term in prison for murder, and committed all sorts of violent crimes that went unpunished. He escaped death at the hands of the law several times in various western states. Turner Jackson had been arrested for vagrancy along with four other members of Soapy's gang in Denver in 1894, binding them together into a firm brotherhood. He was an accomplished bunco artist. Van B. "Old Man" Triplett, a three-card monte dealer, had spent time in prison for his bunco schemes in Ohio, but continued them after he was released. George W. Wilder started in Denver as a real estate speculator, and no doubt helped Soapy concoct confidence schemes in Skagway. These half-dozen and a couple handfuls of more brutish types of men formed a gang of thugs that shared their ill-gotten gains with Smith by working other men's saloons, gambling dens, street corners, and the trails.[51]

No doubt these were the "good men who would help" Tanner if he needed assistance. Primary documents, in addition to the eyewitness statement by Tanner, make clear that the story of Smith's saving Fay was the fabrication of a yellow journalist, before libel suits stymied such creativity. In fact, Frank Clancy, a well-known gambling and sporting man, and associate of Smith in the Pacific Northwest, admitted as much in saying, "There was a murder committed, and the story went out that Smith and his gang prevented the carrying out of justice. That was wrong. It did Smith an injustice. He simply took the position that the truth of the matter should be discovered."[52]

The newspaper that initiated the tale was Portland's *Morning Oregonian*, followed shortly by Denver's *Rocky Mountain News*. The Victoria, Vancouver, Seattle, Portland, and San Francisco papers, and even the newspapers in Skagway's sister city Dyea, Alaska, often exaggerated any report of lawlessness in Skagway in order to discourage people from staying there long enough to stock up on supplies. The ploy of the West Coast newspapers was to get travelers to buy their outfits before they left the ports and to get them to make travel arrangements all the way through to Dawson with a transportation company from whichever city was home to the newspaper. Playing on the travelers' fears of men like Soapy Smith helped the outfitting, transportation, and shipping companies outside of Skagway to improve their sales. Smith had become notorious for petty graft and political corruption in Denver; the con man showing up as a hero in Skagway suited the advertisers in the West Coast newspapers immensely. If this was the best of Skagway, what was the worst?[53]

And what stake did the Denver newspapers have in following Soapy's exploits in Alaska? Soapy hailed from Denver, having left in 1894 when those he was aiding politically lost their elections and the rising tide of moral and political reforms closed down his operations. As is evidenced by a thick newspaper index of stories about Smith in Alaska in 1898, at least four Denver newspapers would chronicle his exploits. Throughout the following months, the Democratic *Rocky Mountain News*, in particular, delighted in publishing accounts of its city's former scalawag. While the articles in this newspaper were not always flattering, they were inevitably humorous, a quality that drew readers who loved to laugh at the criminal element of Denver's tenderloin district. It is difficult to avoid the conclusion that the *News* had a source in Skagway sending it stories of Smith, perhaps even one of Smith's friends. Printing stories filtered through the lens of friendship, poking humor at the misfortunes of others on the edge of the wild frontier, or just trying to make a point—isn't it a good thing we don't have to deal with him anymore?—the Denver newspapers would contribute more to the burgeoning legend of Smith in Skagway than any other group of yellow journalists.

As the West Coast and Denver newspapers embellished the Smith story in Skagway, they seized the double murder as an opportunity to advance an image he had long cultivated as a man who was generous to widows, orphans, and the down-and-out. Early newspaper accounts published in Skagway and repeated along the West Coast praised Smith for passing the hat among his sporting colleagues to raise a fund for the widow Rowan, reportedly securing $700 in the first hour of his drive, and hoping for another $300 before it was over. He was quoted as saying, "Marshal Rowan protected us when he was alive and it is only right that we should help his widow now that he is dead." The author of the article absolved Rowan of any misdeeds by stating that the very idea was humorous under the circumstances.[54]

Because later readers did not understand the Smith stories in the context of Denver politics, they misconstrued Smith's overall importance. It was the *Rocky Mountain News* that named Soapy the "Dictator of Skagway" on February 26, 1898, a claim countered by the *Seattle Post-Intelligencer* on March 5.[55] It becomes clear that the Denver newspaper was using the term in the sense that it had always referred to Soapy and other members of Denver's "gang": criminals who participated in political corruption, as opposed to a democratic form of politics practiced by Skagway's Citizens' Committee. From the sly pen of *Rocky Mountain News* editor John Arkins, a "dictator" or "boss" was a euphemism for a member of the saloon and gambling crowd who deluded himself into thinking he had some sort of political control.

————

Did Ed Fay escape justice? Citizens' Committee member Harry Suydam said so in 1901. Pierre Berton wrote in 1958 that he received a light sentence. According to Ed Fay's court files, he remained in the federal jail in Sitka until November 1898, at which time he was moved to the federal facility in Juneau, where he faced trial for the murder of Andrew McGrath and James M. Rowan. He first went on trial for the murder of Andrew McGrath. That trial resulted in a hung jury. The second one drew a verdict of manslaughter and a ten-year sentence in federal prison at McNeil Island, Washington. His lawyers asked for a third trial, hoping to get a more sympathetic jury. They ended up accepting the ten-year sentence in a plea bargain that dismissed the charge of the murder of James Rowan and sent him to prison only for McGrath's murder. Fay's lawyers understood that he could hang if found guilty of the deputy marshal's murder, so they decided not to pursue their original idea of a third trial for the McGrath murder.[56]

It was not until 2009 that the U.S. Marshal's Office officially listed James M. Rowan as a U.S. deputy marshal killed in the line of duty.[57]

Did Soapy Smith "save" Ed Fay? From the perspective of the legend fabricators and Smith's cronies in the gambling and sporting word, he most assuredly did, and so the story went out to his contacts in Denver and the *Rocky Mountain News*. But it must be understood that there was no power vacuum into which Smith could step in late January 1898. The people of Skagway had a tried and true system, not of "vigilante" justice but of justice by committee supporting the established office of the U.S. commissioner. That system permitted the citizens to speak their minds, but law and order prevailed. If Soapy Smith spoke out at all (and there is no primary historical document to show that he did), he was just one of more than a hundred other citizens who were doing so. Understanding the system of frontier justice, then, it is easy to see how conflicting stories of the events could arise. Justice by democracy often appears messy, but in the case of the killings of Andrew McGrath and James Rowan, the accused was safely detained and never at any risk. Once U.S. Commissioner John Smith arrived from Dyea, and his paperwork could be processed, Ed Fay was transported to prison to await trial, despite what a self-promoting con man tried to make of it in terms of publicity.

CHAPTER TWO

The Committee of
One Hundred and One

Many of the better citizens viewed [Soapy's] activities with
growing alarm and organized a Vigilance Committee of One
Hundred and One members. . . . As its first act this committee
proceeded to throw a bombshell into Soapy's camp by issuing
the following public notice: " . . . All con men, bunco and sure-
thing men and all other objectionable characters are notified
to leave Skagway and the White Pass Road immediately and
remain away." . . . [Smith replied] "The Law and Order
Committee of Three Hundred and Three will see that
justice is dealt out to its fullest extent and no Blackmailers or
Vigilantes will be tolerated."

William Ross Collier and William Victor Westrate,
The Reign of Soapy Smith

The third critical element of the Soapy Smith legend to be tested
for basis in fact is the almost universally accepted premise that
the con man, having established himself as a power to be reckoned
with, became the "uncrowned King of Skagway" in the months that
followed Ed Fay's killing of Andrew McGrath and James Rowan. He
supposedly did this by calling the bluff of the Committee of One
Hundred and One when it threatened to run the gamblers and
other members of the sporting element out of Skagway.

As established earlier, the Committee of One Hundred and One
had first formed on October 14, 1897, to investigate Bernard Moore's
claim to a manufacturing site of 160 acres. On December 4, this committee elected a city council, which in turn appointed a volunteer fire
department, police department, and water and utility committees.

As noted above, the Committee of One Hundred and One reconvened on February 1, 1898, to appoint a judge and jury to investigate
whether there was enough evidence to hold Ed Fay for the murders
of Andrew McGrath and James Rowan.

Soapy was the first to use the term *vigilante* to describe the Committee of One Hundred and One in a broadside he spread about
in March 1898. His objective was to make its members appear to be
anarchists in the face of his more reasoned calm. The journalists who
later wrote Smith's story followed Smith's lead: none of them were
professional historians who evaluated the relative merits of historical documents. They looked only at the saloon and gambling world
and almost universally portrayed the con man as a misunderstood
rascal. They wished to dismiss Smith's crimes in the light of the Robin
Hood–like legend of his generosity to widows, children, and dogs,
and they, therefore, portrayed the townspeople as villains and out-
of-control vigilantes.[1] The situation, however, was hardly that simple.
Rival newspapers that used the term did so to promulgate the perception of Skagway as lawless and out of control. A careful examination of the context of *vigilante* in contemporary reports bears out this
hypothesis.

Having assisted Major Strong and Commissioner Smith in shipping
Ed Fay off to Sitka, J. M. Tanner, Frank Reid, Sam Lovell, and other
members of the Committee of One Hundred and One began to circulate a petition addressed to President William McKinley request-
ing additional law enforcement personnel in Dyea and Skagway.
While they did not specifically ask for army troops, their letter stated
that up to two hundred soldiers would be required to keep the peace
on the border in Dyea and Skagway due to the influx of gold rushers
and immigrants going to the border. They understood that Alaska
was a military district. Law enforcement would have to take the form
of military control.[2]

When Alaska's governor, John G. Brady, visited Skagway in February 1898 and investigated the problems, he found city officials had
matters well under control. Brady reported to Washington that, while
federal troops were indeed necessary, and had been for some time,

they were not needed to control crime in the two cities at tidewater or along the trails. Law enforcement was not the problem. Rather, a general lack of supplies in the interior resulting in starvation had become a concern there over the winter of 1897–98, causing riots in some Alaskan communities. Canada seemed to be making overtures to push its boundaries to the coast. And a British railroad company appeared to be surveying for a railroad (what would become the WP&YR) from Skagway to the headwaters of the Yukon River. The governor concluded that a U.S. military presence in Skagway and Dyea would not be out of order, but for reasons other than rampant criminal activity.[3]

After sending off their citizens' petition, the city council proceeded to take additional steps to curb the growing crime rate in Skagway. In early March, the larger group of concerned citizens that had urged Major Strong to sentence Ed Fay reconvened the Committee of One Hundred and One for a third time. Originally formed by such men as J. A. F. Strong, attorney Samuel L. Lovell, shipper and expressman J. M. Tanner, and town surveyor Frank Reid, they were now joined by Rev. Robert M. Dickey, William Fonda, and Jack Crawford. The newly enlarged committee printed up the posters warning confidence, bunco, and sure-thing men to leave Skagway and the White Pass road immediately, or action would be promptly taken. The Committee of One Hundred and One distributed them around town on March 8, 1898.[4] The threat was leveled at the gambling community as a whole—at Jefferson R. Smith, among others.

Unlike the original members of the Committee of One Hundred and One, Fonda and Crawford were veterans of vigilante justice in California. Given the current crises and Frank Reid's and Si Tanner's previous experience with law enforcement in Oregon and Washington (respectively), these more seasoned men may have been specifically selected by the other members of the committee, if they did not step up voluntarily.

It is presumed that the Committee of One Hundred and One felt it had to intervene at this point because its city council was not fulfilling its mandate to "originate measures for the material and moral welfare of the town [and] arrange for police and fire protection."[5] The city election of December 4, 1897, voted in six council members

and a president who broke the inevitable ties in votes. This city council appeared to be a diverse group of merchants. J. Henry Foster, for
example, owned the Grotto Saloon. Frank Clancy was proprietor of
Clancy's Music Hall and Saloon as well as the building that would
later house Jeff Smith's Parlor. Frank E. Burns was the agent for the
Alaska Steamship Company; J. Allan Hornsby was editor of the *Daily
Alaskan* and an originator of the committee; I. D. Spencer was proprietor of an outfitters and general mercantile company; and Chairman Charles Sperry built and owned a warehouse on the Skagway
Improvement Company Wharf (later the Alaska Southern Wharf
Company), next to Moore's Wharf.⁶ All were respected merchants
who claimed lots within the Moore claim.

Most interesting among this collection of personalities was Frank
Clancy from Seattle. He was one of the six brothers whose syndicate
included saloons, gambling houses, and dance halls all along the West
Coast and Alaska. He was one of three brothers who came to Skagway
at the beginning of the Klondike gold rush, James and John joining
him. He opened his Skagway place—the Clancy Saloon and Music
Hall—in the late summer or fall of 1897, at what would become the
southwest corner of Seventh and State avenues. The place was such a
local landmark that other businesses referred to Clancy's when giving
their location in newspaper advertisements. For example, the Skaguay
Bazaar advertised on February 2, 1898, that it was located on "Trail
just above Clancy's." Gordon, McKee and Noyes, real estate agents,
were in the office north of Clancy's. C. N. Noyes also sold tobacco
from the red door above Clancy's. The Princess Hotel and Saloon
was to be found opposite Clancy's. Eventually, Frank would also own
the Mirror Saloon, the Grotto Hotel and Saloon, Reception Saloon,
Clancy's Café, Jeff Smith's Parlor, and the Skagway Oyster Parlors. So
prominent did Frank Clancy become in the fledgling community's
affairs that when Skagway incorporated in July 1899, he was elected
as one of its first official city councilmen, and he remained a power
in the community until he died in 1901.⁷

Soapy's great-grandson, Jeff Smith, tries to make a case that Soapy
was a "silent partner" of Frank Clancy during November and December of 1897 in Skagway, co-owning businesses such as Clancy's Music
Hall and Saloon and the Klondike Saloon, but he offers no proof, not

even notes or letters with hints as to the connections.[8] Examination of deed records in Skagway and the state archives demonstrate that Clancy alone owned all of those businesses and properties. The first documentary evidence of a business relationship between the two is a newspaper notice that Frank Clancy had sold half the business (not the property) of the saloon at 317 Holly to Smith for use as a saloon in early May 1898.[9]

Later stories would emerge that all city council members had virtually ignored Soapy Smith, and they probably had, in spite of his charm, his gift for conversation, and his donations to causes that would bring him "points." Deed and licensing records indicate he owned no property and no business before May 1898. He simply controlled a band of thugs operating on the trail and street corners. Why should the landowners and merchants pay him any attention whatsoever? True, city councilmen Foster, Hornsby, Clancy and W. F. Lokowitz were all said to be friendly towards Smith. They wanted votes, and so were probably friendly to all of the sporting fraternity. Burns, Spencer, and Sperry, while respectable businessmen, appreciated a drink now and then and were known to visit the saloons, taking a laissez-faire attitude towards the "morality" charge of their administration.

In fact, Smith probably cultivated the sort of relationship with city council members that he had had with Denver's city officials, meaning that he accepted bribes, and exchanged prerequisites and other favors with the influential merchants in Skagway. Rather than "running" Skagway, he was allowed to curry the favor of Skagway's earliest political players. Smith's name would become associated with the names of Hornsby, Saportas, and Clancy through the next few months. Without a doubt, these influential citizens sought Smith's favor in the way that mayoral candidate Wolfe Londoner and Republicans had used Soapy in Denver, hoping eventually to buy votes and threaten those who could be easily scared into "voting correctly."

It is important to note that Clancy, Hornsby, and Saportas had been appointed by the Committee of One Hundred and One in December 1897. They were first and foremost influential businessmen in Skagway at a time when Soapy was out of town doing other business. Any later associations between the con man and members of the city council had very little to do with "control" or influence, but prob-

ably much to do with Smith's background as a vote hustler. Knowing
that future city elections would rely on votes instead of appointments,
and remembering that Smith played a role in manufacturing votes
in Denver's 1889 election, some members of Skagway's city council
might not immediately dismiss Soapy's capability to influence elections. As newspapermen, councilmen Hornsby and Saportas, and
also Frank Clancy, part-owner of a region-wide gambling syndicate,
would have been aware of Smith's participation in political influence-
buying in Denver.

As stated earlier, the confidence men were regarded as quite different from the professional gamblers, one being a petty thief, the
other a professional working a then-legitimate business. The best-
known professional gamblers in Skagway were Frank Clancy, Lee
Guthrie, George Rice, and their employees, Pat Renwick, Phil Snyder, and F. J. "Doc" DeGruyder. They dealt cards at the faro and
roulette tables, and—in the case of Clancy and Rice—ran gambling
syndicates that stretched from Seattle to Dawson, and later, Nome.
All of them were respected artisans of the ancient games of chance.
They also owned property or business buildings and paid the voluntary taxes and license fees. A confidence man, on the other hand,
was one who "designed swindles in which advantage is taken of the
victim's confidence." A bunco was "a cheat or a swindler." A sure-
thing man was one who made a bet he knew he could not lose.[10]
Smith took pride in calling himself a "sure thing man." He boasted,
"When I stake money, it's a sure thing that I win,"[11] and he always
took on men too naïve or simple to know better than to engage in
one of his gambling schemes. The sure-thing men were "fly by night"
operators, here today, gone tomorrow, with no interest in contributing to the welfare of the community

Smith could not resist responding to what he considered a taunt
leveled by the Committee of One Hundred and One in mid-March
1898. Within a very short time, he printed up his own broadsides and
posted them side-by-side with those of the city council. He warned
the Committee of One Hundred and One that "the law and order
society consisting of 317 citizens will see that Justice is dealt out to its

full extent as no Blackmailers or Vigilantes will be tolerated."[12] Soapy Smith, in assuming leadership of Skagway's sporting world, declared war on government by the town's merchants—some of whom were professional gamblers—and labeled them all as "vigilantes" in one fell swoop.

The term *vigilante* gained a negative connotation through the latter half of the nineteenth century, primarily because of its association with lynch mobs in western mining towns. Essentially, Smith, by naming the Committee of One Hundred and One as composed of such, was questioning their legitimacy. The *Oxford English Dictionary* defines *vigilante* as "a member of a self-appointed group of people who undertake law enforcement in their community without legal authority." Although that was not their original function, it was more or less the role the Committee of One Hundred and One had undertaken at this particular point. Again, the term had gotten a bad name from the lynchings undertaken by citizen groups in other western communities before the arrival of adequately staffed U.S. marshal offices and the incorporation of cities and counties. The Committee of One Hundred and One, however, was not a lynch mob.

————

Were there 317 law-abiding citizens at Smith's command? Simply put, no. The number comes from the street address of one of Frank Clancy's buildings, the abandoned First Bank of Skaguay at 317 Holly Avenue (or 317 Sixth Avenue as per a city council edict of March 1898). This was the location of the narrow building from which Smith would run a saloon. It had barely enough room for a mahogany bar and a couple of gambling tables in the back room. Typical of the wood plank dives erected by the early entrepreneurs in this boomtown, this twelve-foot-by-forty-foot hole-in-the-wall would eventually cater to men looking for cheap booze and a quick game of poker. Smith would own neither the lot nor the building, that role belonging to landlord Frank Clancy. In March 1898, it is unknown what the place was called or if it was an active business. Smith would not open Jeff Smith's Parlor until May 14, 1898.[13] It is likely that Frank Clancy allowed Smith to use the building as a place for his gang to gather.

On February 19, in the wake of the McGrath and Rowan murders, the *Rocky Mountain News* called Soapy "the Dictator of Skagway." Despite this claim, it appears that Smith's efforts to rally the sporting community failed. Newspapers from several other cities throughout the following months reported that all was quiet in Skagway and that the criminal element was lying low. On March 5, the Seattle *Post-Intelligencer* stated that it was Soapy who was trying to promote himself as "shah," "boss," and "chief" of Skagway, but it was ludicrous for him to do so. The town was quiet, and the citizens of the community had the gambling element well under control. The *News* editor, John Arkin, was simply making a sly reference to *Denver*'s bad old days when Soapy was a member of the "gang" that assisted city hall in influencing politics. It was not the "gang" that ran city hall. It was city hall that was corrupt and controlled the "gang." But the use of slang words such as *dictator, boss,* and *chief* connoted gangland-style politics rather than a person who controlled a city.[14] It should be noted that the word *king* was not used to describe Smith until after his death.[15]

In fact, so much of vital importance to the lives of Skagway's merchants and property owners was happening in the months of January through June of 1898, that to call Soapy Smith the "ruler" of that town is absurd. Smith's interests, such as they were, were confined entirely to the gambling and drinking world, what was usually referred to as "the sporting world." It is of little wonder that his twentieth-century biographers did not pay any attention to these distinctions.

[By March 1898] Smith was referred to as "The Uncrowned King of Skagway."

Pierre Berton, *Klondike Fever*

Defying the Committee of One Hundred and One no doubt earned Smith a large number of kudos in the gambling and sporting world. Anyone can print up a broadside and post it wherever he likes, but the situation was changing. The federal troops that Governor Brady requested on the behalf of Skagway's citizens had arrived in Skagway on February 25, 1898. By March 15, Soapy Smith, through his blustering, was starting to cause enough trouble that the 14th Infantry issued orders reinforcing the Committee of One Hundred and One's command that confidence men close their businesses. This news was reported in Victoria, San Francisco, Seattle, Denver, and a wide variety of places interested in the Klondike.[16] With such legal backing—Alaska was a military district—the bunco men, bunco bosses or steerers, and confidence men had no choice but to obey orders and close up shop, or move up the trail.

Skagway's citizens turned to other, more important business. Among the city councilmen were Frank Clancy and Henry Foster, owners of saloons and notorious gambling places, but they had made their living selling drinks and running legal gambling tables, not as "confidence, bunco and sure-thing men." Both businessmen, as property owners within the Moore claim, had much greater concerns in February and March of 1898 than dealing with a few con men and petty swindlers, who were just not in their league. Like their fellow merchant councilmen, Frank Burns, Charles Sperry, and I. D. Spencer, they were afraid that Bernard Moore, E. E. Billinghurst, and the Alaska and Northwestern Territories Trading Company (A&NTT Co.) would be taking title to all of the property between tidewater and Eleventh Avenue—virtually every lot that had been recorded by Commissioner John U. Smith.

The Committee of One Hundred and One hired J. G. Price to represent them in a lawsuit against Bernard Moore's claim and the A&NTT Co. Attorney Price filed a protest on February 8, 1898, after that recorded by Emory Valentine and others on behalf of the Skaguay Wharf Improvement Company, which also believed it owned a substantial amount of property in the townsite.[17] By March 31, 1898, the U.S. General Land Office in Sitka was ready to hear the protests. Moore repeated his story that he had recorded claims in 1888 and again in 1896, when he began to live there permanently. Starting in August of that year, he built several bunkhouses, a floating dock measuring thirty-three feet by sixty feet, and he cut piles for another dock and a float.[18]

Moore stated that all of these improvements amounted to about fifty thousand dollars, and that the A&NTT Co. had backed him with the money. In fact, the company now owned his rights with Moore acting as a minority partner. Ernest Edward Billinghurst, of Victoria, British Columbia, was agent and trustee for the company. His distinct British accent seemed to gall the American merchants. While the founding fathers of Skagway objected to the very idea that a company managed and operated by Englishmen could operate and own land on American soil, the law said the company had every right to take out a mortgage on Moore's trading and manufacturing site.[19]

Attorneys Price, Valentine, and Twitchell, in their separate protests, claimed that Moore was being used as a tool of a British company that had incorporated in West Virginia for the sole purpose of getting a foothold in an Alaska port, and correctly stated that Moore would not have been able to develop the site by himself. Skagway's Committee of One Hundred and One, acting through J. G. Price, believed that it could win its case by arguing that the "English Company" had no business taking a trading and manufacturing site in Alaska at the expense of hundreds of American businessmen.[20]

Examination of all lot location notices from August 5, 1897, through Jefferson Smith's death on July 8, 1898, as well as all deed transactions from August 1897 through the time of his death, indicate that Smith did not buy or sell any real estate in Skagway.[21] He had no recorded financial interest in the single most important issue of the winter and spring of 1897–98 to the citizens of Skagway: the land fight with the Moores, the Close Brothers, and the A&NTT Co. No one could be called the "uncrowned King of Skagway" without a pecuniary interest in this one single issue.

––––––––

In addition to the land controversy, another major issue facing the merchants in Skagway was the rights-of-way for the Brackett Wagon Road and the White Pass and Yukon Route railroad (WP&YR). This road had started as the White Pass Trail, but the Skagway and Yukon Transportation and Improvement Company had obtained the rights to develop it as a haul road to the summit of White Pass in October 1897, and, with George Brackett as general superintendent and manager, had begun construction in early November 1897. Most of the merchants and businessmen had grown prosperous on the trade generated from the existence of the wagon road. In January 1898, the United States Congress passed a bill providing for the construction of railroads in Alaska. The Close Brothers' attorney, on behalf of the Pacific & Arctic Railway & Navigation Co., filed an application to build a railroad over the White Pass, a mere twenty-four hours before George Brackett's representative attempted to do so. In a rapid trip to Washington, D.C., Brackett protested the granting of the application on the basis of his improving the road. In compensation, the secretary of interior, Cornelius N. Bliss, granted Brackett the first right-of-way for his road and transportation corridors.[22]

The WP&YR needed a right-of-way from the wharf that the railroad had purchased from William and Bernard Moore at the north end of Skagway harbor through the city of Skagway. Unfortunately, because Brackett had acquired the rights along the eastern bluff, the only other option was to lay the tracks down one of the city streets, at least until such a time that the right-of-way could be purchased from Brackett's company. After lengthy discussions with the Skagway city council—the Committee of One Hundred and One's representatives—in May and early June 1898, officials of the WP&YR convinced the city that it was in their best interest to grant the railroad its requested temporary right-of-way up either State or Broadway. When WP&YR officials E. C. Hawkins and John Hislop left Skagway to inspect their construction project on May 30, they thought they would return to receive the council's signed resolution granting them those rights.[23]

Upon returning from his inspection tour on June 14, Hawkins found that some members of the city council had balked and refused to grant the right-of-way. In a session that lasted past midnight on June 15, Councilman J. Allan Hornsby, supported by Frank E. Burns and Charles Sperry, argued long and hard with the Broadway Street merchants, wearing down their opposition. The moment the resolution passed the city council, Hawkins had his laborers staking the grade. By 7:00 a.m. on June 16, five hundred men were leveling the grade, and a mile had been completed within twenty-four hours of the city council's delayed decision. There was no turning back.[24]

Soapy's great grandson, Jeff Smith, contends that Smith "had an interest in the Brackett Wagon Road," citing as his authority a newspaper article in the *Rocky Mountain News* of April 13, 1899, which quotes Smith's brother, Bascom.[25] Examination of a list of Brackett

Wagon Road investors does not bear out this contention, nor does it make sense that Smith would use his supposed influence on councilman J. Allan Hornsby to persuade the city merchants to grant the right of way to the railroad. Doing so was in the railroad's interest, not that of the wagon road. Logically, Soapy would profit more from the travelers on the wagon road, not the railroad. If Smith invested in the wagon road, why would his compatriot argue to grant a right-of-way to the railroad?

When interviewed by the *Skaguay News*, merchants along Broadway and State streets alike were largely aghast at what their city council had done to them. J. G. Price, who represented himself as the city attorney, and later became Alaska's *ad hoc* delegate to the U.S. congress, said "I am satisfied the building of a road along Broadway will greatly decrease the value of property, and increase the fire hazard along that thoroughfare. It is a serious blow to Broadway property owners." A. M. Laska, a tobacco salesman on Broadway, retorted, "I don't care a hell of a lot about it, still it makes me hot to see the street torn up that way." A. L. Cheney, who owned a clothing store, articulated his concern about increased costs. "I am opposed to the road on Broadway for several very good reasons. First the street is too narrow for business and a railroad, and second, when we are able to obtain insurance in Skaguay, the fact that there is a railroad on Broadway will cause rates to be higher on this street than anywhere else in the city." Joseph Burkhard, through Councilman W. F. Lokowitz, was reported to say, "The property owners on Broadway have been shamefully used after all the expense they have gone to in improving the street. Besides, the railroad will necessarily drive all retail business away from it, as people are afraid to risk their lives by running around locomotives and trains. The value of property on other streets will be enhanced at the expense of Broadway. I have opposed putting the track along Broadway, both as a citizen and as a councilman, and I very much regret the fact that my efforts in that direction were unavailing."[26]

Mrs. L. A. Harrison, who ran the Ladies' Bazaar clothing store, and was a daughter of temperance leaders Thomas and Sarah Shorthill, offered a more moderate opinion. "I think for a year at least, the road will prove beneficial to business. After that time I am satisfied the road on Broadway will be an injury to property owners." E. R. Peoples, the local undertaker, took a more sanguine view. "The road will not benefit the street, but what is the use of kicking. Let 'er go." Most expressed the optimistic hope that the tracks would not remain in town for long, and that the railroad would soon settle the right-of-way issue with officials of the Brackett Wagon Road so the tracks could be moved to the base of the bluff on the east side of town. Although track would be built along the bluff when the company bought Brackett's wagon road that winter, portions of the Broadway track would remain until 1941.[27]

The newspaper does not mention who cast the council's deciding vote that favored the railroad. If one wants to believe that Soapy Smith was involved in Skagway politics, it would have been Frank Clancy. Considering the ample complaints voiced by merchants once the rights were granted, it is highly unlikely that Soapy used his gang to quiet discontent about this issue. If he was "Boss" of Skagway, would he not have been more effective at stifling the discord?

By April 1898, the city of Skagway numbered more than five hundred merchants with a tally of only forty-three saloons, gambling houses, music halls, and brothels.[28] And not a one of them yet belonged to Smith. As for Soapy having been "uncrowned King of Skagway" in the winter and spring of 1897–98, as claimed by Pierre Berton . . . well, there just is not any hard evidence. With his not settling into Skagway until late January, it is likely that he was only the boss of his small sector of the sporting world.

———

Capt. Smith decided that the Alaska Guards should parade through town the evening of Sunday, May 1, 1898, Skagway's first such parade. It started on the waterfront with Capt. Smith, mounted on a white horse heading up the unit. A band, recruited from the various saloons was placed in the middle of the marching men so that all could hear the music . . .

The parade lasted an hour and one-half, breaking up in front of City Hall where several patriotic citizens addressed the group, General Weyler was hung in effigy and Capt. Smith

closed the session with an inspirational address, "You are fine,
brave men, each and every one of you, and I am sure that you
will unhesitatingly follow me anywhere and at any time." With
that he headed for Jeff's Place and followed by a majority of the
"troops were in need of quenching their thirst."

Howard Clifford, *Uncrowned King of Skagway*

Between the fears that they would lose their claims to the lots in
the business district, and that the smoke and sparks spewing from
locomotives would ruin their tinderbox false-fronted wooden stores
along Broadway, few people noticed that Soapy Smith had returned
to Skagway. Other than the brief flair-up between him and the Committee of One Hundred and One in mid-March, and a later legend
that purports that the committee "slunk into hiding," newspapers say
nothing about Smith until May. The anecdotes of Smith's gang's depredations on the White Pass Trail appear to date from this period,
January to May of 1898. Of Soapy himself, not even legend mentions
until May 1. At that time it states that he organized a grand patriotic
parade featuring a number of Skaguay Militia members, which he
had mobilized from among the ranks of the sporting element to go
off and fight for the United States against the Spanish in Cuba.

The source of this tale appears in the *Denver Times*, a newspaper
that, like the *Rocky Mountain News*, enjoyed reporting on the adventures of former Queen City of the Plains's miscreants. They credited
J. G. McCabe, a Leadville Democrat from 1891 to 1894, who had
gone up north, no doubt with Smith, to mine the miners. In May
1899, a Juneau newspaper announced that McCabe had found gold
and copper ore near Haines Mission, a boondoggle that did not pay
out.[29] McCabe was a questionable source, and the tale falls apart when
other sources are checked.

The legend goes that Smith, wishing to capitalize on the out-
break of patriotism following the start of the Spanish-American war,
"recruited" a division of the Alaska militia from among the saloon element and nominated himself captain. In fact, by April 27, Soapy had
received a standard acknowledgment letter from a secretary working in the office of the president of the United States indicating that
his offer of starting a militia unit had been noted, and his letter had

been forwarded to the secretary of war. With appropriate hoopla, the *Daily Alaskan* laughingly commented that Skagway's town spirit would surely defeat the Spanish cowards in Cuba. This sort of "patriotism" had little to do with the man who was organizing the effort for his own promotion, and more to do with making the news amusing for the reading public. Anyone familiar with the tongue-in-cheek style of the editors of both the *Daily Alaskan* and the *Skaguay News* would read their accounts of his efforts to muster a guard as ridiculous and subject to laughter.[30]

When Smith announced that he was holding a public meeting on Fifth Avenue on May 1, 1898, patriotic fervor among men hungry for entertainment took over in the spirit of fun. The *Skaguay News* reported that anywhere from six hundred to two thousand men turned out (when Pierre Berton told the story in 1958, he used the higher estimate, deciding it made a better story). Exaggerating the proceedings, the newspaper continued:

> At half past seven o'clock a procession nearly two blocks in length formed on Broadway led by a carriage containing prominent citizens and Deputy U.S. Marshall John Cudihee and headed by the band. Standard bearer Tanner [*sic*] of Denver, Colorado proudly bore a large silk flag on which was marked the words First Regiment of Alaska Militia, and beside him marched Captain Jeff R. Smith of the Skaguay Guards.[31]

A photograph taken by E. A. Hegg entitled "A Patriotic Parade" captures a carriage full of citizens and the beginning of Brooks Pack Train. A copy of the photograph owned by the Clallam County Historical Society, Washington, has some of the people identified, including city founder William Moore, sitting in the carriage; G. W. Graves, partner of E. O. Sylvester, who owned the Klondike Trading Co., the building before which the parade is standing; Brooks, owner of Brooks the Packer company; C. E. Taylor; and "Soapy." Smith stands next to a flag on a pole, the silk banner mentioned in the newspaper article. He is situated not at the head of the parade, but well behind the band, which led it, the carriage of leading citizens, and a packer. This photograph and the newspaper article authenticate the legend that Smith was involved in a patriotic parade—as was just about everyone else in town. It places him well behind the city leaders and questions the legend that he organized and led the parade.

The author of the *Skagway News* article was Elmer John "Stroller" White, one of the Far North's first columnists. He came to Skagway in April 1898, when J. F. A. Strong went north to Dawson. M. L. Sherpy, owner of the *Skaguay News*, who recognized a legitimate talent when he saw one, immediately hired White to fill in as editor. Born in Ohio, on November 28, 1859, White came from the Puget Sound area where he had been writing for newspapers since 1889. He had developed a prose style that approached that of Mark Twain for humor and colorful exaggeration.[32] White later wrote a humorous version of the May 1 parade that parodied Smith leading a drunken brigade in and out of streets, and up and down alleys, parts of it going different ways, all in a sort of spontaneous response to learning that the United States had declared war on Spain more than a month before.[33]

> There was a parade which was held in the evening as the days
> were growing long at that season of the year. It was Skagway's
> first parade—leaving out the nightly parade from the dance
> floor to the bar while the caller was wetting his callbox—and
> it was probably the greatest parade known in Alaska up to
> that time. It formed up on the waterfront with Captain Soapy
> Smith to lead it on his white horse. Everyone else marched, or
> at least they walked, and there was a brass band to set the time
> and furnish—well, the Stroller was going to say it furnished
> music, but the band had just been organized by Jake Rice, the
> proprietor of the People's Theatre, and its members had never
> had a chance to practice together, so what they furnished may
> not have been music, but at least it was loud. The band was
> placed about the middle of the parade so all hands could hear
> it, and in front of the band and behind it were rank after rank
> of men, tall men and short men, lean men and fat ones, all
> moving along as near as they count in time to Jake Rice's brass
> band.[34]

In view of the actual newspaper articles written by the *Daily Alaskan*, the Stroller's nineteen-teen's version does not sound much different from the truth. Soapy and the sporting world actually tagged along behind the citizens' parade and tried to turn what had started out as a perfectly respectable show of patriotic spirit into a drunken party.

Reinforcing the view that Smith could not have organized and "led" the May 1 patriotic parade is a *Denver Post* account of Skagway's event. According to this version, Allan Hornsby, Dr. Isaac H. Moore, Walter Church, and U.S. Deputy Marshal John Cudihee from Dyea led the parade. Soapy and his lieutenant, John Tener, came near the end of the parade with the Skaguay Guard.[35]

Two weeks after the *Denver Post* published its story about Skagway's patriotic call to arms, the *Denver Times* wrong-headedly noted how influential Soapy Smith had become in Skagway. A week later, the *Denver Post* announced that its correspondent in the north thought it was pure slander to say that "Smith was Deuce High" (a poker term, meaning assuming an arbitrarily assigned high status to a low card or character) in Skagway, a corrective that Smith's later biographers apparently missed.[36] To the writer of this short *Denver Post* note, Soapy was a low-ranking con man momentarily elevated by the war time patriotism. Somewhere along the line, correspondents had missed both Hornsby's and White's notorious tongue-in-cheek style of humor, which made fun of the Gateway to the North, for letting a con man organize a militia, of all things, and call it the Skaguay Guard!

Legend has come down that Secretary of War Russell A. Alger wrote a letter thanking Jefferson Randolph Smith for organizing the Alaska Militia, a letter that Smith posted in his Parlors for all to see. Supposedly it was in Smith's collection of letters stored in a trunk in an outbuilding behind his saloon. Smith's family claims that U.S. Deputy Marshal J. M. Tanner sold the entire collection of letters to *Alaska-Yukon Magazine,* which published them in its December 1907 and January 1908 issues. The only letter that appeared in these issues pertaining to the Alaska Militia and even remotely connected to the secretary of war is one dated April 9, 1898, from John Addison Porter, secretary to the president, acknowledging Smith's minutes and enrollment roster of the Skaguay Military Company and informing him that they had been forwarded on to the secretary of war. Said enrollment lists and minutes were dated March 19, 1898, and Smith had requested arms, accoutrements, and an army officer for the drilling of his troops. He had named himself captain of the troops, and various other ne'er-do-wells as officers, for whom he requested funding.[37]

Smith's biographers fail to realize that neither Congress nor the president had the authority to fund state or territorial militias until the passage of the National Defense Act of 1916.[38] It would have been impossible for the secretary of war to authorize the requisition of arms, accoutrements, uniforms, and a trained military officer to drill militia in Skagway. That was the governor's job. If Smith was as savvy as his biographers made him out to be, he certainly knew that, and this was just another of his many scams. And Governor Brady of Alaska knew Smith's character well enough. He would never have appointed him captain of a militia company.

The fact that the War Department never did authorize Smith's group as a unit of the National Guard is reinforced by the information that the first official unit of the Alaska Militia was formed a year later on February 5, 1899, in Skagway, and celebrated annually after that time, with no acknowledgment that Smith's unit ever existed.[39]

It is true that the *Skaguay News* and the *Daily Alaskan* called Soapy "Captain Jeff Smith" in their May 2, 1898, newspaper articles about the patriotic parade on May 1. Did that mean he had organized a unit of the Alaska National Guard? No. It meant that both J. Allan Hornsby and E. J. "Stroller" White knew how to mock the sporting world. Later authors, reading isolated articles taken out of context, often could not discern their tongue-in-cheek humor. Daily perusal of both papers makes it clear that both Hornsby and White could and would poke fun at whomever they chose, whenever they chose, to make their readers laugh. The sporting world was a particular favorite target for both newspapers, and panning "Captain" Smith and the "two thousand" people he gathered on the night of May 1 probably proved a great source of amusement to startled readers on May 2. Smith himself no doubt enjoyed the game as much as anyone else. That others would take the joke seriously in years to come would not have occurred to a soul.[40]

So what was all of this hoopla really about? Was Jefferson Randolph

Smith a patriotic citizen who could rally a quarter of Skagway citizens into a show of American spirit?

It seems unlikely. Smith, like every other businessman in Skagway in May of 1898, was looking for publicity as the big hoard of summer travelers was starting to come north. Two weeks after the Skagway newspapers poked fun at him for being at the right place at the right time, calling him "Captain" Smith, he opened Jeff Smith's Parlor. He had finally convinced entrepreneur Frank Clancy to rent out a fourteen-by-forty-foot false-fronted shack in the saloon district at 317 Holly Street, a building he may well have been using as an office and a meeting place for his gang.[41] Instead of running his con games from street corners and along the trail, he could set up his three-card monte and bunco tricks in his own place. Who better to protect him than "The Skaguay Guard?"

[T]he Fourth of July, 1898. . . . Down Broadway Avenue
the procession advances, and at its head, mounted upon a
handsome dapple gray, is a pale-faced man with the eyes of
a poet and the beard of a Mephisto, who waves his spotless
white sombrero in greeting to the crowd. And the crowd waves
back and cheers as Jefferson Randolph Smith, the marshal
of the parade and dictator of Skagway, goes riding past. . . .
On the procession moves toward the flag-draped platform
where Jeff Smith, once known as "Soapy," will be joined by the
governor of Alaska himself for the official Independence Day
ceremonies. It is Smith's supreme moment. . . . Now that career
has reached is climax; let him savor it; in just four days he will
be dead.

Pierre Berton, *Klondike Fever*

If the May 1 parade has become confused in legend, Skagway's July 4, 1898, celebration has become even more so in the telling. Through the 114 years since the town's first Independence Day celebration, the role of Jefferson Randolph Smith has become so mythologized that it is almost impossible to cull the fantasy from the fact.

No contemporary newspaper accounts of the Fourth of July parade remain. The Reverend John A. Sinclair, however, kept a diary during his stay in Skagway. For July 4, 1898, he wrote:

> In afternoon took snap shots of the procession. Soapy mounted
> was much in evidence. Went to wharf to hear people speak
> and was called upon to open with prayer on about 2 minutes
> notice; Went lest my refusal should be taken as an exhibition
> of national bigotry [Sinclair was Canadian]. Gov. Brady,
> Dr. Campbell, Church, Humbolt, Everest on platform. Was
> surprised at Gov. Brady's statement that Alaska's yet more
> noted for her agricultural resources than for her minerals. He
> should know.[42]

Curiously, when James Sinclair, the reverend's son, turned his father's diary, letters, and notes into a book entitled *Mission Klondike* in 1977, he misquoted his father as writing:

> I was called upon with less than two minutes notice, to open
> with prayer. For a moment I was disconcerted; but I complied
> lest my refusal as a Canadian should be taken as an exhibition
> of national bigotry. Soapy was much in evidence. He was seated
> on the platform along with Governor Brady, Dr. Campbell, and
> Messers. Church, Humbert and Everest.[43]

The misplacement of the sentence "Soapy was much in evidence," and the insertion of "He was seated on the platform along with Governor Brady, et al." calls into question much of the editing done by James in the rest of the book, and demonstrates the power that the legend exerted between 1898 and 1978, when James published the reverend's memoirs. A perusal of the younger Sinclair's bibliography indicates that the biographies of Smith by Collier and Westrate and Pierre Berton influenced how James Sinclair told the Soapy story.[44]

———

In the days preceding the Fourth, both the *Skaguay News* and the *Daily Alaskan* list "J. Smith" as the leader of the fourth—and last—division of the parade, assisted by one of his known henchmen, William Tener. The fourth division had four entrants: the Skaguay

Guards, the "Fitzhugh Lee," the Man of War Float, and J. H. Brooks's Pack Train. The "Fitzhugh Lee" was the name Smith had given to his live, caged eagle named after the confederate general. The first three of the four entries were all associated with Smith. He appears to have been successful in convincing only one other entrant—J. H. Brooks—to join his portion of the parade. Or possibly, the real organizers wished for the packer, with his herd of horses and all of their manure, to trail at the end—after the con man.[45]

To reinforce the fact that Smith did not lead the parade, both Skagway newspapers indicate that the Grand Marshal was outfitter Charles Everest, aided by Frank Burkhard and A. P. Tonig. All three had been prominent merchants since Skagway's very earliest days. In reality, Smith was the latecomer. The scheduled speakers were Walter Church, a real estate developer, and the new U.S. commissioner, Judge Charles Sehlbrede. The newspapers did not predict a visit by Governor Brady.[46] The governor had been in Skagway in February 1898 and again later while stumping for reappointment to his post. However, as Rev. John Sinclair notes in his diary of July 4, 1898, the governor did speak at the day's ceremonies. Brady had come to Skagway for an unscheduled trip to inspect the progress of the construction on the White Pass and Yukon Route railroad: his words at the Fourth of July celebration in what was then Alaska's largest city were no doubt spontaneous. A letter to his superior, the secretary of interior, is further evidence that Brady was there, as well as his noting that the town had far too many bunco artists.[47]

No contemporary newspaper descriptions of the parade survive. Issues of the *Daily Alaskan* do not exist between July 2 and July 11; the *Skaguay News*, which was a weekly paper at the time, published its first post-parade issue on July 9, a Saturday, holding up its usual Friday printing. By that time, everyone had forgotten the parade. All attention was indeed focused on Jefferson Randolph Smith, but not because he had been the leader of the parade.

Portrait of Soapy Smith, would-be
"boss" of Skagway. From the *Seattle
Post-Intelligencer*, March 5, 1898.

Soapy Smith as he appeared in early summer 1898.
From the *Seattle Post Intelligencer*, July 19, 1898.

Members of Soapy's gang standing in front of his saloon, Jeff Smith's Parlor, on July 4, 1898. Yukon Archives, E. J. Hamacher fonds (Margaret and Rolf Hougen collection), 2002/118, #1132.

The tent used by J. G. Price, attorney-at-law (at left) in Skagway in summer 1897. University of Washington Libraries, Special Collections, PH Collection 273.

People's Theater, Skagway, Alaska, April 8, 1898. Alaska State Library,
William R. Norton Collection, ASL-P226-841.

Drawing of Skagway looking west up Fifth and Sixth Streets. From the
Seattle Post-Intelligencer, March 5, 1898, p. 8.

J. M. Si Tanner, captain of the Safety Committee. Courtesy Skagway Museum.

Frank Clancy, city council member. From the *Daily Alaskan*, January 9, 1900. Drawing by author after a photograph.

Frank Reid, city engineer, town surveyor, and member of the Safety Committee. Drawing by author after a photograph.

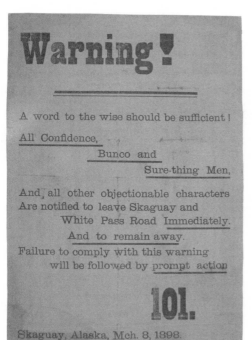

A photograph of the warning posted by the Committee of One Hundred and One on March 8, 1898. Alaska State Museum, Juneau, III-O-86.

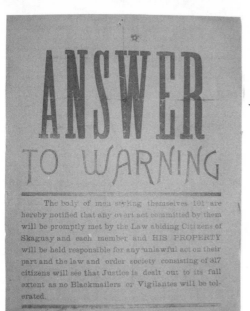

A photograph of the counterwarning posted by Soapy Smith on March 9, 1898. Alaska State Museum, Juneau, III-O-86.

The wharves of Skagway in 1901. J. Bernard Moore Family Papers. Album #1, UAF-1976-35-53, Archives, University of Alaska, Fairbanks.

Laying the railroad tracks down Broadway in June 1898. University of Washington Libraries, Special Collections, PH Collection 561.6, neg. no. UW 29735z.

A drawing of Soapy Smith, a Patriotic "High Mucky-Muck." From the *Denver Times,* June 12, 1898.

Carriage and pack train in a patriotic parade on May 1, 1898, Skagway, Alaska. Clallam County Historical Society, Port Angeles, Washington.

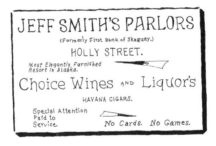

Advertisement for Jeff Smith's Parlor. From the *Skaguay News*, July 1, 1898.

Soapy Smith, July 4, 1898, on the streets of Skagway. Photograph reversed from that usually presented, after careful study of overviews of Skagway to determine correct orientation. Alaska State Library, William R. Norton Collection, Photographs, ca. 1890–1920, ASL-PCA-226-067.

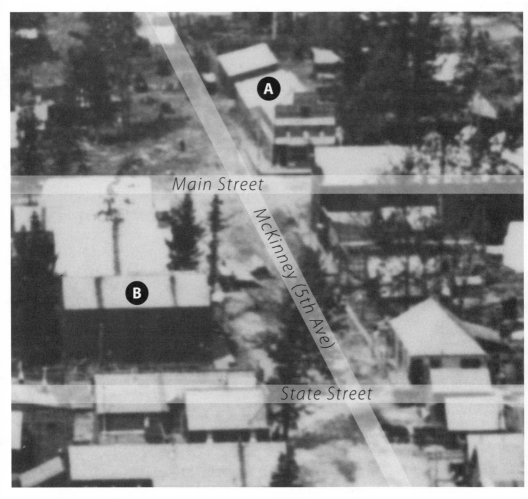

Overview of Skagway in June 1898. Building A is the two-story false-front
at the northwest corner of Fifth and Main. Building B is the two-story false
front at the southwest corner of Fifth and State. Both can be easily located
in the reversed version of the photograph of Soapy on the light gray horse
headed south on State Street. Note also that State Avenue is still blocked
north of Fifth by the mill bunkhouse, which was not moved until the fall
of 1898, thus explaining the black band on the right side of Sinclair's
photo of the mounted Soapy. Having the bunkhouse in the photo would
have raised too many questions about the legend. University of Alaska,
Fairbanks, Frank Barr Collection, 76-151-40, detail.

Smith on his gray horse, at the left, in the Fourth of July parade, riding with J. M. Brooks, the packer, providing further evidence that Soapy did not lead the parade. This photograph was probably taken by the Rev. John A. Sinclair and later sold to Arthur Pillsbury, who operated a photography studio in Skagway in 1900 called the Alaska View and Photo Company. Klondike Gold Rush National Historical Park, donated by Robert T. Whiting, KLGO-00532.

Photograph of Fitzhugh Lee, Smith's eagle, in his cage. Royal BC
Museum, British Columbia Archives, ZZ-95360.

J. D. Stewart with his poke of gold, July 1898. Alaska State Library, William R. Norton Collection, Photographs ca. 1890–1920, ASL-P226-090.

Detail of a photograph of the federal officers convention in Juneau, Alaska, on October 9, 1899: top left, Marshal John A. Shoup; bottom right, Charles A. Sehlbrede, U.S. commissioner. Alaska State Library, Alaska State Library Place File, ASL-Juneau-People.

Officials of the White Pass and Yukon Route railroad in the spring of 1898. Left to right, Samuel H. Graves, John Hislop, E. C. Hawkins, and Michael Heney. Yukon Archives, H. C. Barley fonds, #5409.

CHAPTER THREE

A Con Gone Wrong

[J. D.] Stewart, a native of Vancouver island, was headed home. A simple, guileless youth, he hastened to deposit his gold in the Skagway bank on his arrival, but his approach down the trail had not passed unnoticed. . . . He was . . . persuaded to withdraw his gold and take it to Jeff's Place for an appraisal.

Still clutching the pouch in his hand, he went out into the back lot for a look at Soapy's famous stuffed eagle. The gang crowded around Stewart and someone grabbed the pouch of gold from his hand. The customary fight ensued, and when Stewart picked himself up, the man who had grabbed the gold had disappeared through the hidden exit in the fence. For the boys it was just another day's work; for Stewart, it was a crushing finish to two years of hard labor, and he was not minded to accept it meekly.

He rushed to Marshal Taylor, who asked him if he could identify the man who had robbed him. When Stewart said he couldn't, Taylor told him there was nothing that could be done.

Frank G. Robinson and Beth Kay Harris, *Soapy Smith,*
King of the Frontier Con Men

The best and most authentic version of this incident on July 8, 1898, is the *Skaguay News* account dated that day, but actually published on July 9. It was written by one of the North's most gifted journalists, Elmer J. "Stroller" White, who was then editor of the *News* (appendix B). Almost all accounts authored after that time drew upon White's version as their ultimate source, as well as the elaboration of it by the competing *Daily Alaskan* on July 11, 1898. These stories were picked up by newspapers in Seattle, Victoria, San Francisco,

71

and Denver. Even Harry Suydam, who wrote the first nationally published story in 1901, relied upon the *Skaguay News* version for his account of the events of that fateful day.[1] A careful examination of more than one hundred accounts written since actually turns up no new first-hand testimony until 1952. The one important exception is the Rev. Sinclair's observations in his private papers.

The Rev. John A. Sinclair kept diary notations of what happened on July 8, as well as recorded the events in a letter to his wife three days later. It turns out that he also wrote an account on July 9, which he published on July 22 in the *Toronto Globe* as "'Soapy' Smith's End." Many early authors were probably aware of this important version of the story, but did not acknowledge it. It was not listed in the bibliographies that began to appear after midcentury, but a careful examination of sources reveals that Sinclair's unattributed article had a lasting effect not only on the way people would perceive the facts of the events of July 8 but on the way the legend would evolve over the following years.

Other important eyewitnesses would come forward after half a century had passed. For instance, packer Calvin H. Barkdull, as a principal actor in the events of that day, and as a friend of miner John D. Stewart, added significant detail to that reported by the *Skaguay News* report in his vivid and detailed reminiscence in the *Alaska Sportsman* of June 1952. Most early biographers seemed to have missed Barkdull's story. In addition, none of the biographers seem to have noticed a first-hand account by the victim, miner J. D. Stewart, that appeared in the December 27, 1898, edition of the *Tacoma News*.[2] These five accounts form the basis of the following discussion.

———

Calvin Barkdull worked for packer Charles H. DeWitt on the Brackett Wagon Road, hauling supplies and grubstakes by mule team to the summit of White Pass. On Thursday, July 7, he gave British Columbia miner John D. Stewart a ride down the wagon road, helped the newly rich miner find a good, safe hotel, and recommended he put his gold poke in a strong safe. Stewart had been in the Klondike regions for eighteen months, bringing out a poke of gold dust and nuggets worth a little less than three thousand dollars.[3]

Stewart took Barkdull's sage advice and deposited the poke, minus one hundred dollars for expenses, at Kaufman's Store, located at 509 Broadway, next door to the Burkhard Hotel where he was staying. Then he went out to get a bath, a good meal, and to celebrate a little.[4]

Stewart himself admits he made the biggest mistake of his life the next morning. He wandered up Sixth Avenue and into Jeff Smith's Parlor. There he met two men who introduced themselves as the "Reverend" Charles Bowers and John D. Foster. Unknown to Stewart, these men were prominent members of Soapy's gang from the Denver years. Both seemed anxious for news of the Klondike region, and they plied him with drinks for information. At one point, they urged him into the backyard to watch the bartender feed the pet eagle named the Fitzhugh Lee. This animal had been used as an entry in the Fourth of July parade. According to Stewart's first-hand account in the *Tacoma Times*, he refused.[5]

At this point the small group was joined by a third Smith confederate, Van Triplett ("Old Man Tripp"), who had been with Smith in Denver since the 1880s. Triplett complained that he had lost money gambling, but he had paid the dealer five dollars to show him a winning trick, and he was ready to teach the three of them for the same privilege. Stewart, wisely, passed on this offer, but pulled out the $87 left in his pocket. Foster took it from him, placed it in a box, and announced that he had won it from the miner.[6]

In the newspaper reporting of the December 1898 trials of Charles Bowers, John D. Foster, and Van Triplett, John Stewart testified what happened next.

> I told Foster I should hold him for the money, and the old man, Van Triplett, said we acted as we could not trust him, and gave some of the money back;
>
> And then said he would give us a chance to win it, so Foster turned the right card and started to give him the money, but [Triplett] said, "Supposing you had bet that in earnest, did you have the money to put up?"
>
> Foster said, "No," and [Triplett] turning to me said, "You have the money."
>
> And I said no, I did not have any money: that he [Triplett] took it all;
>
> But he [Foster] said, "You have some dust," and wanted me

to get it just to show the old man that we had the money in case
the bet had been a real one.

Bowers and I went to Kaufman's store to get the money and
Van Triplett and Foster remained behind. We came back with
the dust and I unrolled it and showed them the sack, and the
old man [Triplett] said he did not know if it was gold, and:

Bowers said, "Open it and show it to him, as he don't know
gold dust when he sees it."

But I did not open it, and [I was] just about to roll it up
again, when Foster grabbed it and handing it to the old man
said, "Git!"

And I started to grab the old man when they held me and
said if I made any noise it would not be well for me.

I pulled away from them and started after the old man, but
could not see him;

And then went across the street and asked a party where
there was an officer: that I had been robbed of $3,000 by some
men over there.[7]

It turned out that Stewart had $2,670 in his gold poke. He quickly
demanded to be taken to the law enforcement authority in town.[8]

U.S. Deputy Marshal Sylvester Taylor had been assigned to Skagway in the wake of the murder of Andy McGrath and James Rowan,
with Deputy Marshal D. H. McInness still stationed in Dyea. Taylor, unfortunately, had as wretched a reputation for incompetence
as Commissioner John U. Smith. All commissioners, marshals, and
deputy marshals at the time made their living off the fines and fees
assessed prisoners who pleaded guilty, or those who were fined when
found guilty at a trial. The officers were not paid a salary. Therefore,
prison or death sentences were not very lucrative, as they yielded no
cash fees. Arrangements with the local sporting community, sometimes, could be more lucrative for an unscrupulous law enforcement
official, who could be bribed to look the other way.

A number of Skagway and Dyea citizens had become concerned
about Commissioner Smith's misuse of his fee schedules. He had
been investigated by a U.S. Justice examiner, James S. Easley-Smith,
in March 1898, and removed from office. His replacement, Charles

Sehlbrede, arrived in Dyea in May 1898 and had been making considerable headway in gaining the respect of the law-abiding community. He had not yet gotten around to having U.S. Marshal John Shoup in Sitka replace his deputy in Skagway, but that was on his agenda.[9]

At the marshal's office, the corrupt Taylor took Stewart's complaint, but then explained that there was nothing he could do about it. The gold was gone. He advised the miner to go back to the Klondike and dig up another three thousand dollars. Taylor left and was later seen supervising some carpentry work being done on his new house.[10]

J. D. Stewart looked around for help and saw none. He was in a strange town among strange people, and all of the money he had made in the last eighteen months was gone. Then he saw the only man he knew, Cal Barkdull, the packer who had given him a ride down the mountain from White Pass. Perhaps Barkdull would listen.[11]

Captain Tanner, one of the pioneers of Skaguay, was chairman of the Law and Order Association. He called a committee and sent for "Soapy." Full of bravado, "Soapy" appeared. Captain Tanner told him that the robbery had taken place in his saloon, that he was responsible for it, and must disgorge the money. Smith refused. The Captain expected nothing better.

"'Soapy,'" said he, "let me tell you something. Your reign in this town is over. This isn't a camp, but a city; and the citizens mean to clean you out of town."

"Soapy" shut his square jaws. "Do your damndest," he growled. Then the fight was on in earnest. Work came to a standstill. Able-bodied citizens were organized into militia. Guards were posted, and no "Soapyite" was allowed to leave town while a thorough search was made for the Klondiker's gold.

Harry L. Suydam, "The Reign of 'Soapy' Smith"

After being brushed off by Deputy Marshal Sylvester Taylor, J. D. Stewart did not give up. Encountering the only other man he knew in Skagway, he described the crime that had been committed upon

him. Packer Calvin Barkdull did not know what to do by himself, but
he knew people who could take action. He walked his new friend to
his boss's office, that of packer George DeWitt. When he heard the
story, DeWitt took Stewart and Barkdull down to Charles Sperry's
dock for yet another recital.

Sperry owned the warehouse where DeWitt stored the goods he
packed over the trail to Lake Bennett. There the men who had been
heading north could build boats and begin floating them down to
the Yukon River. Sperry was also chairman of the city council, as well
as one of the original members of the Committee of One Hundred
and One. Hanging around Sperry's warehouse on this fateful morning were two other founding members of the committee, Frank Reid
and J. M. Tanner, as well as grocer John Kalem, who owned the store
across the street from the Burkhard Hotel. All four influential members of the community heard the story at the same time.[12]

Kalem dashed off to spread the word. Sperry, Reid, and Tanner
immediately organized an executive meeting of the Committee of
One Hundred and One. By 10:00 a.m., thirteen members of the
committee met behind closed doors to figure out how to handle this
latest dereliction of duty by the ineffective federal law enforcement
officials of Alaska. The committee was joined by four new members:
WP&YR construction superintendent Michael Heney; chief engineer
Erastus C. Hawkins; and Hawkins's assistant, civil engineer John Hislop; as well as visiting official Samuel H. Graves, who was general vice
president for the American branch of Close Brothers Company, the
British corporation that was building the railroad. The committee
members promptly pressed into service the one newcomer and outsider as a supposedly neutral party to officiate at their meeting: Samuel H. Graves. He had been in Skagway only three days.[13]

The recent conflict in trying to get the right-of-way approved down
the middle of Broadway had left the city council, and the merchants,
many of whom ran the Committee of One Hundred and One (including Tanner), at serious odds with each other. The choice of Graves,
a total stranger to town, but soon to be a very important business
leader, seemed, at the time, to be a brilliant move. It is doubtful that
any committee member objected.[14]

Graves, himself, was the only dissenting voice to his being chosen as the chairman of the meeting. He recognized the fact that he did not have a clue as to what was happening. He had stopped briefly in Skagway for only a day on July 2, and then had gone up the line to inspect the progress of the railroad construction. He had been back in Skagway since July 6, and the only people he knew were "the three H's"—Heney, Hawkins, and Hislop. He would take all his cues from those three men.[15]

The group of seventeen voted that midmorning of July 8 to call for a general meeting of all concerned citizens at eight o'clock that evening: that is, they reconvened a citizens' meeting, what had once been termed the Committee of One Hundred and One. They set the meeting place at E. O. Sylvester's building at Third and State, known as the Klondike Trading Company. This was a meeting hall they ordinarily used for city council meetings when they expected an audience. They adjourned and sent out the word.[16]

Jefferson Randolph Smith was about to make a very big mistake.

———————

J. M. Tanner, who had remained in the background until now, began to emerge as a real leader of his community. Someone placed a telephone call to Dyea and summoned U.S. Commissioner Sehlbrede. The town waited for the judge to find a boat and come to Skagway. Fearing another lynch mob, not of a bartender but of three sure-thing men, they could do nothing but talk directly to Smith, at whose saloon the gold was taken and who was known to have some influence over the three confidence men. Si Tanner, Frank Reid, and other members of Skagway's Safety Committee (that is, its *ad hoc* police force) had ideas about how to diffuse the powder keg burning around Soapy Smith. Harry Suydam described the confrontation between Tanner and Smith in the quotation at the beginning of this section.

Suydam became the first of the legend-makers to infuse Smith with an aura of kingliness, in his 1901 article for Frank Leslie's Popular Monthly. Putting the words "Your reign in this town is over" in the mouth of Si Tanner lends weight to the assertion that Smith had more power than he actually possessed. As shown earlier, Smith and other members of the sporting element had by this time largely been robbed of their power—if they ever had any—and any rule that he managed was strictly within the boundaries of his own sector of the community: the dance halls, gambling dens, and dives on Fifth and Sixth avenues, a demographic Suydam was perhaps more familiar with than others of the business community. Suydam had, in fact, not lived in Skagway since February, and could only repeat second- or third-hand hearsay in his version of events—or, more probable, invent dialogue that was never spoken.[17]

By four o'clock that afternoon, Commissioner Sehlbrede had managed to navigate Lynn Canal and arrive in Skagway. Meeting with representatives of the city council, the Committee of One Hundred and One, and the Safety Committee, the commissioner was briefed on the day's happenings. He placed Sylvester Taylor under house arrest for dereliction of duty. Although he did not have the authority to deputize the Safety Committee, Sehlbrede could appoint a special federal officer, and promptly named Si Tanner. Hoping that Smith would pay more attention to himself than he had to members of the Safety Committee, Sehlbrede paid a visit to the proprietor of Jeff Smith's Parlor. He took half a dozen members of the ad hoc police force with him, probably Captain Tanner included. The commissioner met with the same results as Tanner, with Smith repeating that he would "stand by the boys" and not return what had been fairly won in a game of chance.[18]

By this time, Soapy Smith was uncharacteristically drunk. Later chroniclers state that he encountered Frank Reid in a crowd during the afternoon and called him out, wishing to shoot him down. According to the legend, Reid smiled and indicated he was unarmed. Smith swore and shoved his way off through the crowd, continuing to work up his bravado.[19]

This portion of the legend first appears in the *Denver Times*, a newspaper notoriously "soft" on Soapy. Its source was Louis Pratt, identified as a Denver attorney. Pratt could not be located in any of the contemporary city directories, but he was placed in a sensational gun battle between police and religious fanatics on December 8, 1908, in Kansas City, Missouri. Supporting a "holy roller" named John Sharp who called himself "Adam God," Pratt and his five children were caught in a hail of gunfire with police. His thirteen-year-old daughter, Lola, died on the scene; Pratt passed away of gun wounds two days later. This self-styled religious group had been in Colorado before coming to Kansas City and causing trouble.[20]

Louis Pratt, the *Denver Times*'s source for the anecdote about Smith meeting Reid earlier in the afternoon, was not a real estate and corporate attorney, but probably a defense lawyer. If he was a friend of Smith's, as suggested, the report is biased, like many of the stories that came from Denver newspapers showing Smith to be a legendary figure.

Back in Skagway on July 8, 1898, promptly at 8:00 p.m., the Close Brothers Company vice president, Samuel Graves, called the mass public meeting to order in E. O. Sylvester's Klondike Trading Company building at the southeast corner of Third and State. It was an order that even Graves's commanding presence—big build, square jaw, resounding voice, and air of authority—could not control. Although Smith had wisely chosen to stay in his saloon, his cronies riddled the audience, and soon had the hall in a state of chaos, peppering Graves with irrelevant questions and bringing up issues with no bearing on the theft. Cooler heads quickly brought the meeting to an end. Because the hall was too small for the large crowd that attended the meeting, it was proposed that they reconvene at 9:00 p.m. The new meeting place was located on the wharf at the southern end of State Avenue, in a warehouse owned by E. O. Sylvester and Emory Valentine, the brother-in-law of J. M. Tanner. It was here that most goods were transferred to ships going to Juneau, earning the wharf the nickname of "Juneau Wharf."[21]

A few executive members of the Committee of One Hundred and One, seeing that Samuel Graves's lack of knowledge of Smith's cohorts among the spectators at Sylvester's hall kept an orderly city council meeting from occurring, managed to appoint a new chair. Choosing Tom Whitten, the manager of the Golden North Hotel, also a relatively neutral citizen, to conduct the meeting, the committee thought they could have better control. Thoroughly tired of meetings altogether, Special Officer Si Tanner and Safety Committee member Frank Reid volunteered to stand guard at the entrance to the wharf. They would allow only solid citizens to approach the warehouse. They took with them railroad laborers Jesse Murphy and John

Landers, as guards. Reid armed himself with a revolver. Between the four of them, the Committee believed that most honest community members would be recognized, and that the disruptive characters would be kept at bay.[22]

Still drunk, and not understanding how badly outnumbered he was, Smith gathered his loyal followers together and decided to attend the 9:00 city council meeting himself. He started for the Juneau Wharf.

Describing Soapy's march toward his fate, the Reverend described the scene for the *Toronto Globe*:

> "Soapy" became more and more desperate as he saw that
> the time had come "to bluff the people or get," stiffened up
> his nerve with whiskey and morphine, and about 9:30 seized
> a Winchester and started for a wharf where an indignation
> meeting of the citizens was being held. As he passed down
> State street, swearing that he would "teach these damned sons
> of b——" a lesson, he presented a terrible sight. Remembering
> the often expressed conviction during the day that the leader
> of the gang must be dealt with to-night, seeing the excitement
> of the people, and Soapy's own sense of danger as evidenced by
> his frequent presentation of his gun and warnings to the crowd
> following him to keep back or he'd shoot, I felt that "Soapy"
> was making his last terrible bluff.[23]

———

Soapy advanced toward Reid. The two men stood close to each other, only an arm's length apart. Not a word was spoken as they waited to see who would make the first move.

Then Soapy yelled, "I should've got rid of you months ago."

At the same moment, he brought the Winchester down off his arm. Reid grabbed the muzzle with his left hand, and with his free hand he drew a .38 from his pocket.

"My god, don't shoot!" screamed Soapy.

Reid pulled the trigger. The hammer fell with a distinct click, but there was no explosion. The cartridge had been faulty.

With that reprieve, in a single moment that seemed to stretch on forever, Soapy jerked the rifle from Reid's hand, as he pulled the trigger, Reid fired, too. Two shots exploded, but they sounded as if they were one.

Soapy's bullet smashed in Reid's groin. Reid's hit Soapy in the arm.

But the two men were still on their feet, still firing, still right on top of each other. Gun barrels flashed, once, twice, three times. The noises were rapid and large.

All at once there was silence. Reid had fallen facedown, breathing but with blood and life itself rushing from him. Soapy was on his back surrounded by a spreading circle of blood, a bullet in his heart. The king of Skagway was dead.

Howard Blum, *The Floor of Heaven*

The Rev. Sinclair wrote his observations within twenty-four hours of watching Soapy killed. Howard Blum wrote his version of the death 112 years later. This event does not vary in the telling in more than a hundred versions of it mostly because they can all be traced back to one version, that which appeared in the July 8, 1898, publication of the *Skaguay News* (actually published on July 9). Supplemented in its next issue on July 15, the expanded story took up eight columns spread over two pages. Even Harry Suydam's 1901 publication in *Frank Leslie's Popular Monthly* and Samuel Graves's report written to his superiors in the days following the killing of Smith recount the events essentially the same as they were told by editor E. J. "Stroller" White in the *Skaguay News*. The version told by the *Daily Alaskan*, when it resumed publication on July 11, 1898, added no new details and reiterated virtually the same information. When newspapers around the country picked up the story, they all copied or paraphrased the *Skaguay News*.[24]

One of the most succinct accounts, and probably the most accurate because it was vetted by lawyers on both sides of the conflict, was recorded in the appeal case of *U.S. v. Turner Jackson*, one of the men who accompanied Smith to the Juneau Wharf that night.

> The record shows that soon thereafter [9:30 p.m.] Smith
> and his associates, including the plaintiff in error, Jackson,
> arrived at the approach to the wharf, where they came to a
> halt, and then started forward,—Smith being in the lead, with

a Winchester rifle in his hand, cursing and swearing, using
violent and obscene language,—and ordered the assembled
citizens to get off the wharf, and with oaths, threatened to
drive every one off. Smith continued right along through
the center of the wharf (which was about 16 feet wide) for
about 60 feet, going by Tanner and Murphy, and when he got
opposite Reed [*sic*] he wheeled around and struck at Reed with
his gun. Shooting immediately occurred between Reed and
Smith, resulting in the immediate death of Smith, and mortally
wounding Reed.[25]

A little more than two weeks after the summer solstice, the light at
that time of the evening in Skagway would still have been sufficient
to read a newspaper without the aid of artificial light, but the sun
would have set below the mountains to the northwest. Approaching
the wharf, Smith, by his actions, apparently saw only Frank Reid, for
he ignored the other guards and walked straight up to the man he
had challenged earlier in the afternoon. Reid had fought the Nez
Perce for the Army in the 1870s in Montana and Idaho, had served
as a deputy marshal in Idaho in the 1880s, and had killed a man in
self-defense in Yamhill, Oregon. He knew how to handle a firearm.
He also knew how to conduct himself when threatened by a man that
he regarded as a criminal. Reid challenged the con man, telling him
he could go no farther; Smith held his ground.[26]

Reid grabbed the barrel of Smith's rifle, pushed it towards the
ground, and drew his pistol. Smith fired his rifle, the ball passing
through Reid's groin and right hip.[27]

Up to this point, all accounts agree. The *Skaguay News* and most of
the later versions cited above state that Reid and Smith fired two or
three shots at practically the same time, one going through Smith's
heart, and the other through one of his legs. Both men fell, Smith
dead; Reid mortally wounded.[28]

An alternate and rarely told version states that another shooter
was involved in the killing of Smith. Another important witness, Samuel H. Graves, president of the American branch of Close Brothers
Company, which owned the WP&YR, said he was fifty yards from the
entrance to the wharf when Smith "passed near enough to touch me."

He saw Soapy's men following about twenty-five yards behind the con man. As these men passed, they "shut out my view," so he climbed up on the boardwalk "and saw Soapy go up to Reid."[29] Graves, following the lead of the newspaper article, then detailed the number of shots fired, indicated that Soapy pumped a couple of shots into Reid's stomach, that one of Reid's bullets went "clean through" Soapy's heart. He stated that it was impossible to tell who fired first, and declared that everything happened in an instant.

Graves then observed a railroad laborer, Jesse Murphy, spring forward. Murphy "snatched Soapy's Winchester from the dead man's hands," and swung it back as Smith's men approached. With the rifle trained on first one and then another of the gang, the gang's rush to attack the wharf was stalled, and then they "broke and fled."[30]

Sam Graves was not the only man to notice Jesse Murphy grab up Soapy's rifle. The Rev. John A. Sinclair, who stood about seventy-five yards up State Street, provides a third, and perhaps more accurate, description of events. He noted in his July 8 diary entry:

> Soapy had come down State St armed with a Winchester to
> disperse the meeting and show them who he was. He struck
> Reid one of the guards who fired but his revolvers missed
> fire. Soapy then shot him in the groin and before falling Reid
> fired three shots at him, one taking effect in the leg. Murphy
> another guard wrenched Soapy's rifle from him & shot him
> through his heart & Soapy's followers froze for a moment.
> Before the friends & dispersed on hearing on all orders the cry
> to "all citizens get your arms."[31]

Was it really Jesse Murphy who shot and killed Soapy Smith? Jeff Smith, Soapy's great-grandson, who has spent his entire life researching his ancestor, believes it was.[32] Besides citing Portland newspapers, Smith also points to a communication by Samuel Steele, commander of the Northwest Mounted Police at the Canadian border, who on July 11, 1898, confirmed Sinclair's eyewitness account. He wrote his commanding officer saying that the man who killed Soapy Smith was Jesse Murphy, not Frank Reid as had been reported in the newspapers. Steele's source was J. M. Tanner, by then universally accepted as the new U.S. deputy marshal of Skagway.[33]

Who was Jesse Murphy? The *Portland Oregonian* called him a carpenter from Portland. Sam Graves claimed he was an Irish railroad laborer, and depicted him as having a heavy accent.[34] That suggests he may have been a recent immigrant. He cannot be found in any U.S. censuses or genealogy databanks. Nothing more of substance can be determined about him. His very anonymity marks him as one of the hundreds of working-class men that the WP&YR hired in the spring and summer of 1898 to build the railroad from Skagway to Whitehorse.

As the years went by, rumors continued to surface that someone other than Reid had killed Smith. In the 1930s, tourism promoter Martin Itjen hinted that the bullets in Smith's heart were a different caliber than the one in his groin. Eyewitness Matthew Sundeen, forty-three years later in 1941, stated that he was in a hardware store at the head of the Juneau Wharf at the time of the shooting. He said he saw Jesse Murphy fire the fatal rifle shot, corroborating the early accounts.[35] Biographers Robertson and Harris in 1961 noted that some people believed the caliber of the bullets dug out of Smith did not match those fired by Reid. Howard Clifford, in his 1997 biography of Smith, named Murphy as Smith's possible killer.[36] It was a story that would not be laid to rest.

———

With Samuel Graves, Rev. Sinclair, and Soapy's gang as witnesses, why did none of them name Murphy as Smith's killer? Dr. C. W. Cornelius, who conducted one of the two autopsies of Smith's body for Skagway's coroner's jury on July 9, 1898, wrote to his Portland partner, dentist H. R. Littlefield, that it was Reid's bullet that killed Smith. He stated that although Murphy did indeed fire at Smith, the bullet was not fatal.[37]

The "Smith-Reid" gunfight was over in about twenty seconds. The shots—who fired them and the actual number of them will forever be in dispute—had all been fired, and the event had become history. At this point, all of the eyewitnesses would repeat what little they did see to the reporters of the *Skaguay News:* it was a shoot-out between Soapy Smith and Frank Reid.

———

Whoever killed him—Frank Reid or Jesse Murphy—Soapy Smith was dead. As all of this was happening, Smith's followers had confronted Murphy and the other two guards. Si Tanner later told his family that the barrel of the gun that Smith cohort Jackson Turner stuck in his face looked as big as a stovepipe. He did not back off. When they heard the gunshots and saw Smith crumble to the wooden planks of the wharf, Jackson and the rest of Smith's men turned tail and ran. Tanner rolled Smith's prone body over to find a gaping hole in his side and sightless eyes staring up at him. He then fell on his knees next to the fallen Reid, and turned him over.[38]

"I'm hurt bad, Cap," Frank told him, clutching a stream of blood to his belly.[39]

Jesse Murphy and John Landers joined Tanner and Reid at the foot of the Juneau Wharf as Matthew Sundeen ran up from the hardware store near the wharf. The crowd from the meeting at the end of the Juneau Wharf came out to see what had caused the commotion. Sam Graves and the Rev. Sinclair crowded near the fallen body almost immediately. Frank Reid was a much respected man about town, a founder of the community, the city surveyor, the person who had done a yeoman's job of laying out the townsite, making it possible for them all to stake town lots. He was a founder of the Committee of One Hundred and One and the Safety Committee. He was a man who had helped maintain law and order and resolve inevitable conflicts, and he had sacrificed a great deal of personal time and money for the benefit of the community. Blood soaked the ramp leading up the wharf built by Si Tanner's brother-in-law, a wharf that benefited the entire town with its lucrative trade from Juneau and points farther south, trade that would not have been possible without the entrepreneurial leadership and gumption shown by Frank Reid in the early days of Skagway's formation.[40]

"You got him, Frank," Tanner assured Reid. "Smith's dead."[41]

According to Tanner family tradition, Si glanced at Murphy, Landers, and Sundeen—and possibly Graves and Sinclair—daring them to call him a liar.[42]

According to all first-hand accounts, Tanner quickly took charge, ordering Cal Barkdull and A. L. Remick to carry Frank Reid to the White Pass hospital. Looking around the crowd, he named his deputies, and ordered them to get arms. Tanner headed north along State Street towards the Moore Hotel to borrow a Winchester rifle from Captain William Moore, a neighbor at Fifth and State. At Clayson's Hardware Store at the corner of Fourth and State, he asked the owner to loan out rifles and pistols to his new deputies. Si Tanner began to round up Smith's gang and clean out Skagway, once and for all.[43]

Although in future years, Tanner would refuse to take any credit as Skagway's hero in the days that followed the shooting, it was clear that more than one man had been involved in bringing Smith to his end, just as many more than one would be involved in creating a legend out of the death of a petty confidence man.

CHAPTER FOUR

A Lie Agreed Upon

That said Smith came to his death by reason of a pistol wound piercing the heart.

That said wound was the result of a pistol shot fired by Frank H. Reid who now lies in the Bishop Rowe Hospital of Skaguay, dangerously wounded from shots received at the hands of the deceased, the said Smith.

That such shooting on the part of the said Reid was in self defense, and in the opinion of this jury entirely justifiable.

Findings of the Coroner's Jury convened at 9:00
a.m., July 9, 1898, under the jurisdiction of U.S.
Commissioner C. A. Sehlbrede, Skagway, Alaska

One of the major schools of American ideology after 1870 held that this country derived its moral power from its populist character. A group of writers emerged around the turn of the century called the "red-blooded realists"—among them were James Fenimore Cooper, Owen Wister, and Bret Harte—who espoused masculine violence in literature and journalism as the legitimate monopoly of the privileged class, and the idea that middle- and upper-class native-born, white males constituted America's "natural aristocracy."[1] Their objective was to legitimize democracy but discourage the masses of immigrants and anarchists from gaining control. The well-educated, prosperous, and morally superior made better leaders of men than those who spoke English with an accent or did unskilled labor.

Richard Slotkin voices this turn-of-the-century trend in popular writing when he states:

The West of the Progressive Era was recognized by
contemporary journalists, sociologists, and red-blooded
novelists as a particularly useful setting for the exploration of

such matters as [race and labor wars] . . . What made western
class struggles important were their high levels of violence,
their combination of agrarian and industrial aspects, and
the fact that the opposed classes were led and predominately
constituted by native-born whites.[2]

That ideology should be kept in mind as one considers what the
respectable businessmen of Skagway were thinking when they took
matters into their own hands on July 8, 1898. They believed that
anarchists in the form of the town's gambling element were exerting too much influence on Deputy Marshal Sylvester Taylor and the
Daily Alaskan. In the newspaper story that followed Smith's death, the
violence that redeemed or restored order to Skagway took the form
of a shoot-out between a brave Skagway city founder and a notorious
con man instead of a struggle between several town factions over the
control of City Hall. Because the American frontier myth could not
allow an immigrant Irish laborer to redeem the lawless Skagway (the
wilderness), the native-born white male, the gunfighter, and interme-
diary between lawlessness and civilization (Frank Reid), could and
did overcome the forces of chaos (the Soapy Smith Gang).

This ideology was so deeply ingrained that the editors of the Skagway newspapers, the *Toronto Globe*, the West Coast and Denver newspapers, and the legions of reporters that followed espoused the legend
and the myth it supported wholeheartedly: Frank Reid liberated lawless Skagway from gang leader Soapy Smith. Skagway now was free of
crime.

————

One of the first people to write the story of Soapy Smith's death,
other than the newspaper reporters in Skagway, Alaska, was the Rev.
John A. Sinclair. Besides being an impeccable and independent witness, a man who had not taken any position on the townsite controversy or the right-of-way issue, Sinclair kept a faithful diary and wrote
prodigiously. He was a superb amateur photographer. His interest in
reforming those who were sinful, combined with his flair for captur-
ing images on paper and photographic negatives, provides us with
some of the best first-hand evidence of Jefferson Randolph Smith
in the last two months of his life. It is from Sinclair that we have

accounts independent of the local and coastal newspaper stories, a number of newspaper clippings predating July 8, 1898, that would not otherwise exist, and four photographs of Smith and his friends at the Fourth of July parade.

The Reverend Sinclair came to Skagway from Spencerville, Ontario, arriving on May 20, 1898. He worked for the British Presbyterian Ministries, his initial assignment to relieve the Rev. Robert M. Dickey, who had been serving in Skagway preparatory to work in British Columbia and Yukon territories. His duty in Alaska dismayed him; he had little love for Americans or for American clergymen, finding them coarse, greedy, and selfish, as is readily evident by his diary entries and letters to his wife. He presided over the funeral for Jefferson Randolph Smith when two other ministers declined to do so. That he had refused to meet Smith and begin the con man's reformation preyed on his mind to such an extent that the gambler became almost an obsession with the clergyman in the later months of 1898 and 1899.[3]

Sinclair wrote his first eyewitness account of the July 8, 1898, events in his diary, meant obviously as a personal record and reminder for later writings. These later writings took three forms: a letter to the editor of the *Toronto Globe* detailing the events of July 8, along with some background material; a letter to his wife on July 11; and a longer, more detailed manuscript for the London-based magazine, *The Strand*. An analysis of these four versions, from the same author, shows an evolution in the community's understanding of events, as well as Sinclair's influence on the town's moral conscience, a province over which he believed he had a right.[4]

Sinclair's July 8 diary entry, quoted in chapter 3, is the first, and most important account of the event. In it, he names Jesse Murphy as the man who killed Soapy Smith.

On Saturday, July 9, 1898, Sinclair penned a letter or article to the editor of the *Toronto Globe*, the newspaper nearest his hometown, and he promptly sent if off on that day's ship, before public opinion could change his mind. Significantly, of the biographies that provide bibliographies, none mention this article, including even Sinclair's son, James M. Sinclair, who published a much-edited version of his father's diaries and letters. Because Sinclair's article was published in a Canadian newspaper, it is possible that most later authors missed it.[5]

What is important about Sinclair's version is that it does not copy from the *Skaguay News* account dated July 8, 1898 (published on July 9, after Sinclair mailed his article). It is a fresh and independent version by an eyewitness. When taken together with his diary entry and the letter he wrote to his wife on July 11, we see an account untainted by the impressions given by what other eyewitness thought they saw. Sinclair tells the story eloquently in the following excerpt:

> But "Soapy" became more and more desperate as he saw that the time had come "to bluff the people or get," stiffened up his nerve with whiskey and morphine, and about 9:30 seized a Winchester and started for a wharf where an indignation meeting of the citizens was being held. As he passed down State street, swearing that he would "teach these damned sons of b——"[6] a lesson, he presented a terrible sight. Remembering the often expressed conviction during the day that the leader of the gang must be dealt with to-night, seeing the excitement of the people, and Soapy's own sense of his danger as evidenced by his frequent presentation of his gun and warnings to the crowd following him to keep back or he'd shoot, I felt that "Soapy" was making his last terrible bluff. In a few moments I saw the flashes and heard the reports of four or five shots in quick succession. "Soapy" had encountered a guard of five men that had been detailed to hold the approach to the wharf where the indignation meeting was being held and struck Frank Reid over the head with the barrel of his rifle. Reid warded off the blow with his left forearm, in which the stroke made an ugly wound, drew his revolver and aimed at his assailant. But the revolver missed fire. In an instant a bullet from Soapy's rifle entered Reid's groin and passed through his body paralyzing his right leg.
>
> ### Reid Brings Down His Man
>
> But Reid, standing on one leg, shot "Soapy" three times before he himself fell, once in the leg, once grazed his arm and once in the chest. The last shot penetrated the left [and] side

punctured both lungs, passed through the descending aorta near the heart, causing instant death. Both men fell to the ground at almost the same instant, and just as another shot was fired at "Soapy" from his own rifle, which had been wrenched from his grasp.[7]

What is interesting about this account is its difference from the one Sinclair had penned just the night before in his diary. In less than twenty-four hours, Sinclair went from naming Jesse Murphy as the man who had wrenched away Soapy's rifle and had fired the fatal shot to an anonymous person wrenching the rifle from Smith's grasp, and the possessor firing a nonlethal shot at Smith's corpse. The story had already started to change as Sinclair talked to other eyewitnesses.

To whom had he listened on the morning of July 9?

According to his first diary entry of that day and a letter he wrote to his wife on July 11, he went to the coroner's inquest, where it was determined that Smith had died of a wound "the result of a pistol fired by one Frank H. Reid." That was the official, legal finding of the six court-appointed jurors. As a minister of the church, Rev. Sinclair, no matter what he personally or morally believed, could not say otherwise. He had to take the official line. As Napoleon once said, "History is a lie agreed upon," and those six businessmen of Skagway, on the testimony of the witnesses called before the jury, decided that the killer of Soapy Smith was a man who acted in self-defense and now lay dying of his wounds.

The six jurors were Frank F. Clark, manager of the Burkhard Hotel; Antone Laumeister, owner of the Alaska Meat Market; Godfrey Chealander, who operated a tobacco store on Broadway; Alfred E. Cleveland, owner of a freighting company since August 1897; and citizens William O. Henn and C. F. Niece. The people who testified to the jury were eyewitnesses J. M. Tanner and Jesse Murphy; D. C. Brownell (who operated Clayson's Hardware Store); O. F. Laird; J. F. Smith; undertaker E. R. Peoples; and physicians C. W. Cornelius and Fenton B. Whiting, who had examined Smith's body.[8]

It is obvious that during that morning of testimony, after hearing the testimony of eyewitnesses Si Tanner and Jesse Murphy and two doctors who conducted autopsies, the six jurors concluded that

Frank Reid's bullet—not Murphy's—killed Soapy Smith. Although Murphy had claimed to fire the fatal bullet, and Rev. Sinclair had named him as the shooter in his diary, not to mention that Si Tanner told Sam Steele that Murphy had killed Soapy, the jury decided otherwise.[9] Two possibilities exist for this finding: Murphy indeed fired a nonfatal shot; or Murphy did indeed kill the unarmed Smith, but the jury, made up of Reid's peers, wished to recognize Frank Reid as Smith's killer.

Ignoring for a moment the first possible reason, why would twelve leading citizens of Skagway—Commissioner C. A. Sehlbrede; J. M. Tanner, a man who would shortly become a U.S. deputy marshal; two physicians with impeccable reputations; a minister of God; and six jurors sworn to carry out justice—agree to lie to the newspapers and the public about what happened on the night of July 8, 1898? What purpose did it serve to determine that Frank Reid, not Jesse Murphy, was Smith's killer?

There were a number of very good reasons, all of which made sense to the middle-class businessmen that constituted the coroner's jury.

1. Smith led a gang that numbered anywhere from about twenty to forty members, and all of whom felt themselves above the law. Toughs, in particular, would not be above threatening or harming the person who had killed their leader. Lengthy vendetta trails were widely known for Billy Atrum Bonney, better known as Billy the Kid, and his killer, Pat Garrett; Jesse James and his assassin, Bob Ford; Wyatt Earp and the killers of his brother, Morgan; and a whole host of lesser known figures. Even as heroic a figure as Wild Bill Hickok had died at the hands of a glory-seeker who simply wanted to be known as the man who killed the famous Wild Bill. Si Tanner, Jesse Murphy, and the good people of Skagway did not need to be in harm's way, fleshing out the legend as accidental targets of assassins. Frank Reid was clearly dying and Jesse Murphy was not. A tough could not seek revenge on a dead man.

2. Soapy Smith had clearly gotten more than he deserved for the long list of petty crimes he had committed over the

months since he had been in and out of Skagway. If the
coroner's jury found that he had been killed by a man while
unarmed and unable to defend himself, that would mean
a trial, putting up bail for his gang, who were witnesses
to his murder, and having undesirable members of the
Smith gang in town for several more months. A dead hero
required no trial. To the people of Skagway, justice would
be served by going after real criminals, not the man who
had just administered a sort of poetic justice.

3. Frank Reid, middle class, white, native-born male, was
regarded as a founding member of the community. He
had surveyed the townsite, he had served on the Safety
Committee and was a member of the Committee of One
Hundred and One, the body of citizens that determined the
unofficial bylaws and code of behavior for the community.
As is evidenced by the diary entries, letters to his wife, and
Rev. Sinclair's article published by the *Toronto Globe* in the
days that followed, Reid was much admired by the middle-
class citizens and merchants of Skagway. He had testified
on their behalf during the lawsuit trials in Sitka over the
townsite, and it appeared he would help the community
secure title to their lots. No one wanted to think of Reid's
death as meaningless. In contrast, Jesse Murphy was an
immigrant Irish laborer, someone considered in the same
league as blacks at the time. He was not hero material.

As to the last reason, it should be remembered that J. M. Tanner
had assured Reid that he had "got Soapy" on that wharf.[10] In addition, Reverend Sinclair remembered "the almost savage satisfaction
[Frank Reid] showed all that first night [July 8] in saying whenever
he remembered that he had 'finished that fiend in Hell.'"[11] Sinclair
would not have been the only witness to these utterings. Reid was
attended by three doctors, two of whom testified at the coroner's jury
on July 9. Both Dr. Cornelius and Dr. Whiting would have told the
jury that Reid believed he shot Smith.

———

Did Jesse Murphy kill Soapy Smith?

Officially, no. The duly constituted coroner's jury convened on July 9, 1898, did not mention Jesse Murphy in its discussions of the shooting except for witness Dr. Cornelius's letter to his partner in Portland. They determined that Frank Reid killed Smith in self-defense. The others testifying at the coroner's jury gave their acquiescence to the tale by their silence or simply by signing concurrence with the findings. In his writings after July 9, Reverend Sinclair, Presbyterian minister, dropped his accusation of Murphy and verified the "fact" that Reid killed Smith; Sam Steele, commander of the Northwest Mounted Police, changed his story and echoed the "fact" that Reid killed Smith when he wrote his memoir in 1915; and Samuel Graves, vice president of the American branch of Close Brothers Company, an eyewitness to the shooting, verified the "fact" that Frank Reid killed Smith in his 1908 memoir. Even the *Oregonian* immediately backed off claims that Murphy was involved in the shooting, and claimed only that he had fired a nonfatal bullet.

And so the legend that Frank Reid killed Soapy Smith became fact. Perhaps it was a lie tacitly agreed upon. Nonetheless, it is now history. Sinclair's turn-about on the tale is most intriguing, in that his July 8 diary names Murphy as the killer, his July 9 newspaper article names an anonymous person, but his July 11 letter to his wife names Reid. Sinclair had just spent three days with the dying Reid and had time to change his story. His sermon at Smith's funeral would name "the heroic Reid" as the man who took Jeff Smith's life as the will of God, as part of the preacher's first lesson on "The Way of the Transgressor."[12]

The hero could have been Si Tanner, Charles Sperry, Tom Whitten, or Sam Lovell, maybe even Captain William Moore. Any American-born, middle-class male member of the Committee of One Hundred and One or the Safety Committee would have done just as well. But not John Landers or Jesse Murphy, laborers for the White Pass and Yukon Route. The hero had to have been a founder of Skagway, a man who had built the town from the bottom up, someone who had saved it from the British capitalists, and now, had saved it from an unsavory reputation: a symbolic hero for a symbolic act.

———

By this time guns were popping in all directions, members of
the Vigilance Committee were scouring the hills, the wharves
were guarded, and the boundary watched by the Mounties,
so that escape was impossible, and by 6 o'clock the following
evening fourteen suspects were rounded up at the city hall
and placed under guard. There was talk of lynching, but
soon a troop of soldiers from Dyea arrived, which prevented
drastic action, and in order to prevent martial law the
citizens' committee gave assurance that, after deporting the
undesirables, those remaining would receive fair trials. This
was arranged and no further bloodshed ensued.

Harriet Pullen, *Soapy Smith, Bandit of Skagway*

To their credit, the followers of Jefferson Randolph Smith recognized that they were no longer welcome in Alaska's gold rush port
city. They quickly discovered that Tanner used his new authority as a
federal special officer to contact the Canadian Northwest Mounted
Police, closing the border to them; the ships and boats in the harbor
were all watched, and the trails over the passes were all guarded. With
forty to sixty men at his disposal (accounts vary)—he probably used
only about a dozen trusted men, mostly of those members of the
original Skagway Safety Committee—Tanner searched the saloons,
restaurants, hotels, and known habitués of Smith's gang.[13]

Van Triplett, "Old Man Tripp," one of the principals in the theft of
the gold, had been hiding in the hills northeast of Skagway without
any food. With nothing to eat since Friday, he reappeared in town
on Sunday in the Pack Train restaurant, gorging himself on beef-
steak. Allowed to finish his dinner, he was then taken to the City Hall,
where he was placed under heavy guard. Using information given by
Triplett, Tanner sent thirty armed men out to search for the remaining wanted men.[14]

Among them was Tom Ward, co-owner of the Burkhard Hotel, the
businessman who had approached Jake Rice about turning over Ed
Fay to the Safety Committee back on February 1. Based on Triplett's
information, Ward led a posse up the Brackett Wagon Road. Three
miles from town, he and his posse encountered "Slim Jim" Foster,

John Bowers, and George Wilder, who had been hiding out in an abandoned cabin in the woods. Faced with starvation, they had decided to risk coming into town for food. Ward kept his head as he had back in February; he calmly brought in three of Smith's most notorious gang members.[15]

At noon on Sunday, Tanner asked Calvin Barkdull to take three men up to Liarsville, a string-town paralleling the Skagway River, haunt of cheats and con men. Van Triplett had said that three of the remaining men they wanted could be found there. The posse rousted out ex-deputy Taylor from under his bed to the sound of his two small daughters crying in the arms of their mother.[16]

By this time, the posse had Hank Brown (also known as Blue Jay), Allan Hornsby, and Billie Saportas under lock and key in a makeshift jail at City Hall, as well as ten other Smith supporters. The building was not made to hold that many.[17] Men like Hornsby and Saportas had committed no crime except by implied association, and were being held simply for questioning of any knowledge they might have of the whereabouts of J. D. Stewart's gold poke. Others, like Van Triplett, would be held over for arraignment and possible trial.

By midafternoon on Sunday, as the City Hall grew more crowded, the mob outside on Fifth Avenue grew more unruly. From outside the walls of the makeshift jail could be heard calls for the hanging of Hank "Blue Jay" Brown and "Old Man Tripp" Triplett. In an act that clearly demonstrated where he stood back on February 1, 1898, and where his sense of justice lay, Tanner climbed up on the seat of a wagon parked on Fifth and addressed the crowd.[18]

"Don't hang the evidence," he warned the crowd. "If you want to hang someone, hang me!" The shocking statement quieted the mob.[19]

Then, before anyone had time to rile up the crowd again, he instructed the guards to take the loads out of their weapons, fearing gunshots would cause a riot. As Calvin Barkdull tells the story, Tanner personally conducted Triplett and Brown "boldly across the street to the entrance of a two-story building [the Burkhard Hotel], and up the stairs to a hall on the second floor." Barkdull states, "I was dumb-founded. Not a hand was laid on any of the three while they forced their way through the mob."[20]

Slim Jim Foster and George Wilder were also placed in the sec-
ond-story garret room when they were apprehended later in the day.
According to an unpublished account by WP&YR physician Fenton
B. Whiting, Tanner continued to "plead for . . . peace and harmony
and to let the law take its course." As Whiting checked out the situation for his friend Michael Heney, "Slim Jim" Foster escaped through
a back window.[21]

Concerned that the mob was getting out of control, Commissioner
Sehlbrede telephoned to Dyea and asked Captain R. T. Yeatman of
the U.S. Army to bring over troops and take control of the town. At
3:00 p.m. Sunday, word passed through the crowd that the army had
arrived, and the mob began to press the guards in the corridor of
the hotel. Preoccupied with controlling the mob now trying to take
over the Hotel Burkhard, Tanner and his deputies were helpless to
pursue the escaping prisoner. In a 1929 unpublished account, Whiting claimed to have rounded the corner of Broadway into the alley,
covered Foster with his newly purchased six-inch Colt, grabbed the
prisoner by the coat collar, and dragged him out of his hiding place
next to a shed in the alley. In his excitement over his capture of the
criminal, Whiting turned around to bump into Captain Yeatman,
thereby knocking him down.[22]

Curiously, in his 1933 published version of these events, Whiting
does not give himself any credit in the capture of Slim Jim Foster, nor
does he name Si Tanner in any role, except an occasional mention
of the unnamed "new marshal." It is difficult to determine whether
Whiting feared that others would question his version of the event,
or he was simply being modest. The *Daily Alaskan* merely stated that
almost a hundred men started shooting at Foster when he escaped,
but that "Captain Tanner again came to the front in a manner that
could not be misunderstood. He recovered his man and quietly
marched him back to the guarded room."[23]

In Whiting's unpublished version, by the time he had helped Captain Yeatman to his feet, Tanner arrived on the scene and retrieved
the prisoner who had escaped through the garret window. Yeatman
asked if he could be of assistance, and Tanner assured the captain
that he, as special officer, together with the Safety Committee and
the Town Council, had matters well under control. Yeatman offered

to stay available if they should need him, before retreating from the scene.[24]

According to his own report on the matter, Yeatman was just as happy to stay uninvolved. He was in the course of investigating charges of Tlingit restlessness in Chilkat country near Haines, Alaska, something he believed had more to do with his mission in Alaska than settling the law enforcement issues of the boomtowns of Skagway and Dyea. In his mind, the sooner that the U.S. Congress got around to revising the Organic Act for Alaska and giving its cities the power to incorporate and form civil governments, the better for all concerned.[25]

Later that Sunday afternoon, Tanner climbed on top of a wagon in front of City Hall and once again addressed the crowd. According to the *Daily Alaskan*, he asked,

> if the citizens of Skagway would support him and his deputies,
> or if they desired to have the military quartered in the town—
> not for a day or a week, but for a long season. It goes for
> citizens to know Captain Yeatman had been here and seen the
> situation and returned with his men to Dyea. He had only done
> so upon the solemn assurance of the acting marshal and the
> leading business men that order would be maintained, and that
> the men arrested would be protected and have a fair trial.[26]

Tanner threatened that Yeatman would come back and declare martial law if they proceeded to act like vigilantes and hanged anyone. The acting deputy assured the crowd that those who were guilty would be punished and that they would clear the town of "the disorderly element." The *Daily Alaskan* made Tanner's stance clear: "If people wanted violence they would have first to overcome him and his deputies." To that announcement, the crowd cheered.[27]

The threat of martial law acted like a bucket of cold water on the collective heads of the lynch mob. With mutterings and grumblings, the crowd dispersed.[28]

Tanner's authority to call upon the military was clearly established in law at the time. He was an officer of the federal court, a U.S. deputy marshal hired by John Shoup, the U.S. marshal appointed by President McKinley on June 26, 1897. The marshal and his hired deputies had the power to conscript a *posse comitatus*, a volunteer posse, even when U.S. military troops were in the vicinity, in order to keep the peace. The courts and their enforcement arm, the U.S. Marshals Service usually preferred the *posse comitatus*, over the military as the chain of command was much more clear and forward, and the posse could be disbanded when the emergency was over. The Judiciary Act of 1789, which created the federal court system, gave the courts the authority to decide when and if they needed military assistance. The decision to use a civilian posse legally rested on Commissioner Sehlbrede and Deputy Tanner as officers of the federal court. This is why Captain Yeatman left Skagway when Tanner assured him that he had the matter under control, and why Yeatman reported to his superiors that he was not needed during the affair.[29]

Before the day ended, special officer Tanner set up an advisory committee of a dozen "of the most cool-headed men of the city," charged with the task of recovering J. D. Stewart's gold and returning it to him; finding out who the accomplices of the robbery were; and ending the campaign of vengeance for the wrong without spilling any more blood. He also meant to completely rid the town of any men who had collaborated with Jefferson Randolph Smith.[30]

All of this action was reported by a newspaper seeking to redeem itself in the eyes of a public that thought it had been wronged. J. Allan Hornsby, accused of being one of Smith's sympathizers, worked for the *Daily Alaskan*. This daily afternoon newspaper had failed to report the theft of the gold on July 8, and had not issued a paper between that day and July 11, when it announced that Hornsby had been fired and that editor George W. de Succa would be writing the articles until Weston Covney, a previous correspondent for the *New York Herald*, would arrive to write the copy. The reporting from that day on proved detailed and thorough.[31]

Now, Hornsby was in jail, awaiting questioning along with twenty-six other Smith associates.[32]

At least in these early days of Skagway's history, Tanner was well-appreciated. The *Skaguay News* paid him tribute in its Friday morning, July 15 edition:

> Marshal J. M. Tanner has shown in his every act since Friday
> night that he is the right man for the place but never were his

honest convictions more ably defended by his true courage
than Sunday night, when for nearly an hour he valiantly
labored with the enraged crowd for the protection of his
prisoners in the name of the law.[33]

Before the Soapy Legend became entrenched by legend-mongers
like Harriet Pullen, the citizens of Skagway knew the identity of their
heroes. Pullen would forget that Tanner existed and fail to mention
his name.

––––––––

The committee decided to deport ten men on the steamship
Tartar: [including] Allen [sic] Hornsby and W. F. Saportas
. . . When they reached Seattle, Saportas, and Dr. J. Allen
Hornsby, identified as the editor of the Skagway *Daily Alaskan*,
proclaimed their innocence, and complained that they had
been railroaded. At two in the afternoon, Thursday, July 14,
John Bowers, W. F. Foster, and Van B. Tripplett [sic], the three
gang members accused of robbing Stewart, appeared before
U.S. Commissioner Sehlbrede. Three other gang members,
Henry Jackson, George Wilder, and John Clear were arraigned
on charges of assault with a deadly weapon. In spite of his long
association with Soapy, John Clancy was never shown to be
involved in the unlawful activities of the gang. The stolen gold
was found in a trunk in the back room of Soapy's saloon, minus
about $600.

Jane G. Haigh, *King Con*

The final premise of the legend goes that Skagway became free of
crime after Smith was killed. That required the purging of the Smith
gang.

––––––––

J. M. Tanner would not actually become a U.S. deputy marshal until
July 11, 1898, when Marshal John Shoup finally arrived from Sitka.
There being no telegraph from Skagway to the outer world, it had

taken three days to get word to the marshal and for him to attend to the crisis occurring in the northern part of his district. One of his first acts on arriving in town was to formally appoint J. M. Tanner as Skagway's U.S. deputy marshal. The occasion passed with little fanfare. The townspeople had already accepted Si as their marshal.[34]

The citizens' committee appointed by acting deputy Tanner on Sunday, July 10, included business executive Samuel H. Graves, railroad engineer C. E. Hawkins, wharf owner E. O. Sylvester, steamship agent Frank Burns, businessman H. E. Battin, blacksmith Sam Freemand, hotel proprietor Thomas Whitten, and Mr. Humbert of the Humbert-Yukon Outfitting Company. As the names were announced to a crowd assembled on the street, cries rang out "good," and "he's all right." Someone in the assemblage suggested the addition of A. L. Remick, another popular member of the Safety Committee.[35]

By the following Saturday, July 16, five additional members had joined the original eight, including major players in the Committee of One Hundred and One: Leslie Butler, a grocer; George Brackett, builder of the Brackett Wagon Road; Drs. C. W. Cornelius and Fenton B. Whiting; and John L. Sperry, partner in the real estate firm of Sperry and Varig at Main and Sixth. Over the course of the previous five days, these committee members interviewed seventy-three witnesses, including the twenty-seven men they had taken into custody. They believed they had enough evidence to convict Van B. Triplett, W. E. Foster, John Bowers, and Harry Bronson of larceny; George Wilder and J. D. Jackson of assault with a dangerous weapon; Al White of larceny and being armed with a dangerous weapon; and Charles Butler of inciting to riot. They recommended that the other persons held by the Safety Committee be released. All were encouraged to leave town.[36]

On the afternoon of July 15, preliminary hearings were held in City Hall before Judge Sehlbrede. He bound over George Wilder and Turner Jackson for $5,000 each; Charles Butler was held for $10,000, and Harry Bronson for $20,000. Charged with neglect of duty, ex-deputy Sylvester Taylor was bound over for $5,000. A search was being made for Mrs. Michael J. "Vie" Torpey.[37]

An earlier attempt to deport Mrs. Torpey had failed. On Wednesday, July 13, the Citizens' Committee had chosen those in Soapy's gang not charged with crimes to be deported that day on the steamer *Tees* as undesirable citizens. They included William Tener, the man who had stood by Smith in the May 1 patriotic parade and served as Smith's second at the head of the Fourth Division in the Fourth of July parade; Billy O'Donnel, Jim Hawkins, Bert Markinson, and Mike Torpey. Vie Torpey, the latter's wife, had refused to be shipped out. A warrant for her arrest was issued, charging her with keeping a house of ill-fame, the first person to be so accused in Skagway.[38]

This deportation was the second in so many days. On Tuesday the 12th, "an immense crowd" had gathered to see the first group of Soapy's gang leave on the steamer *Tartar*. Sentenced merely to leave town and not come back, J. Allan Hornsby led the group, followed by W. F. "Billie" Saportas, Nate Pollock, C. S. Hussey, Bradley O'Brien, Charles Bromberg, J. Swain, J. Leary, Hank "Blue Jay" Brown, and Henry Smith. The crowd handled itself well, refusing to jeer at the miscreants. At approximately 2:00 in the afternoon, photographer W. H. Case posed the ten men on Moore's Wharf and snapped their picture. At the gangplank, Commissioner Sehlbrede asked each one if he was leaving of his own free will. Nearly all of them "expressed a disinclination to go but preferred to do so rather than stay and face the music." Hornsby was the most vociferous in his objection, but finally relented and said he went of his own consent.[39] When asked if he was going of his own accord, Hank Brown said, "Yes, and I want to say that Captain Tanner is a perfect gentleman."[40]

"No bouquets, please," interrupted Tanner, not wishing to be praised by the likes of Brown. But "Blue Jay" knew who had saved his neck from a lynch mob, indeed, who had saved Skagway from living up to an undeserved reputation already beginning to circulate. It would be one promulgated by Canadians eager to build up Dawson's character at the expense of Skagway's, a reputation as "the roughest place on earth" (a quote from Canadian Sam Steele); a place "conceived in lawlessness and nurtured in anarchy," as depicted by Canadian Pierre Berton.[41]

Among those being deported by Tanner and the members of the committee investigating the robbing of Stewart were two city council members, Hornsby and William Saportas, both of whom, as members of the press, had been expected to be more forthcoming with news of

Smith's evil doings about town. Fairly or not, the people of Skagway believed these two individuals had had privileged information about what Jeff Smith and his cohorts had been doing all along, and had not shared those facts with the public. In particular, they thought that Hornsby, as editor of the *Daily Alaskan,* had not reported the theft of Stewart's gold, nor had he used his influence with Smith to discover the poke's whereabouts. The investigating committee alleged that these two individuals, above all others, had failed in their civic duties to Skagway.

The very fact that these two gentlemen of the press had reported little about Smith in the months leading up to his death seems at first glance to be ample evidence that the con man was actually doing very little in Skagway. Some writers hint that Smith paid both to stay quiet about his doings. However, as is suggested by articles in newspapers throughout western North America, Smith was not even in Skagway most of this time, much less causing enough trouble and exerting enough influence to become the city's uncrowned king. It is fairly obvious that, other than setting up his business and starting up the Skagway Guard, the only other activity he may have been engaged in was trying to trump up a baseball team in June, something many of the saloon owners tried at one time or another.[42]

Upon reaching Seattle, Allan Hornsby and William Saportas both protested vociferously—and probably justifiably—what they believed was their unfair eviction from Skagway. Interviews of the two journalists made their way into the Denver newspapers, and therefore into mid-twentieth-century biographies of Smith. The first news report in Denver appeared in the *Denver Times* on July 16, denying that their native con man had been killed, rumors notwithstanding. Billy Saportas's version of events appeared in the *Rocky Mountain News.* He noted that Smith had indeed been shot on June 19—an inaccurate date—and went on to state that Soapy had held the town in a state of subdued terror for a year, ignoring the fact that Skagway had existed for less than eleven months, and Soapy had resided there only since January. The next day, the *Rocky Mountain News* announced that the town had been "rid of the leader of as desperate a gang of toughs as ever infested a frontier city." It went on to tabulate Smith's misdeeds in Denver before he went to Skagway, thus expanding on a legend

that had little basis in fact. Other Denver newspapers took up the
theme later in the month when, on July 20, 1898, the *Denver Times*
printed an interview with Louis K. Pratt, friend of Smith's from the
Denver days who claimed to have witnessed the shooting, telling the
story essentially the way it appeared in the July 9 issue of the *Skaguay
News*. Clearly, this is the primary source for most later chroniclers. By
August 1, the *Denver Times* eulogized Smith as a "square gambler" who
had risen from a bellhop in a St. Louis hotel to mayor of Skagway,
clearly a falsehood, and clearly in an attempt to make a hero out of a
misanthrope.[43]

It was after Saportas and Hornsby arrived in Seattle that the
"Uncrowned King" story got aired across the nation. An article in the
Seattle Post Intelligencer on July 19, 1898, entitled "I am the Uncrowned
King," written by a staff reporter who interviewed the two correspondents made a point that Smith had given himself that name. The
reporter countered rumors coming out of the North that made Smith
a ruthless villain. He admitted that Smith was king of the grafters in
Alaska, but he could not make him any worse than that. Although
Soapy had been accused of murdering eight men, the journalist
found no evidence for a single killing by Soapy. And the reporter
pointed out that Frank Reid's one previous killing had ended with
a trial and an acquittal for self-defense. Neither man was a vicious
murderer.[44]

Less than a week later, the *Denver Times* fell all over itself with a
three-column obituary praising Smith as the "Con-King of the West."[45]
This article alone, which was obviously written by an admirer, may be
most responsible for the outrageous legendary deeds attributed to
Smith, both in Denver and in Alaska, in which his petty crimes were,
according to the reporter, ameliorated by charitable works and acts
of kindness.[46]

It was in this Denver obituary that the legend-makers went to work.
Jeff Smith's shack of a saloon became well-furnished, opulent parlors,
where he was always the gentleman; it was in this article that he delivered a Memorial Day parade address and was elevated to the Grand
Marshal of Skagway's Fourth of July parade. Here we first learn that
men shrank from him in terror on the day that J. D. Stewart's gold
was stolen.[47] We can only assume that the *Denver Times* source was

someone like Louis Pratt—a friend of Smith's who conspired with the con man to make him something larger than he had ever been in life. Whoever he was, later writers believed the legend, parade, speeches, philanthropy, and all.

———

Back in Skagway, city reform continued at a lightning pace. With the guilt of city council members Billie Saportas and J. Allan Hornsby established, Skagway's Committee of One Hundred and One no longer trusted anyone on the city council. A public demand for resignation of the entire council resulted in a special council meeting at 10:00 a.m. on Monday morning, July 11. The remaining members were chairman Charles Sperry, I. D. Spencer, W. F. Lokowitz, Ed Foster, and Frank E. Burns. Spencer did not attend, and all present councilmen but Sperry immediately submitted their resignations. By the following Saturday, Spencer had resigned, as had Billie Saportas and Allan Hornsby by proxy. Perhaps feeling that his part in the clean-up of the town did not warrant his removal from the council, Charles Sperry clung to his post until the end of July, at which time his brother, John, replaced him on the new council. The only person who ended up serving on the first, 1897, council, the interim summer 1898 council, and the December 1898 council was Frank Clancy, the real power behind the underworld in Skagway. One of the ways that Clancy ingratiated himself with the influential citizens, especially those who counted themselves among the Committee of One Hundred and One, was to recover the six hundred dollars missing from J. D. Stewart's gold poke. He and H. E. Battin, a member of the investigative committee, traveled to Sitka where Clancy convinced Van Triplett to sign over a personal note on a Tacoma bank for that amount. Clancy, in turn, reimbursed those funds to Stewart.[48]

———

On November 11, 1898, J. D. Stewart arrived in Juneau to testify at the trials of the Smith gang. J. M. Tanner, as deputy marshal, attended the entire November and December session of the federal court in Juneau. The Grand Jury soon found that there was not enough evidence to try Harry Bronson, Al White, and Charles Butler. Charges against the three were dropped. Vie Torpey pleaded guilty to keeping a house of ill-fame, paid her one hundred dollar fine, and left southeast Alaska. All interest turned to the remaining defendants.[49]

The *Skaguay News* speculated that the defense would contend that Stewart had lost his gold while gambling; the district attorney charged that it had been stolen. Observers had not counted on the charges the court would bring against Smith's men for pulling a gun on an officer of the law. George Wilder and Turner Jackson were each charged with the assault of special officer Josias M. Tanner.[50]

As listed on the court documents, W. E. Foster, Van B. Triplett and John [Charles] Bowers were all charged with larceny, committed at Skagway, Alaska, on July 8, 1898, where they "feloniously did steal, take and carry away with intent to steal or purloin . . . property of John D. Stewart to wit: one hundred and fifty-eight and 14/17 ounces of gold dust and nuggets of the value of twenty-six hundred dollars." In addition, Foster and Bowers were charged with assault and battery of Stewart, at which time they "did beat and ill-treat" him.[51] The town and courts had not forgotten Smith's gang, and they still sought their vengeance.

The gang's lawyers, W. T. Hume and W. E. Crews, worked valiantly to convince the juries that the defendants were just honest gamblers trying to make a day's living. They presented Wilder and Jackson as being in the wrong place at the wrong time, with no proof that Smith knew them or that they knew Smith. They argued that Tanner's testimony that they were in Smith's company on the night of the killing did not make them Smith's friends. Simply because George Wilder and Jackson were found with loaded pistols in their pockets thirty-six hours after the shooting did not mean they were armed on the wharf. Nor should the jury trust the testimony of an officer of the law, who is sworn to convict a man he is convinced is guilty. The defense attorneys tried to convince the judge that Tanner was not an expert witness and could not judge whether cartridges had been sitting in a gun for one hour or thirty-six hours.[52]

The judge would have none of this reasoning, and struck all of the defendants' proposed instructions to the juries along these lines, as well as their later petitions for writs of error.

Likewise, Crews and Hume tried to convince the juries in the trials of Foster, Bowers, and Triplett that Stewart was simply a poor loser in a poker game. Again, the judge would not allow their long lecture on the sins of gambling and on how to lose gracefully, a point that the defense later tried to argue when it threatened to appeal. The judge stood firm. He, and the jury, believed that Stewart's gold had been outright stolen.[53]

Bowers and Foster each received a prison sentence of a year for the larceny charge and another six months for the assault and battery. Foster had to pay an additional one thousand dollar fine for the robbery, which he could not do, so additional time was added to his sentence. Van Triplett went to federal prison for a year for the robbery. Wilder drew a prison sentence of seven years for his assault on Si Tanner on the wharf.[54]

Turner Jackson appealed his ten-year sentence to the Ninth Circuit Court of Appeals on fourteen counts, many of which were simply matters of semantics used in Alaska courts of law. Only one count was struck down, that of being sentenced to ten years of hard labor in a federal penitentiary, as the appeals court deemed the sentence to be redundant. The words "at hard labor" were stricken from his sentence, and he was sent to McNeil Island to serve ten years for his assault on Tanner. He was released in September 1905, for good behavior, having served seven years.[55]

––––––––

The legend repeatedly states that Skagway was lawless and violent, whereas the Yukon Territory was relatively safe for travelers. Real data suggest otherwise. Besides the murders of Andy McGrath and James Mark Rowan on January 31, 1898, Soapy Smith on July 8, and Frank Reid on July 21, historic documents for Skagway and Dyea indicate that three other people were killed in the vicinity of those two towns in 1898. A prostitute named Ella D. Wilson was tied and strangled, and her throat was cut by unknown assassins believed to be members of Soapy Smith's gang in late May 1898. W. S. Gregg was shot by Pat Malone on the Dyea Trail on May 23, 1898. Frank Clement was shot and killed at Sheep Camp by Gotitko Sneider on March 14, 1898. In addition, bartender Sam Roberts was reported to have been killed at a saloon in Dyea.[56] That makes a total of eight homicides in the two towns and over the two trails in the year 1898, an area with an estimated 20,000 population. That translates to a homicide rate of 40 per 100,000.

In comparison, Samuel Steele's 1915 memoir provides some anecdotal information on homicides in Yukon Territory in 1898. Major Steele was on his way to his post on the border between the United States and Canada in January 1898, spent most of February in Skagway, was stationed at Lake Bennett until midsummer, and stayed in Dawson the rest of the year. He personally investigated or reported eight homicides in a territory with an estimated population of 20,000 people. A check of the Canadian Archives verifies that there are surviving records of eight homicides in that year.[57] That translates to a homicide rate of 40 per 100,000.

Clare V. McKanna, Jr., who has studied homicide in the American West between 1880 and 1920, states that measuring homicide rates per 100,000 population is the best way to track the incidence of death by violence. He notes that the homicide rates for the three counties he studied in some depth averaged 6, 34, and 70 for Douglas County (Nebraska), Las Animas County (Colorado), and Gila County (Arizona), respectively, over a forty-year period. During the year 1900, their homicide rates were 4, 39, and 78, respectively.[58] Each time, the Las Animas County data compares favorably with both Skagway's and Yukon Territory's rate. Incidentally, during the same time period McKanna notes low homicide rates in Boston, New York, and Philadelphia, which averaged less than 5 per 100,000, comparable to that in the urban Douglas County, Nebraska. Roger McGrath, using similar data and statistics, found homicide rates of 116 and 64 per 100,000 in Bodie and Aurora, California, respectively, for the years 1880 and 1863, during the height of their gold rush booms.[59]

The comparisons are instructive when looking at the Skagway and Yukon cases. Both Skagway and Yukon were in the middle of a mining boom. Apparently, the vigilantism and violence studied by McGrath did not exist in Skagway. While a homicide rate of 40 is nothing to be proud of, it was not nearly so high as the 116 and 64 in California mining towns of twenty and forty years earlier or the 78 in the copper mining area surrounding Globe, Gila County, Arizona, of 1900. The latter area was plagued by Anglo-Apache warfare, a high murder rate, and three lynchings. In contrast, the coal mining communities of Las Animas, Colorado, with a lower homicide rate of 39, experienced violence from labor disputes as well as drunken brawls.[60] Their working-class laborers resembled Skagway's miners, railroad workers, and businessmen, thus accounting for an admittedly high homicide rate, but one that was comparable to the North Country's rate of 40.

The point is that what statistics are available indicate that Skagway was no more violent than similar working-class communities of its time. The legend of a chaotic Skagway grew out of a need to bolster an American frontier myth, not out of real data.

The Rev. John A. Sinclair, ca. 1900. Royal BC Museum, British Columbia Archives, I-67820.

Special Officer J. M. Tanner, on the far right, and his deputies on July 9, collecting at the Manila Saloon on Fifth Avenue. Klondike Gold Rush National Historical Park, George and Edna Rapuzzi Collection, Rasmuson Foundation, #000346-K/C-A.

Volunteer harbor guards, July 1898, Skaguay, Alaska. J. M. Tanner is on the far left. Anchorage Museum, John Urban Collection, AMRC-B64.1.46.

The Burkhard Hotel, where members of Smith's gang were confined while J. M. Tanner held off a lynch mob. Yukon Archives, H. C. Barley fonds, #5006.

Nine men shipped out of Skagway on July 12, 1898. Alaska State Library, Case and Draper, Photographs, 1898–1920, ASL-P39-0843.

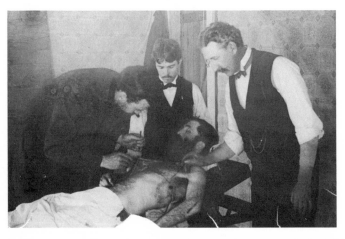

The body of Soapy Smith at the coroner's inquisition on July 9, 1898. Alaska State Library, William R. Norton, Photographs, ca. 1890–1920, ASL-P226-786.

PART 2

The Legend

CHAPTER FIVE

The Local Legend-Makers

Wister's very popular [1901] version of the Frontier Myth was
that "civilization" . . . can be defended from the forces that
menace it only by an armed and virile elite that is willing and
able to take the law into its own hands and substitute itself for
the will of the people.

Richard Slotkin, *Gunfighter Nation*

Whether or not the gun-bearer was really an outlaw or just
some fool full of testosterone and alcohol, wild wielding meant
violence—just as the controlled wielding of the lawman did.

Michael L. Johnson, *Hunger for the Wild*

It was not so important what actually happened on July 8, 1898, in
Skagway, as how it was interpreted. The results of the coroner's
inquiry supported the beliefs of white, native-born, middle-class
merchants of Skagway that only a member of the Safety Committee,
one of the original Committee of One Hundred and One, could
have killed Soapy Smith. Likewise, the killing of a man who had
done nothing worse than cheat petty gamblers going to and from
the Klondike needed to be explained in the context of perceptions
about themselves as a community and their place in the larger world.
As journalists began to write about the event, they drew upon popular images and concepts to symbolize the conflict that lead to the
deaths of the two men.

By the end of the nineteenth century, journalists and other popular writers in America were lamenting the end of the frontier or the
mythic West, which symbolized for them an environment in which

people could be free to achieve their highest potentials. While historian Frederick Turner Jackson announced the end of the frontier, author Owen Wister articulated an encroaching civilization on the frontier in a popular format in his best-selling 1901 novel, *The Virginian*. This novel made a hero out of a vigilante who tamed the lawless frontier by taking the law into his own hands. Both writers showed how ingrained the frontier myth had become with most Americans. In their view, the wilderness and the lawlessness that existed there remained only in the sinful cities and in the wild and wooly mining camps of the West.[1] The opening of Alaska to mining seemed to open a new frontier wilderness to conquer.

Michael Johnson, in discussing Americans' obsession with the untamed West, notes that most of the violence of the late-nineteenth and early-twentieth-century West was more often social than personal. It consisted of vigilantism, social banditry, range wars, race conflicts, and union struggles, but stories about the violence were usually couched in terms of personal, open conflict. When consigned to narrative, the stories generated a symbolism that took the form of gunslingers acting on their own personal initiatives, inside or outside the law.[2] These gunmen, according to Kent Steckmesser, "served as a surrogate for all those other westerners who disliked industry, corporations and progress." As westerners romanticized the gunmen, they began to obscure whatever caused the outlaw's sociopathy and to turn his violent characteristics into virtues. He became a legend praised for his independent derring-do rather than his antisocial pathology.[3]

Gunslingers were recognizable as American heroes from historic figures such as Wild Bill Hickok, Wyatt Earp, and Bat Masterson to their fictional counterparts in the twentieth century ranging from the Virginian to Matt Dillon, Zane Grey's Lassiter, and a whole host of Louis L'Amour gunfighters.

So it was that as soon as Soapy Smith and Frank Reid pulled their triggers in the remote western town of Skagway, Alaska, journalists immediately recognized the American western myth come to life. Stalwart middle-class leaders of a community on the edge of the wilderness, fighting for law and order, take matters into their own hands. By violence, they regain control of their town and retame the wilderness. Frank Reid fit the Wild Bill, Wyatt Earp, and Bat Masterson mold. Jesse

Murphy did not. Obviously, a working-class, Irish worker could not have been the one to shoot and kill Smith.

The first reports of the shooting came from journalist E. J. "Stroller" White, writing for the *Skaguay News,* and his colleagues at the *Daily Alaskan.* The spin, that of a morality tale, of good redeeming evil, came within three days. And who better to teach that moral than a preacher?

> God . . . inspired heroic Reid with courage, steadied his
> nerve, and directed his fire so unerringly that the leader
> of lawbreakers had not one breath to call his followers to
> violence. By His intervention no life was lost but that one which
> alone could have put any great obstacle in the way of Skagway's
> liberation.
>
> Rev. John A. Sinclair, July 11, 1898

As noted earlier, John A. Sinclair was the only minister in Skagway to agree to preside over Smith's funeral. In both his diary entry of July 9 and his July 11 letter to his wife, he wrote that two other ministers had declined the request, fearing that it would hurt their reputations. In his July 11 sermon, Sinclair admitted, "When Jeff Smith was alive I refused an introduction to him. But today if he were alive and suffering, I would be at his bedside for the same reason as I conduct these sad obsequies."[4] The writings in his personal papers dating from July 1898 through the following spring suggest that Rev. Sinclair became obsessed with the fact that he had not taken on the reform of the living sinner. It is obvious that his conscience bothered him. Sinclair, when he sat down to write Smith's funeral sermon, hoping it was not too late to redeem his own soul, decided to make the con man's life an object lesson. He took his text from Proverbs 13:15: "The way of the transgressors is hard."[5]

In his July 11 sermon, Sinclair first made Smith into a devil by "lament[ing] that in the career of one [Smith] who has lived among us there is so little that we can look back upon today as unmistakably good or heroic." He next warned that "the work of reform will not be complete when every member of the 'Smith gang' has been punished or deported," suggesting that Skagway was still infiltrated with evil. He called the still-living Reid brave and heroic for being the only one to step forward and offer his blood in the service to his community, and cautioned that such sin as Soapy's could only be cleansed with the blood of both the sinner and the martyr.[6] That is, after all is said and done, a basic Christian concept.

Then, Sinclair taught the tragic lesson:

> Let us learn from poor Smith's mistaken career and awful end, what a curse even great and cultivated talents may become to the possessor and to others, if devoted to unconsecrated ends in life. Let us learn from the unhappy fate of his associates, and from the fears of those who lent countenance to his wrong-doing, that in the future and larger liberation of Skagway, by the liberation of Divine truth and Christian woes, all who today countenance what will then be cast aside as unfortunate elements of pioneer life, will find the way of transgressors hard.[7]

Through the blood shed by sinner Soapy Smith and the martyr Frank Reid, the town of Skagway had found redemption. The city that had been so fraught with evil had been scrubbed clean. Good had triumphed over evil. Travelers would once again be safe.

Sinclair also used the morality framework when he wrote his article for the *Toronto Globe* on July 9:

> So one great barrier is removed Skagway's progress, but by resolute citizens, and perhaps at the cost of the life of her heroic city surveyor, Reid, who in simple self-defense had to take their lives in their hands and establish order that the United States government has lamentably failed to establish in this territory. "Grafters" and "confidence men" had now better give Skagway a wide berth, and travelers may now come and might, almost, if they choose, leave their "dust" on the streets while taking meals and feel perfectly safe.[8]

So confident did Sinclair feel in Skagway's redemption that he omitted the words "and might, almost"—words that the editor of the

Globe later added to make the statement a little more believable. Sinclair obviously believed the community had been wholly restored to grace with the symbolic self-sacrifice of the heroic Frank Reid and killing of the archetypal sinner Soapy Smith. With Smith gone, anyone could leave his gold in the streets and feel perfectly safe.

————

Frank Reid died on July 20, twelve days after being shot by Soapy Smith. The self-sacrifice theme of Rev. Sinclair's funeral sermon and *Toronto Globe* article became one of martyrdom. As the years rolled by, others would take up the morality theme. The legend was short; it was simple; it was easy to tell. A dead villain, a martyred hero, a redeemed town. How could anyone top a story like that? Both Americans and Canadians of the turn of the century could understand the moral immediately, and it struck a chord.

Fiddling with the story began at once, at the hands of the editor of the *Globe*. He did what Sinclair had already started, as he edited Sinclair's piece: made Smith worse than he actually was.

When Sinclair sent his manuscript to the *Globe*, he also sent some supporting materials, in the form of newspaper clippings he had collected about Smith while he had been in Skagway. A comparison of the original manuscript and the published article makes it clear that the *Globe*'s editor chose to insert information from those clippings into the final article for clarification, not understanding the local politics.

For instance, Sinclair originally wrote, "I was not an hour in Skaguay until this desperado was pointed out as one who in early days had 'terrorized Denver & several other mining camps into submission by his dictates, and who now runs Skagway along the same lines.'"[9] The *Globe* changed this sentence to read, "I was not an hour in Skagway until this desperado was pointed out as 'Soapy' Smith, who terrorized Denver and several other mining camps into submission to his dictatorship, and who now runs Skagway along the same lines."[10] In the evolution of a legend, the change of the word *dictates* to *dictatorship* could easily lead to words such as *reign* and *kingdom*.

Likewise, Sinclair had originally written the following, poorly constructed sentence: "I was not long in town until I found that the wisest way to mention the name of Soapy was in an undertone as influence was felt not only in the gambling houses, but in the city council and I had strong suspicions at times that I could see indications of it in church affairs." The *Globe*, hoping to make Sinclair's intention better understood, changed it to: "Nor was I long in finding his influence not only among the gamblers and confidence men but in the administration of justice in the City Council and even in the church circles was so great that it was wise to speak his name in an undertone."[11] The newspaper, by its change in emphasis, suddenly gave Smith a much greater role in the courts and church than Sinclair had even hinted at.

In fact, Sinclair's diary and letters to his wife make it clear that he was more concerned over the squabble he was having with Dr. Rev. Campbell of the Episcopal Church than about Soapy's influence in Skagway. That is the meaning of the unclear sentence in Sinclair's draft to the *Toronto Globe*. Campbell had taken over as head of the board of the Union Church, a position that rightly belonged to the Presbyterian Church and was Rev. Sinclair's by right. Campbell had locked the doors of the Union Church, and refused to let anyone use the church, which was meant to be nondenominational. Rumors that Smith had donated to the building of the Union Church disturbed Sinclair, and may have prompted his belief that Dr. Campbell was sympathetic to Soapy Smith. In later years, Rev. Dickey, who had been the Presbyterian minister in Skagway and had the Union Church built, sent Mrs. J. A. Sinclair a letter stating that Soapy Smith had nothing to do with contributing to the building of the Union Church, thus laying to rest that portion of the Smith legend in Skagway. It dispelled any thought that Smith had any influence on church matters.[12]

In Sinclair's eyes, the town of Skagway knew it was being delivered of a great evil. On July 9, when he wrote for the *Toronto Globe*, he described the crowd that emerged from the mass "indignation meeting" finding Smith's body. The scene was clearly meant to stage the redemption theme:

> A weird, but pardonable scene took place when not far from
> the corpse of "Soapy," lying where it fell and beside the
> prostrate and agonizing form of heroic Reid, a group of men
> threw up their hats in the air and gave three soul-thrilling
> cheers. So long had this baneful rule insulted Skagway's best

citizens, so indignant were Skagway's business men over the hurtful reputation that "the gang" were giving Skagway that all felt that a new era had dawned on the city. This made the tragedy not a personal altercation but a Waterloo, and it was felt that cheering did not desecrate the dead.[13]

Baneful rule? Is this where the legend of "The Reign of Soapy Smith" began? Not with Harry Suydam's title of that name in the pages of *Frank Leslie's Popular Monthly*, but from the pen of a clergyman sorry that he had not saved the soul of a transgressor?

Rev. Sinclair's eulogy was published in the *Skaguay News* on July 15, 1898, and was available to a growing body of readers. It was reprinted in part in the *Portland Oregonian* of July 22, 1898. The *News* continued to sell copies of the July 8 and July 15 issues long after Soapy's body was laid to rest in its grave. In fact, reprints continue to garner a brisk tourist business to this day.

Did Soapy rule Skagway, the new "Sodom?" Were his dark days as evil as those of the rogues of Gomorrah? He had to rule as an evil villain, then have his fall, an unredeemed sinner; the town's surveyor, Frank Reid (or any founding member of the Committee of One Hundred and One), became the symbol of good, dying for Skagway. He would be immortalized that way, the epitaph on his large gravestone reading, "He gave his life for Skagway." The town was now redeemed. And Sinclair's eulogy put into words the North's great morality tale.

The Reverend John A. Sinclair recorded his thoughts of the events of July 8, 1898, on the day it happened in his diary, and then wrote a newspaper article that he sent to the *Toronto Globe* on the morning of July 9, 1898. In Skagway, news of the death of Soapy Smith blared from the headlines of the *Skaguay News* by midday on July 9. It had missed its usual Friday publication date, delaying by several hours so that its editor, Elmer John White, could get as much information into his weekly newspaper as he could find. He did a job that no one, in more than 114 years, has been able to top.

When asked thirty-five years later what his greatest story was, "Stroller" White replied without hesitation, "The shooting of Skagway's robber king, Soapy Smith, and the cleaning up of his gang."[14]

He, of course, referred to the lead article of the July 8 issue, published on July 9, entitled "Soapy Smith's Last Bluff and Its Fatal Ending."[15]

E. J. "Stroller" White came to Skagway in April 1898, when J. F. A. Strong went north to Dawson. M. L. Sherpy, owner of the *Skaguay News*, who recognized a legitimate talent when he saw one, immediately hired White to fill in as editor. Born in Ohio, on November 28, 1859, he came from the Puget Sound area, where he had been writing for newspapers since 1889.[16] For all of the tall tales and wild imagination that went into "The Stroller's" tales of the North, his account of the shooting of Soapy Smith was one of the most factual examples of serious journalism of the time. How any editor could have rounded up the eyewitnesses and pulled together such a straightforward, lucid story in such a short time, a story that has stood the test of time so well, is a credit to his serious journalistic skills. His account is quoted in its entirety in appendix B.

Copycat articles ran in the Seattle, San Francisco, Denver, and Victoria, B.C., newspapers, and in cities connected by news cables, which literally plagiarized the *Skaguay News* copy and the later version printed by the *Daily Alaskan* on July 11, 1898.

By August 1898, the local hullabaloo was largely over, and the Alaska papers would not print another story about Smith until the trials of the arrested gang members in November and December. Snippets like the following would appear over the next couple of years, quoting Soapy in a humorous vein or referring to the bad old days when Soapy ran riot in Skagway. "I owe my success in life to the free advertising I have received in newspapers by the number of lies they have written about me," was a quote attributed to Smith in Juneau's *Alaska Mining Record*, and was intended to be a condemnation of the press, not a commentary on Smith's cleverness.[17] Likewise, an editorial comment noted that the corrupt British Columbia government could give "the Soapy Smith outfit cards and spades."[18] In October 1901, when Skagway decided to district its prostitutes, the Juneau newspapers gloated that the town up north had not seen such excitement since the Soapy Smith days.[19] These types of references were generally meant to disparage the person or organization being compared to Smith. The only other mention of Smith and his gang members came when Foster was pardoned by President McKinley in December

1899, and Van Triplett died in prison in May of 1901.[20] Except for the latter two stories, the Skagway newspaper eschewed mention of Soapy entirely.

———

It was not until 1901 that Harry Suydam, one of the town founders and the city's first assessor, wrote an article about Smith for *Frank Leslie's Popular Magazine*. Published in its January issue, "The Reign of 'Soapy' Smith" dealt mostly with Smith's depredations on the White Pass Trail during the winter of 1897–98, and the murders of Andy McGrath and James Rowan on January 31, 1898. Only the last four pages of the eleven-page article recounted his supposed rise to power and last days in Skagway, during which time Suydam was not in Skagway.

Suydam assisted city engineer Frank Reid in 1897, shared an office in the city hall with U.S. Deputy Marshal D. H. McInnes as city assessor in the winter of 1897–98, and was a member of the Safety Committee. He left Skagway early in the spring, after the McGrath and Rowan murders, and was in Circle City, Alaska, when Smith was killed. He states that he "had the particulars" from a single copy of "the newspaper" from Skagway (the *Skaguay News?*) and spoke to a friend who was also a friend of Soapy's in Seattle, where he could have picked up a copy of Rev. Sinclair's funeral sermon, published on July 15. Suydam would have had to pass through Skagway on his way to Seattle. In Skagway, he would surely have talked to others, including those influenced by the reverend's redemption theme. His account of the shooting is necessarily brief; he adds only a conversation between Smith and J. M. Tanner as head of a citizens' delegation. There he states that Tanner told Smith that his "reign in this town is over." Because Suydam was not a witness to the conversation, he could only have repeated it second-hand or invented it.

Suydam referred to Smith's "reign" of Skagway, as Sinclair did to his "baneful rule." Where Sinclair spouted allegory, Suydam repeated the narrow worldview of a friend of Soapy Smith. Suydam relied on these men—most probably the newspaper writers Alan Hornsby and Billie Saportas—who between May and July had helped Smith engage in a self-promotion campaign to advertise his business and to support his not inconsiderable ego. That ego had been dealt a serious blow when, in late 1894, reformers in Denver closed the saloons and sent him a strong message that his brand of political patronage was not appreciated.

Away from Skagway in the spring of 1898, Suydam wrote that he visited with a friend of Smith's in Seattle. Of course, this friend would state that Soapy was in charge: Soapy ran his small sector of the world. Had Suydam consulted with Charles Sperry, Tom Whitten, Sam Graves, Mike Heney, or J. M. Tanner, he probably would have gotten a very different viewpoint, and Soapy would have been far from the top of the list of who was running Skagway.

Taking their lead from the redemption portion of Rev. Sinclair's message, and no doubt alarmed at the negative press that the theft of J. D. Stewart's gold had generated for their community, Skagway's promoters worked hard to establish the port as a respectable city in the months following the killings of Jeff Smith and Frank Reid. But it had never been all that violent, despite the efforts afterwards to make it seem so. In all of 1898, only four men were killed by gunshot in Skagway: Andy McGrath, James Rowan, Jeff Smith, and Frank Reid.[21] In the special edition of January 1, 1900, the editor of the *Daily Alaskan* printed the crime statistics in Skagway for the year 1899. No murders and no gambling cases appeared on the list. With a population of 3,110 souls and tens of thousands more pouring through on the White Pass Trail, the thirty-one cases of assault and battery, thirty-one cases of larceny, and thirty cases of disorderly conduct during 1899 hardly seemed worth mentioning.[22]

John Troy, who had edited the *Daily Alaskan* as early as 1899, became chief editor of the paper in 1902. When the city was incorporated in 1901, he headed the nominating committee of the Citizen's Party, the group of businessmen who won the first city election and would dominate city politics for the next six years. Troy would become one of the town's greatest promoters. He believed that in order to make Skagway grow, it was incumbent upon all businessmen to cast the city in the best possible light to attract new business, new investment, and new energy. Anything negative said about the town did it a disservice. Reminding anyone of the chaotic Bad Old Days of '98 was strictly forbidden. An examination of eight years of Troy's newspaper articles proves that he would not print any story that put Skagway in a negative light. No mention of Soapy Smith was allowed.[23]

Not so in other Alaskan communities. As in the period between 1898 and 1901, sporadic items appeared mentioning members of Smith's gang, Skagwayans who had run them out of town, or the bad old days when Smith lived in Skagway. More press was devoted to the first topic than any others. Joe Brown, a Soapy gang member, was arrested in Skagway for drunkenness at the Board of Trade Saloon in April 1902; gang member Joe Moore tried to sue district Judge Brown for incompetency in July 1902. In October 1902, "Long Shorty" Bigelow was sentenced to ten years at McNeil Island for robbery of a Klondiker's gold. Joe Young, another Soapy colleague, was given a "blue ticket" out of Seattle in May 1904 for trying scams in the tenderloin area of that city. A report came out in November 1904 that George Wilder had been released from prison. And Kid Preston, also known as The Mysterious Kid, was given a fifteen-year sentence for housebreaking in Walla Walla, Washington, in December 1904.[24]

Of less interest to the newspapers outside of Skagway were the town heroes of Skagway. Only two articles appeared during that time period reminding folks of the men who cleaned up the town: in July 1902, the *Juneau Daily Alaska Dispatch* announced that John Stanley, who became mayor after Soapy Smith's alleged regime was ended, had returned from Nome. And in May 1906, Frank Burns, "head of the anti-Soapy Smith force at Skagway," was mentioned as one of the passengers on *The Dolphin*, a local steamship.[25] Of course, Burns had merely been a member of the city council at the time. On the other hand, the Juneau newspaper twice referred to the rough and ready frontier days of Skagway as "the days of Soapy Smith."[26] Only once did it cite Smith's humor to make a point. Or rather, the newspaper quoted Judge James Wickersham, who quoted Soapy Smith, as he debated a rival politician. "Be a good loser and a reasonable man," shouted the judge, who, as the *Juneau Dispatch* pointed out, was "echoing the admonition of the late Honorable 'Soapy' Smith to the astonished Argonaut who had been sandbagged and relieved of his money and effects." Wickersham meant only that his political rival was just as slick and corrupt as the now legendary con man.[27]

Being the possessors of a picture showing scenes attending the last acts in the life of "Soapy" Smith, which is annually looked upon by thousands; having been called upon hundreds of times to relate the story of the career of "Soapy" in this city, coupled with requests from all parts of the country that the facts be put into print, has caused us to publish this little book. No pretense is made towards literary ability. Our effort has been to give a plain, unvarnished recital of the affair, and in such form it is herewith presented to the public from whom we trust it may receive such consideration as it may deserve.

Shea & Patton to readers of *The "Soapy" Smith Tragedy,*
1907

By 1906, Smith's story had stayed outside Skagway, at least in print. That did not keep it out of the back rooms of the town's saloons. That year, Chris Shea, part owner of the Pack Train Saloon, started the Labor Party "as a joke but taken up seriously" and ran for city councilman against the businessmen of John Troy's Citizen's Party. The Labor Party endorsed two of the Citizen's candidates and offered up five other candidates, including Shea himself. Five of the candidates endorsed by the Labor party won, with Shea losing by only twelve votes. The election concerned *Daily Alaskan* editor John Troy, who saw the near loss of his Citizen's political party to a saloon keeper as a blow against the respectability that he and others of Skagway had been building so carefully ever since "cleaning up the town" in July of 1898.[28]

Shea did not give up. In April 1907, he gathered the working class and fought that much harder for his Labor Party, this time sweeping all of the remaining Citizen's candidates off the slate and bringing his entire party to victory. That included himself, who came in seventy-three votes ahead of the highest scoring candidate of the Citizen's Party. With Shea as the only businessman, and a saloon-owner at that, the rest of the new council consisted of working-class men.[29] Jesse Murphy's colleagues could now interpret the Smith legend.

Troy had badly misgauged the issues and interests of his readership. One of his biggest mistakes was ignoring a railroad strike that had lasted from December 1906 through April 1907 in a town where the WP&YR was the major employer. Shea, as part owner of the working man's preferred meeting hall—a saloon—knew all about their labor issues and concerns, and subsequently rallied the vote. Troy's efforts to distract the voters with threats that Shea would reintroduce gambling to a town that had made it illegal in the fall of 1906 backfired. The working men in Skagway probably wanted those gambling tables, not petty con games conducted by the likes of Soapy Smith but faro, black jack, poker, and roulette run by saloon owners like Chris Shea, George Rice, Robert Smith, and Lee Guthrie, and honest gamblers such as Phil Snyder, Frederick "Doc" DeGruyder, and Pat Renwick. The workingmen certainly thought discussing issues such as wages and working hours was more important than talking tax rates.

As spring wore into summer 1907, Shea decided that he could not count on the working class alone to maintain him in control of Skagway's city government. He needed to consolidate his power with both the working class and the middle class. As a businessman, he had originally been interested in tax issues, and he began to court other middle-income merchants, pushing forward some of his plans to cut real estate taxes while raising taxes on store inventories. This plan would—and did, in 1908—restructure the taxes in Skagway, putting the burden on the big companies such as the Moore Wharf Company and WP&YR, so that he could cut taxes for homeowners and small businessmen.[30]

Shea's plan was successful. He joined forces with Si Tanner's Taxpayer's Party—which had been active since 1903—got new support from the middle-class businessmen in town, became mayor, and effected his restructuring of the tax code, all in 1908.[31]

It was during the summer of 1907, while Shea was contemplating his 1908 election campaign, that the Skagway Chamber of Commerce began to consider how to celebrate its first decade as a city. A number of projects were put forward, and Shea hit upon the idea of a booklet that showed how much the town had changed since the wild and chaotic days of the gold rush.

Ever since taking over the *Daily Alaskan* in 1901, John Troy had depicted petty crime waves as reminders of "the days of Soapy,"[32] suggesting a mythical time before law and order set in, before his Citizen's Committee controlled City Hall. These were the only references Troy would make to Smith or the lawless times of the gold rush days. On the other hand, Shea believed celebrating Soapy's legend would show how far Skagway had come out of the mythical wilderness.

Because Shea and his partner, Fred Patten, owned several photographs depicting the violent episode, their bartenders were constantly questioned about the early days. They thought they could serve the public by putting the story to print. If it helped give the politician, Shea, some publicity, so much the better.[33]

It is patently obvious why Chris Shea, city politician, would choose the popular Soapy Smith "Tragedy" for his subject matter. The possession of eleven Case and Draper photographs in a collage (including the Rev. Sinclair's picture of Soapy on a prancing horse) gave him a decided visual advantage and a platform from which to tell the story. The morality play—a villain taking over a town in the face of political chaos, a hero purging the town of its social ills, and the community's redemption—fit clearly into his political plans. The story was perfect for the type of humor and political satire common in the working-class saloon of the time. In fact, as a bartender Shea had probably been rehearsing most of the funniest lines in his story for years.[34]

Shea had come to Skagway in the fall of 1897 and was registered in the Mondamin Hotel in January 1898. He may have been the "Shea" who was one of Ed Fay's guards on February 1 and 2, 1898. As a bartender and member of the sporting world, he had plenty of opportunity to become acquainted with Soapy Smith. If he was not in Skagway at the time of the killing, he certainly would have known many of the people involved in the affair. In later years, he ran for councilman as a "Taxpayer" with Si Tanner. Their party was, in fact, called "Shea, Tanner & Co." by their opponents. Tanner would certainly have shared his version of events with Shea.[35]

The owner of the Pack Train Saloon had every reason to include himself in the Smith story, but chose not to, wisely it appears. In fact, a careful reading of his version shows it—at face value—to be the classic, legendary version: one hero, one villain, and a fully redeemed Skagway. Read aloud with a dead-pan face, it must have given everyone in town who had been in Skagway on July 8, 1898, a very big chuckle. Not a sentence in the story could be argued . . . or taken at full face value.

The satire in *The "Soapy" Smith Tragedy* can best be understood in the context of the politics of the time, and according to the bias of the narrator. When read aloud by Shea or one of his party sympathizers, a bald statement like "The members of the vigilance committee straightway crawled back into their shells where they remained until the tragedy that freed the community"[36] would send the entire audience into gales of laughter. Of course the customers of the Pack Train Saloon knew that the Committee of One Hundred and One had been alive and well all through the spring and early summer of 1898. But picturing those uptight "citizens" hiding in the face of Soapy's bluster appealed tremendously to the awakening working-class Labor Party that gathered in Shea's saloon.

And so it was that the other exaggerations in the booklet were likewise recognized and laughed at. Shea's customers knew that Soapy postured about his "Law and Order Committee of 317," but when Shea called it the "Law and Order Committee of Three Hundred and Three," the exaggeration merely sounded funny, and so they laughed. The working class was equally delighted to hear Soapy promoted from marshal of the Fourth division of the Fourth of July parade to simply "marshal of the day." And although most of them knew that Soapy hated his nickname, when Shea asserted that the appellate "Soapy" was used with affection, the reader or listener no doubt doubled up with laughter. All of these quips appear on the fifth page of the booklet. They are as telling as the reversed photograph of Soapy on the prancing gray horse, printed as the frontispiece. Anyone living in Skagway in 1907 would have been able to figure out where the photograph was taken, and that Soapy was not headed north to his saloon, but south to the end of the parade. The photograph, like many of the sentences in the booklet, was just the opposite of what it appeared to be.

Every paragraph of the booklet, if not every sentence, contains a similar sly joke. Enough information is correct that the Chamber of Commerce could not toss it out as blatantly wrong.

The *Daily Alaskan* announced on August 6, 1907, that *The "Soapy"*

Smith Tragedy, compiled by Chris Shea, had been submitted to their printing house, and it promised to be "the most authentic story of the affair that has ever been published."[37] Throughout November, the newspaper advertised copies of The "Soapy" Smith Tragedy, for seventy-five cents a piece, and by November 4 five hundred copies had been sold. It was a hit.

And Shea's motivation seems wholly political. He wished to demonstrate his pride in his city by showing how advanced it had become. He ended his tribute to Skagway by describing Frank Reid's grave, "a granite shaft surrounded by a low wall—a sturdy monument to the man who gave his life to free Skagway from organized anarchy."[38] It is Sinclair's redemption theme restated wholesale.

Much of the legend outlined by Rev. Sinclair was given full flesh here, in this seemingly harmless tribute to the pioneers of Skagway. Skagway's founders could not be brave and fearless without a cunning, conniving villain on whom to test their courage. That is why, in Shea's retelling of Sinclair's story, Smith became "a sharper of wide reputation on the frontier and a masterful man," an archrascal, the head of a gang of rogues who organized a reign of terror in Skagway.[39] How else could Frank Reid rise to such heroic status, except by killing the villain on the Juneau Wharf?

It is from Shea's Irish wit, with his tongue firmly imbedded in his cheek, that the legend first emerges that Soapy's Law and Order Committee of Three Hundred and Three (not 317) forced the "vigilante" committee "back into their shells" and that the War Department backed Smith's "Alaska" Guards. Shea points an unwavering finger at "weaker-kneed business men who feared to offend the uncrowned king by absence" in the parade. It is the first time since the Denver and Seattle newspaper obituaries that we see the term "uncrowned king."[40]

What is this? Hidden meaning in such a simple story? So maybe it was not quite so simple after all. The most telling paragraph of Shea's booklet, full of meaning for the people who were in Skagway in July 1898 and August 1907, but almost indecipherable to anyone not in the know, comes right before the shoot-out on the wharf.

> During the later hours of the afternoon [of the 8th] the feeling
> that the time for a crucial test of strength between decency
> and crime was at hand became general. The bluster of Soapy

and his gang found counterpart in the quiet but determined
demeanor of the vigilantes, while the conservative business
element was on a nervous qui vive to so trim its actions that
the cause of the party that might come out on top could be
espoused with becoming grace.[41]

Shea appears to blame the conservative doubters, those of the business element who would not involve themselves in the controversy,
the friends of Allan Hornsby and Billie Saportas who insisted on riding the fence, and who had probably continued to do so ever since.
Could that mean people like hotel owner Harriet Pullen, who had
gone on to make a profit off the Soapy Smith story?

There can be little doubt, as the story continues, of Shea's irony,
the way he firmly keeps his tongue in his cheek as he describes Smith.
Especially when he talks about Smith's funeral and the lack of attend-
ees. He notes, "The Honorable Jefferson Randolph Smith, the free
hearted 'Soapy', the generous good fellow and acknowledged leader
of the town, worshiped by his gang, courted by the business people
and tolerated by everyone, had none to do him honor when he
fell."[42] It appears that the saloon owner's twisted humor was never
more obvious. This was councilman-cum-mayor Shea's way of laugh-
ing at Smith, making fun of a man who thought he owned the world.
Smith's biographers, unfortunately, thought Shea was being serious.
The customers and voters in Shea's Pack Train Saloon knew otherwise.

There are definite parallels between the writings of Rev. Sinclair
and Chris Shea, suggesting that the latter saw some of the manuscripts
of the former. Sinclair wrote of Smith's grave in the draft of an article
he prepared for the London-based *Strand* magazine in 1901. "The
rough, ungraded stump & stone 'city of the dead,' the monstrous
roar of the mountain stream, broken only by the rattle of the passing
freight wagons on the way after gold seemed to me to be fitting sym-
bols of the Wild West life he chose to lead."[43] Whereas in 1958 Pierre
Berton would come right out and steal these words ("Sinclair took
the body out to the little cemetery along the White Pass trail, where
to the monotonous roar of the mountain streams and the occasional
passing freight wagon, it was committed"),[44] Shea found another way
to borrow the concept.

> Out of a dark forest, that mingles with the clouds when the rain
> falls, over the brink of a mountain, plunges Reid's Falls, to the
> bench above the river where the people of Skagway have laid
> their dead, rest the victims of the double tragedy. The dirge of
> the wind in the spruce trees, the murmur of the river and the
> roar of the falls alone break the stillness of the quiet spot, save
> when a passing locomotive shrieks a reminder that civilization
> now reigns the route to the great gold fields.[45]

Updated to account for both Reid's and Smith's deaths and the subsequent construction of the railroad past the cemetery, Shea's passage still makes the same point. The fallen lay among Nature; mankind rushes on to the gold fields. Rev. Sinclair's redemption message did not bypass Chris Shea.

Shea's mention of Smith as the "uncrowned king" in the passage with the businessmen is significant, as it is only the third time in which the term was used. The *Denver Times* of August 7, 1898, had labeled Smith a "Con King," but that newspaper, which catered to Denver's sporting crowd, paid homage to him as a master of the confidence game, not as a boss of Skagway. Contemporary newspaper articles had spoken of Smith using the political slang of the time, usually as a "boss," "chief," or once, even a "shah." In those contexts, they implied that he enabled influence buying during political elections. Shea's shift to the word *king* was a natural outgrowth of both Rev. Sinclair's and Harry Suydam's use of the word *reign*, without the word *king*.

Significantly, Shea himself had been called "King of Skagway" before he wrote his Smith satire. On August 11, 1907, the *Juneau Alaska Dispatch* wrote, "Councilman Chris Shea, the king of Skagway municipal politicians, baseball team backer and prince of sports, was in the city yesterday with his wife and daughter. Shea led the reform forces to victory at the last Skagway election." The following May, the editor of the *Skagway Interloper*, a weekly newspaper that catered to the working-class crowds, ran a political cartoon showing Mayor Shea with a crown on his head. It did not have to label him as "King of Skagway," because voters had already made him their ruler.[46] Shea, to the delight of his working-class readership, indirectly wrote himself into his Soapy Smith tragedy with his reference to the King of Skagway.

Shea's depiction of Soapy as the uncrowned king of Skagway, a man who rallied weak-kneed businessmen, evoked a comical political image that appealed to Shea's working-class clientele as well as to his more liberal-minded middle-class associates. Shea won more votes than any other city council candidate in the 1908 election, and became mayor of Skagway. The editor of the *Daily Alaskan* attributed his success to his ability to get out the vote among the saloons and working class, leveling a charge of Denver-style bossism and political corruption.[47] Shea turned it into an inside joke, one that would ultimately feed a local legend.

———

Did Chris Shea intend to become one of Soapy Smith's legend-makers? Probably not. On August 6, 1907, the *Daily Alaskan* noted that Shea and Patten intended to share the booklet with their friends, indicating they had not originally thought of selling it to the public at large. They had not yet decided what would be done with the other copies. Shea probably meant it as a local political joke, and the entire thing was to be taken with a big round of beer and peanuts and lots of laughter, with the guys in the bar considering who wrote it. The complete lack of mention of Si Tanner (no one joked about Tanner), and no discussion of Jesse Murphy, both of whom most people in town knew a lot about, is a dead giveaway as to the nature of this version. The booklet was no doubt intended to promulgate jokes, laughter, and barroom conversations about local politics. No one, especially its creator, meant for it to be taken seriously, much less to promulgate a legend.[48]

CHAPTER SIX

The Journalists and the Memoirs

Soapy Smith was a bad man, to a degree, in externals only. Inwardly he possessed the open-hearted characteristics of a child, but these were often used to tone down and modify in a way, the lurid criminality of his acts. He tempered his sand-bagging and robbery many times with a benevolence and "square deal" reaction that frequently gained him immunity from prosecution or mob law. That was the object he sought. Even his naturally generous instincts were used as a bluff.

Don Steffa, "'Soapy' Smith, Bad Man and Bluffer," 1908

When Rev. Sinclair established Soapy Smith as an irredeemable villain, he set the stage of the morality play for all sorts of permutations on Smith's character. If in some future versions, he would become "uncrowned king," in others he would become a loveable rascal, capable of redemption, but one who chose the "way of the transgressor." Various legend-makers would choose their own variation on these two themes.

The earliest writers, Cy Warman and George Buffum, promoted Soapy's generosity. It is true that Smith had often tried to buy his way out of fixes, after the fact, tempering his criminal acts with generosity to widows, orphans, dogs, and the homeless by making token donations to charitable causes with the money he had stolen from gullible shills. It was a common device of magicians and sleight-of-hand manipulators throughout the ages to deflect attention from their true object—robbery. Smith no doubt viewed his charitable donations as business expenses, much the same way heads of corporations have done throughout the ages.

Jefferson Smith, largely due to his undeniable charm, had indeed been treated as a "character" of the West even as early as 1898. Cy Warman briefly mentioned Soapy in his tale of the killing of Bob Ford, the assassin of Jesse James. In setting the scene for Ford's assassination, Warman describes Creede, Colorado, in 1892. One of the colorful characters in the background is Soapy Smith, who made a donation of five dollars to a collection for a dead prostitute. Smith's Rival matches that donation and quips, "Charity covereth a multitude of sins."[1]

Likewise, George Buffum mentions Smith in passing in his collection of stories about wandering in the West. Although entitled *Smith of Bear City and Other Frontier Stories* (1906), the Smith of the title is another character, and the short chapter on Soapy Smith is devoted entirely to his Creede days. Buffum plays up the petty con man's generosity to clergymen and prostitutes, and dismisses his tendency to scam men who had recently won their fortunes in the gold mines.[2] This Robin Hood theme would dominate later accounts of the thief.

The next four journalists to write about Smith—Don Steffa, Will Irwin, Barkalow Barnacle, and Guy Forsney—made an indelible impression on future researchers, and it is important to understand both their motives and their credentials in order to appreciate the evolution of the Soapy legend.

An early creator was Don Steffa, once a journalist with Portland's *Morning Oregonian*. In October 1908, Steffa published an important article in the *Pacific Monthly* entitled "Soapy Smith: Bad Man and Bluffer." Now more than ten years after Smith's death, Steffa compared Smith to the outlaws of Dodge City and Billy the Kid, saying the only difference between the earlier villains and the confidence man was that Smith was "a bluffer as well as a bad man." He bluffed his way through his career, his last bluff not working out the way he intended.[3]

The bulk of Steffa's story deals with the Colorado years, but when Smith finally gets to Skagway, the con man finds the city to be without a code of law, a condition well advertised in the newspapers on the West Coast in 1897 and 1898 by Puget Sound outfitters who were trying to convince Klondikers to buy supplies from them before heading north. It is in Steffa's version that readers first learned that Smith "preserved law and order" by preventing the lynching of Ed Fay. "It was pure bluff, but it bore fruit." The fact that Smith was not charged with the murder and robbery of a woman strangled and shot in her room—an act probably committed by Smith gang member Turner Jackson—indicates that he was "immune from punishment."[4]

In Steffa's version, the robbery of J. D. Stewart took place through the guise of a shell game, not a con. Afterwards, the law-abiding citizens conducted a secret meeting, slipping quietly through the night to gather at Sylvester's Wharf. The three guards with Frank Reid were unnamed in Steffa's story, and Smith did not fear them. Smith and Reid bandied words; Smith broke his rifle over Reid's head; Reid misfired several empty shells at Smith before one finally caught and killed the unfortunate bluffer.[5] In the days after the killing, it took a dozen posses to hunt down Smith's gang. Echoing Rev. Sinclair's, Chris Shea's, and the Skagway Chamber of Commerce's message that the Bad Old Days were over and Skagway was now crime-free, Steffa ended his tale with the lesson: "Soapy Smith's death rang down the curtain on Skagway's reign of lawlessness. With this bad man out of the way, the little city thrived in its hopeful orderliness."[6] Steffa further promulgated the theme of Skagway's redemption.

At the time this article was written, Don Steffa was a journalist for a Portland newspaper. He often appeared in the society pages of the *Portland Oregonian* between 1905 and 1910, when he was writing for that paper.[7] Steffa once owned the *Crook County Journal* in Princeville, Oregon, and the *Bend Bulletin* at Bend, Oregon. He and his wife moved to San Francisco in about 1910, whereupon he took up a variety of occupations, including lumbering and mining. He died in Fresno, California, on December 23, 1960, less than six months short of his eightieth birthday.[8]

As an Oregon reporter at the time of the Soapy Smith killing, Steffa had access to the newspapers that arrived on the West Coast through Portland and Seattle, probably the primary source for most of his material on Smith's Alaska days. Also, being in Portland, Steffa was biased by the viewpoint of the West Coast ports, which tried desperately to capture the trade of the Klondikers before they got to Skagway.[9] It was very much in the interest of the Seattle, Vancouver, Tacoma, and Portland newspapers to exaggerate any report of lawlessness in Skagway and Dyea in order to discourage people from staying in those cities long enough to stock up on supplies. The West Coast newspapers battled to get travelers to buy their outfits in local cities before they left the ports and to try to get them to make travel arrangements all the way through to Dawson with a local transportation company. Playing on travelers' fears of murderers and con men like Soapy Smith helped the outfitting, transportation, and shipping companies achieve their goals. A typical article was published in the *Tacoma Daily Times* on February 21, 1898, three weeks after the murders of Andy McGrath and James Rowan. It advised parties going to the Klondike to buy their outfits in Tacoma, where a party of sixty-five men from back east just did so, and reminded their readers, without pause, that Skagway had just organized a vigilance committee.[10]

Steffa, reviewing ten-year-old articles in the Portland newspapers, doubtless saw only alarmist articles to shade his story. And of course, if he saw Shea's 1907 work, he had no reason to understand the political satire underlying the tongue-in-cheek criticism of the merchants who could not keep the railroad from taking over the main street of the town or assessing a quarter of the value of the downtown properties. The simple morality play was the obvious and easiest story to grasp. Steffa swallowed it whole.

———

Also in 1908, the *Saturday Evening Post* published a series of stories entitled *Confessions of a Confidence Man as Told to Will Irwin*. In 1909, these stories were collected and reissued as a book under the title *The Confessions of a Confidence Man*, Irwin sharing credit with Edward H. Smith. This Smith is not to be confused with Soapy's cousin, Edwin B. "Bobo" Smith. Any of Soapy's friends who might have expected the story to be about the Denver and Skagway con man were to be disappointed. The confidence man of the title was A. B. Stafford, who started on his life of crime at the age of seventeen in a midwestern city and gave it up in his mid-forties after discovering that crime does not pay. The narrator, Stafford, was a friend of Jeff Steers, who claimed to have worked alongside Soapy in Alaska for a few weeks during the spring of 1898, and the reader is treated to about six pages of the Smith story in Alaska.[11]

Through Stafford's narration about Steers's time with Soapy, Irwin has very little to say about the actual killing of Smith, having left Skagway before that important event. Steers does accuse Alaskans of exaggerating the villainy of the Smith gang by making them into robbers and killers. He goes on to deny that was the way they operated. Robbery and murder were too risky, and the money came too easily with just the petty con games. There was no need to resort to such crimes as robbery and murder.[12] Apparently, Steers did not consider the con games thievery.

The only reason this source is important, other than the fact that later biographers reference it, is due to the confusion of Edward H. Smith with Edwin B. Smith. Later biographers would make much of the fact that E. B. Smith worked for the *Washington Post*.[13] This connection added supposed authenticity to the legend because of the association between the nationally famous author, Irwin, and Soapy's supposed cousin. Or so it seemed.

According to the Library of Congress, Edward H. Smith, who co-authored the *Correspondence of a Crook*, lived from 1881 to 1927. The 1900 census places an Edward H. Smith with a birth date of 1881 in Washington, D.C., living with his parents, Charles B. Smith and Mary L. Smith, and sisters Bella W. and Ethel Smith. He was eighteen years old at the time and was working as a clerk at an art store. In 1910, he still lived with his parents, although he had acquired a wife, Ellen, and he was considered the head of household, with his parents as dependents. He was now working as a draftsman at a typographical business. By 1920, his mother had passed on, but his father still resided with him. He had a new, younger wife, and still no children. Still a draftsman, he worked for the federal government. In 1923, he published a modified version of *Confessions of a Confidence Man*, subtitling it *A Handbook for Suckers*. He died in 1927; that same year, he or his widow published *Mysteries of the Mystery* and *Famous Poison Mysteries*. His widow published *You Can Escape* in 1929.[14] These titles suggest he was a popularizer.

An important contribution to the Soapy Smith legend was Will Irwin, the main author of *Confessions of a Confidence Man*. Irwin wrote regularly for the *Saturday Evening Post, McClure's, Colliers* and other national magazines, and was a well-known author by the time Edward H. Smith approached him to write *Confessions*. Born on September 14,

1873, to middle-class New Yorkers, Irwin had spent his childhood in Leadville, Colorado, at about the time Soapy was learning his sleight-of-hand tricks. Irwin often passed himself as being born a westerner, and he loved to recreate the curious characters of the "wild" West to his largely eastern audience. Publishing almost forty books in the early twentieth century, most of them novels, Irwin practiced a style that has been called "fluent, easy and epigrammatic." He won recognition as a novelist, a short story writer, a newspaper and magazine editor, a dramatist and a poet, but most importantly as a reporter. He has been called one of the greatest reporters in America, a distinction he earned during World War I.[15]

Irwin's gift for fiction is readily evident in *Confessions*. As stated earlier, the story is actually about A. B. Stafford, a reformed confidence man who claimed to know Soapy during his Alaska days. At the time, few people believed the book was about a real con man. Irwin's biographer places the early work in the author's "muckraker" days, and it is possible that in later editions Irwin decided to share credit with Edward H. Smith because he felt the work was substandard. In fact, a 1913 edition does not carry Irwin's name. Nor does Irwin refer to Smith in his autobiography.[16] Clearly, as demonstrated by Soapy's great-grandson Jeff Smith, Edwin H. Smith was *not* the man who was born in Georgia in 1859, was an orphan, grew up with Soapy Smith, and lived in Washington, D.C., until 1941.[17]

The two points of this tangent are simply this: (1) the person who really did know Soapy Smith, A. B. Stafford, did indeed have a valuable contribution to make in clarifying the legend. Soapy himself was no grand larcenist and he was no killer. Having no stake in the redemption tale about Soapy Smith and Frank Reid, Stafford had little reason to exaggerate Smith's villainy. And (2) the ones who did not know Soapy—Edward H. Smith and Will Irwin—were later credited as having an expertise they did not have, simply on the strength of national recognition. Their book, despite the weakness of its authority, appeared in later bibliographies, giving it an authority that it did not deserve.

———

The next article of any note about Soapy Smith appeared in *The*

Trail, a monthly publication of the Sons of Colorado, which was a pioneer organization that published between 1908 and 1928. Coming out in 1920, Barkalow Barnacle's "'Characters' of the Early Day: 'Soapy' Smith, The Gambler," devotes less than one page to the Alaska days. Smith is exonerated from stealing Stewart's gold, but he believed he could retrieve it from the unidentified thieves. He made the mistake of getting drunk and thinking he could control the miners' meeting. The wharf guards tried to keep him out of it; he and Frank Reid struggled, with the result that both died. Barnacle states that if Smith had stayed out of politics, he would never have been kicked out of Denver and would not have gone to Alaska in the first place. He takes the tack that Smith was redeemable, but chose to be a transgressor.[18]

Barnacle claims to have known Smith slightly, but states that he knew Smith's cousin, the aforementioned Edwin B. "Bobo" Smith, better. It was from Bobo that he got most of his information, and therefore, with that authority, he claims it is correct.

According to Jeff Smith, Soapy's great-grandson, Edwin B. Smith was raised by Smith's parents as a brother to Soapy, and they spent their childhood together. Parting when teenagers, they did not meet again until November 1897 in Washington, D.C., when Soapy visited for the purpose of acquiring permission to open a business on the military reservation near St. Michael on the Yukon River.[19] It is not clear how long Smith was in Washington—it could have been two weeks or two months—and all other knowledge "Bobo" had of his cousin would have come through letters.

The personal testimony of the Jeff Smith family could indeed be a valuable viewpoint of the events of July 1898; unfortunately, Soapy did not survive to tell his version of events. As it is probable that "Barkalow Barnacle" is a pseudonym, it is possible that the 1920 publication in *The Trail* was actually written by "Bobo" Smith, a tack he may have taken to avoid breaking his contract with the *Evening Star,* his newspaper in Washington, D.C. At the very least, the story is told from Edwin B. Smith's perspective. In this account, readers of Soapy Smith's life learn that he was a family man, that he cared for his wife and children (although he did not live with them), that he quickly and easily made friends with people of influence, that he passed for a scholar (he

used Latin phrases and spouted Shakespeare, as did many miners at
the time), and that his characteristics ranged from love of gambling
to generosity to those in distress. While a ringleader of more desperate men, he managed to keep worse criminals under control; and his
undoing was his mixing in politics rather than crime.[20]

Although Edwin tried to talk him out of returning to Skagway,
Soapy felt he belonged in the port city to the Klondike, so he went
there after his visit with his cousin. Bobo, through Barnacle, tells a
straightforward version of Soapy's Alaska story, in which Smith had
no hand in the stealing of Stewart's gold, tried to retrieve it for him
due to his leadership position in the community, and was wrongfully
killed by one of the wharf guards when denied his rightful place at
the citizens' meeting. His belongings were seized and his wife was left
penniless in St. Louis. His character was besmirched by the disrepu-
table character of the friends he kept.[21] As would be expected from a
family account, the words *charming* and *entertaining* appear far more
frequently than *swindler* or *criminal.*

Perhaps it is only fitting that the title of this very positive portrayal
also appears in the bibliographies of all of the major biographies of
Soapy Smith.[22]

––––––––

Of final note in this trail of journalists in the first three decades of
the twentieth century was the 1927 publication of Guy Forsney's article in the *St. Louis Dispatch* and almost simultaneous reprint in a Sunday supplement of the *Rocky Mountain News.* It recounted Smith's last
months in the Far North, told from the often erroneous reports in
the two newspapers. From Forsney, the reader learned such inaccurate "facts" that Smith's "gambling establishment in Skagway was one
of the most elaborate the northwest ever saw. It had only one rival
for size and none for ferocity or double dealing." Readers discovered
that Smith gave a widow $500 when she said she needed $117 to get
home; that Soapy and Reid were on good terms and that Reid was the
only man Smith feared; that Smith himself broke up a mass meeting
of the Law and Order League run by Frank Reid on July 1 (the Committee of One Hundred and One?); that Smith broke up another
meeting on July 4 and that Frank planned a third one for July 8; and

that Frank Reid stood up alone against Smith and four hundred of his followers. Readers in Denver "learned" that President McKinley sent flowers to the dying Frank Reid while children were taught to spit on Soapy's grave. Since then, Skagway had "carved" a monument to Smith, a great grinning skull at the mouth of the harbor to remind all who approached of the follies of lawlessness.[23] Forsney freely invented details to elaborate on the evolving mythology of the lawless town ruled by the uncrowned Smith, redeemed only by the deaths of Smith and Reid. Skagway continued her spirit of contrition by constructing a lasting, grisly monument to remind sinners of what would happen to them if they tried similar acts of lawlessness in the rehabilitated community.

Thus the legend evolved, springing not so much from facts but from moral lessons taught by authorities with dubious credentials or by friends and relatives who fondly remembered a fallen comrade. The legend grew because it struck a resonant chord, one with which both Americans and Canadians identified: lawlessness inevitably must give way to law and order; good must inevitably triumph over evil; self-sacrifice always results in the betterment of society. Or, the dead must be remembered fondly. These sentiments found expression in the American frontier myth, more recently articulated by Richard Slotkin.[24] Civilization could be regenerated by violence; evil could be redeemed by the blood of the sinner, Soapy Smith, and the martyr, Frank Reid.

While correspondents for national magazines might be excused for finding a redemption legend easy to consume and pass on to their readers, why would eyewitnesses falsely remember the exploits of Jefferson Randolph Smith? When it came time to commit their memories to pen and paper, why would such dignitaries as the president of the White Pass and Yukon Route railroad, the commander of the Northwest Mounted Police, and the physician who examined Soapy Smith's body after his death recall the legend of Smith's great villainy at the expense of Skagway's moral reputation? And all for the sake of perpetuating a legend? Does it make sense?

Indeed, Samuel Graves, the president of the British-owned railroad, and Samuel Steele, the Canadian commander at the border between Alaska and British Columbia, did have good reasons to exaggerate the lawlessness and chaos of Skagway, compared to the law and order in the British colonies. The WP&YR was interested in obtaining licenses, rights-of-way, and franchises at a time when the exact location of the border had not been determined; Major Steele had been sent to the border to protect British interests in the region. Both Canadian and British nationals, especially those of the upper-middle and upper classes to which Samuel Graves, Samuel Steele, and Fenton Whiting belonged, felt superior to the working and middle-class Americans who swarmed into Skagway the winter of 1897–98. The theme of the redemption of a sinning Skagway taken up by the British-Canadian Rev. Sinclair was much to the liking of men who wrote memoirs of their days in the Far North in the decades that followed the publication of first generation American and working class Chris Shea's political satire. Whereas Shea was a first-generation working-class American who made sly fun of the legend, these elite white males embraced the theme of a lawless town ruled by a lawless "uncrowned king." They showed how either the railroad or the Mounties alone were superior to the crude vigilantes who were incapable of controlling him.

––––––––

> The criminal element, though numerous, were in the minority,
> but they had the advantage of being thoroughly organized
> and armed, and skillfully led by a man named "Soapy" Smith,
> who was the uncrowned King of Skaguay. He was not a
> constitutional monarch, but his word was all the law there was.
>
> Samuel H. Graves, *On the White Pass Payroll,* 1908

The first important memoir to recount the Soapy Smith story was that of Samuel H. Graves, the British-born representative of the White Pass and Yukon Route, who operated out of the company's Chicago office. He arrived in Skagway on July 2, 1898, to investigate the expenditure of investors' funds for the Close Brothers, who owned the railroad. He readily admits that his advisors in all matters were construction superintendent Michael Heney, chief engineer Erastus C. Hawkins, and Hawkins's assistant, civil engineer John Hislop. He says that he sent his account of the Soapy Smith affair to WP&YR headquarters "at the time," an assertion which may be called into question because his note dated July 11 states that Reid had died, an event that did not take place until July 20.[25]

Graves was born in London in 1861, but became an American citizen in 1885 in order to serve as the American head of the British-owned corporation. He spent most of his adult life in Chicago, although he traveled extensively to London and the Close Bros. field headquarters in Vancouver, British Columbia. In fact, he was visiting Canada when he died of a heart attack on November 13, 1911.[26]

Like many of the later eyewitnesses, Graves places himself foremost in the action near the Juneau Wharf, along with the three railroad managers. He states that Reid was one of three men guarding the entrance to the wharf, one of them including railroad laborer Jesse Murphy. He does not mention Si Tanner at all, even by position as the man who replaced the U.S. deputy marshal. Graves does not refer to the presence of the U.S. Army, either. In fact, he alludes to the deputy marshal in quotation marks, as if questioning his authority, stating that there was no duly authorized law in Skagway.[27]

This attitude to law enforcement and authority in Skagway was to the White Pass's and Close Brothers' advantage. Trying to gain a monopoly on transportation services between tidewater and the navigable waters of the Yukon River, Graves would shortly be negotiating a license for railroad and other transportation rights with the British government. He had far more faith in the Northwest Mounted Police than he did in the U.S. Marshals Service, and any effort he could make at showing how little control the latter had in Skagway was to his distinct advantage. The Soapy Smith affair could not have happened at a better time, from Graves's standpoint.

One of the most interesting aspects of Graves's account is the detailed description of Jesse Murphy's actions on the wharf after the killing. While ignoring Tanner's presence on the wharf, he praises the railroad laborer's quick action in seizing Smith's rifle and holding off Soapy's bodyguards or "Tigers."[28] The combination of Graves's repeated refusal to recognize Si Tanner's role in any of the events

leading up to and the days after the killing, combined with his tribute to Jesse Murphy, the only employee of the railroad at the scene
of the killing, reinforces the probability that Murphy actually shot
Smith. The likelihood that members of Soapy's gang interfered
with Graves's view of the fast-occurring events, or that the struggle
between Murphy and Smith over Smith's rifle occurred so quickly
that Graves could not see exactly what happened, probably explains
why he would credit Reid and not Murphy with the killing of Smith.
Then, too, Graves, like everyone else, was ready to accept the legend
as it was evolving into fact, because it reinforced his preconceived
idea that lawlessness ruled in any American town.

Furthermore, Graves was a member of the white British upper-
middle class, which saw itself as superior to Americans in general and
the largely immigrant working class in particular. While he could not
acknowledge the efforts of "vigilantes" such as Si Tanner, he could
show himself in a central, positive role in leading the forces of civilization against the forces of chaos and criminality. As has been discussed
previously, this class believed it had both the right and the privilege
to exact justice. In Graves's view, the Irish laborer Jesse Murphy could
assist in bringing down the violent criminal Smith, but only those of
class and privilege had the means and authority to administer true
justice. The "truth" could be told only by those of sufficient position
and rank to re-establish civil order.[29] With leaders and memoirs such
as these, it can be seen how historic fact was warped from the very
moment it happened, and later perpetuated.

———

The town of Skagway at this period of its existence [February
1898] was about the roughest place in the world. The
population increased every day; gambling hells, dance halls
and variety theatres were in full swing. "Soapy" Smith, a "bad
man," and his gang of about 150 ruffians, ran the town and
did what they pleased; almost the only persons safe from them
were members of our force. Robbery and murder were daily
occurrences.

Samuel Steele, *Forty Years in Canada*, 1915

Major Samuel B. Steele, born in Simcoe County, Ontario, on January 5, 1849, was commander of the North West Mounted Police at the border between the United States and Canada at the time that Jefferson Randolph Smith was killed on July 8, 1898. Widely respected throughout the region, he had been stationed at Lake Bennett since late February 1898. His primary responsibility was to ensure that any party passing into Canada had sufficient supplies to stave off starvation, a condition that had threatened many lives the previous winter. Steele, commanding a better outfitted and better paid force than the U.S. marshals, was contemptuous of the Americans' custom of dealing with the criminal element through miners' meetings and kangaroo courts. Perhaps not considering the difference between a military district and a formal U.S. territory, Steele could not understand why the U.S. marshals had little or no authority—indeed, few Americans understood the distinction, including the marshals and the army officers, who squabbled over limited funds. In the absence of reliable government response, U.S. citizens did as they always did in the mining frontiers: they resorted to miners' committees.

Steele devoted very little space to Skagway in his 1915 memoir of the forty years he spent serving the North West Mounted Police in Canada, and all of his impressions of the town and its citizens were negative. The page and a half describing the town consists mostly of slurring verbiage about the noise and the sporting world, suggesting that Skagway engaged in a continual drunken party, in which gunshots, murder, and robbery were common occurrences.[30]

Significantly, Steele was in Skagway in February and March, 1898. Unlike him, the Seattle and Victoria newspapers assert that Skagway saloons, gambling dens, dance halls, and bunco operations had been shut down at this time (see chapter 3). Had Steele's seventeen-year-old memory failed him? Or did he want to remember a lawless town ruled by a dire sinner in need of redemption?

It seems likely that Steele, like the Canadian Pierre Berton forty-three years later, was interested in inventing a contrast between American and Canadian ways of enforcing the law, to make himself and his organization appear more "civilized." It certainly is to Steele that we can trace Pierre Berton's description of Skagway as the sort of town in which saloons and gambling halls stayed open around the clock and gunshots could be heard at any time of day. It does not seem a coincidence that both Canadians would wish to make Dawson appear more sophisticated that its American counterpart.

William R. Hunt in *Distant Justice*, his study of law enforcement in Alaska during the late-nineteenth and early twentieth centuries, concludes that neither the criminal activities nor the systems of justice in Alaska were different than those in any other American territory at the time.[31] His study of hundreds of criminal cases and contrasts to ones in Arizona and New Mexico indicate that the Northern Frontier simply was not that lawless, despite its reputation in legend and popular literature. And, as shown in the statistical analysis of the homicide rates in Skagway, Dyea, and the Yukon Territory at the end of chapter 4, there really was not that much difference between Alaska and Yukon in terms of violent deaths. Steele and Berton, for nationalistic reasons, found the Skagway version of the American frontier myth to their liking.

————

The next memoir is mentioned only because it epitomizes so many of the old timers' stories that began to crop up in the 1920s. Arthur T. A. Walden, writing in 1928, was a dog sledder, taking his dogs over the Chilkoot into the Yukon in 1896 and over the White Pass Trail in the spring of 1898. During the telling of the latter crossing, he relates a second-hand and badly warped version of the Soapy Smith story. He claims to have known Smith, and been proud of it, but obviously had heard the showdown story so distantly as to get it all wrong.[32]

In the Walden version, Smith "was the leader of about the most desperate gang of criminals that Alaska has ever known." At some time during his "regime," Smith broke up a meeting in a dance hall just by showing up, standing at the back of the hall of the "so-called respectable element" with his Winchester on his shoulder, and saying, "Gentlemen, I think you had better disperse." The telling of this story does not make it clear whether it happened on the occasion of the McGrath and Rowan murders or at one of the early Committee meetings on July 8.[33]

On July 8, Walden has the townspeople electing a guard for the foot of the wharf, and a "stranger" volunteering for the position because he had a score to settle with Smith. Smith showed up with a sawed-off shotgun, both barrels of which he emptied into thin air. He killed no one, but he himself was killed by the stranger. The stranger was later spirited away on a boat so that Smith's gang could not seek revenge.[34] In this way, the unknown hero symbolically cleanses the evil community of its tainted blood by killing its greatest villain.

While the worst of Smith's gang escaped unscathed, Charles Bowers turned himself in and "fairly blackguarded himself out of being lynched." Walden admits to never having heard what happened to Bowers and the others. Smith's widow and orphaned children arrived two months later with letters proving what a good father and husband Smith had been. Walden continues with his fabrication that the citizens of Skagway raised a purse for her two years later.[35] In Walden's imaginative version, the town completed the redemption story by making restitution to Soapy's widow and children.

Because of its many errors, Walden's memoir, especially in the case of the Smith story, is of little value. Its only importance to this study is that it epitomizes a rash of similar stories that followed over the next several decades in which old-timers who claimed to have encountered or known Smith related their own somewhat warped version of the tale. Whether they obtained the original story from the *Skagway News*, the *Daily Alaskan*, Chris Shea, one of the journalists, or someone else who claimed to be an authority, everyone who went north seemed to "know" the legend as it grew. And it continued to thrive, largely because the morality tale was so easy to remember, and so easy to recapture in spirit.

———

"Soapy" Smith, the one biggest man in town by long odds, proudly emphasized that fact by proclaiming himself the "Uncrowned King of Skagway." Many more or less prominent citizens hobnobbed with him, partly through fear, but also for financial gain, indirectly, and winked at his depredations, although well knowing of his depredations. He presented a striking appearance a few days later as he rode a prancing dapple gray horse at the head of the Fourth of July parade, in front of a noisy brass band playing patriotic airs. Dozens of cameras snapped him as he passed, much to his satisfaction and pride. He was killed four days later as an outlaw, by the vigilantes.

Dr. Fenton B. Whiting, *Grit, Grief and Gold*, 1933

Thirty-five years after Smith's death, another employee of the WP&YR decided to join those who were compiling their memoirs of the Far North. Fenton B. Whiting was not only one of the physicians who examined Smith's body but was also among those who hunted down his gang. Whiting wrote *Grit, Grief and Gold: A True Narrative of a Pathfinder in Alaska*, which recounts the time he served as the railroad physician in Skagway from 1898 through 1901, and in other parts of Alaska.[36]

Not published until 1933, the book shows that Whiting's memory had failed in some details. He writes of Ed Fay's acquittal as if it were fact, but does not mention (nor apparently realize) that the man served time for the murder of Andrew McGrath. He called the grand jury "a picked coroner's jury" that acquitted Fay as a case of self-defense, something that did not occur. He implies that this inaccurate verdict, suggesting Skagway's reputation for lawlessness and miscarriage of justice, contributed to stampeders avoiding the White Pass and Skagway for the Yukon River route.[37]

Whiting later asserts that the first "vigilante" meeting was called because Smith's men had stolen a load of liquor off the dock on July 7, and also because of an incident with "an unsophisticated Australian . . . with a fair-sized poke of gold."[38] He had obviously forgotten that J. D. Stewart was from British Columbia, not Australia, and no one had ever mentioned the stolen liquors being of concern to the Committee of One Hundred and One before.

It is understandable that Whiting should get many of the details of July 8, 1898, incorrect. He states that he was at Rocky Point, a railroad stop, six miles out of Skagway, on that day. His description of the shooting matches that of the *Skaguay News* and *Daily Alaskan*, no doubt his primary sources to jog his memory in his later years. He fails to mention the name of any of the "several" guards at the wharf except Frank Reid's. And, critically, he follows Graves's lead, and does not mention Tanner by name: he simply refers to "the new Marshal."[39]

In fact, other than Smith, "Slim Jim," Frank Reid, Mike Heney, and certain other employees of the railroad, Whiting does not provide many names. The author was a good friend of Mike Heney, who was the superintendent in charge of the construction of the railroad. Whiting dedicated his memoir to Heney and included a photograph of the construction superintendent in the frontispiece. The book is devoted to Whiting's memories of the railroad days in Alaska.[40] He worked for the political party that favored the railroad. Si Tanner, on the other hand, spent his entire thirty-year political career in Skagway working with the party that opposed it.

Evidence of Whiting's bias is evident in the scene where "Slim Jim" Foster is recaptured outside the Hotel Burkhard on July 10. In this sequence, a "large man" makes the capture of Slim Jim and turns him over to the U.S. Army. No mention is made of Tanner's role in the episode, which was told in the *Skaguay News* of July 15, 1898.[41]

As in the case of Graves, it is impossible that Whiting did not know of Tanner's part in guarding the wharf and the later clean-up of Skagway. Whiting's private letter to "Georgia," written six years before he published *Grit, Grief and Gold*, praised Tanner as an old friend. "He proved to be a mighty good man. I knew him well, and he always treated me with every Courtesy, even in 'pinches.'" In this letter, he described Tanner holding Van Triplett, John (Charles) Bowers, and Jim Foster at the Hotel Burkhard. Tanner begged the crowd "with crocodile tears in his eyes for 'peace and harmony,' and to 'let the law take its course,' in the language of the officer who is faced with the mob bent upon lynching. . . . Yes, Si was bringing into play every inch of his unnatural eloquence—and he never was borne to be an orator."[42] Perhaps not flattering, but at least Whiting, privately, was willing to acknowledge the role Tanner played in keeping the mob from lynching anyone on the days following the killing of Smith. Why he would not do so publicly can only be due to the local politics: because men like Si Tanner and Chris Shea represented a political party that opposed issues near and dear to the economic good of the WP&YR railroad. Rather than belittle them, Whiting, like Graves, ignored the fact that Tanner was involved in the wharf incident.

Looking back through time made it much easier for Whiting, like Steele and Graves before him, to remember Skagway as a brutal, lawless place, full of sinners and vigilantes, controlled by a con man, and out of the control of good men like Frank Reid and Si Tanner. In these nationalistic memoirs, personal ambition and politics—the British-owned corporation vs. the home-grown merchants—encouraged the growth of the legend that Smith ruled Skagway and that the real heroes of the town—universally labeled "vigilantes"—had to regenerate civilization through violence and redeem the town's reputation.

CHAPTER SEVEN

Skagway Tourism

His lawless word was law in the wild days of the Klondike rush.
Like any feudal baron he ruled Skagway when it was a boom
town. He levied tribute on the hardboiled pilgrims of the
Chilcoot [*sic*] Pass and Heartbreak Trail. His gambling and
drinking joint was the pirate isle of that terrestrial Spanish
Main. And now . . . high on the gray limestone cliff it looms,
the skull of Soapy Smith . . . keeps on grinning through the
deepening dusk, a mammoth, eerie death's head. . . . Surely
one of the most singular monuments by which a liberated
community ever exprest [*sic*] its hatred and mockery, mingled
with grim satisfaction over the downfall of its former despot.
Elsewhere in America, eminent sculptors hew statuary out of
mountainsides in honor of heroes and patriots; on the Alaskan
coast the brow of a cliff is wrought into a ghastly skull to
commemorate the misdeeds of a "bad man."

"Soapy Smith's Skull: An Ironic Monument to a Two-
Gun Tyrant," *Literary Digest*

Tourism: what a vehicle by which to perpetuate a legend. Skagway was forever cleansed of crime by the killing of Skagway's
only criminal. How better to advertise that "fact" than make com-
mercial capital of it?

By the late 1920s and early 1930s, tourism was becoming increasingly important to the economy of Skagway. The fame of its gold
rush days had always been a big draw, and the Smith-story-made-leg-
end, now resolving itself into myth, could not be resisted. Indeed,
why should it be? It was classic, retold from tales as old as Beowulf,
the Trojan War, and the Arthurian cycle. By forfeiting himself, Reid

redeemed not only himself and the vigilantes, but his community. Reid was seen as Christlike after his death.

Although Skagway's tourism promoters did not articulate their love of the Smith story in those exact words, they were quick to see its potential. What had been for them a side business in the 1910s became an increasingly important part of the economy in the 1920s. Helping it all along was a German-born immigrant, Martin Itjen.

In 1880, at nine years old, Itjen immigrated to the United States. At the age of twenty-eight, he came to Skagway, almost a year after Soapy Smith was killed. He worked for the WP&YR as a laborer until about 1905, when he became an express man, one of the many jobs he held through ensuing years. Skagway's economy began to fail in the 1920s, and like so many of the few remaining people in Skagway, Itjen turned to tourism as a way to diversify his economic opportunities during the hard times.[1]

Like Chris Shea, who owned the saloon where Itjen liked to hang out, Martin was a great practical joker. He and several fellows from the YMCA had long had their eyes on a curious rock formation above Moore's Wharf, where he lived while working for WP&YR during those early years in Skagway. One day he and his friends headed out with some cans of whitewash, and together they touched-up what they had all been seeing in the formation: a skull. Like Chris Shea's photographs and booklet of two decades before, the stories about the painted skull proved an endless source of amusement.[2]

The skull-painting party was meant as a joke among the high-spirited young men of Skagway, but none of them anticipated what the national magazines would do with the story. Perhaps what followed is merely coincidence: in fact, it probably is. Guy Forsney's article, which mentioned the skull "carved" into the cliff at Skagway's harbor, was published on September 3, 1927. The *Literary Digest* published an article about the skull the same day. J. M. Tanner died of a heart attack on September 20, 1927, less than three weeks later, about the time both articles would have found their way to Skagway. The old marshal could not have been pleased that a national magazine had brought up the old story that Smith had once "ruled" a lawless Skagway.

Less than two years later, tourist hotel owner Harriet Pullen published her version of the Soapy Smith story. She heroically tried to correct the inaccuracy of the Forsney account, but in doing so, only added to the legend, and, unfortunately, cast it in concrete. By inserting herself into the story and focusing on details, she neglected to address the most salient points of all: Smith did not rule Skagway; Reid alone may not have killed Smith; Skagway had not been a den of iniquity; and the story was not about one hero and one villain.

Indeed Pullen had little interest in disabusing her tourist customers of the legend, because by 1929, the most important point was supplementing Skagway's sagging economy. That could only be done through tourism. And Soapy's morality play, after all, could help boost Skagway's economy by attracting more sightseers.

Over Skagway's first decade, an emerging tourist industry began to grab the attention of its Chamber of Commerce. Seven articles in the *Daily Alaskan* of 1900 featured the way tourism contributed to the economy in the town, with four hundred tourists on one ship in July 1900. By April 1901, the WP&YR openly advertised for tourists, and two years later, the railroad boasted that it expected its biggest year yet. In one day in June 1908, all of Skagway's hotels were packed and the town was filled with five hundred tourists.[3]

By the fall of '97 "crook" rule was thriving in Skagway, the town being split into two factions, the "Skinners" and the "Skinned." The skinners had the better organization and stuck together so that those who were degraded were unable to obtain redress. What an ideal setting then for the re-appearance of "Soapy" Smith; everything arrived to his liking and nothing to prevent his proclaiming himself leader of the rougher element which, I assure you, he lost no time in doing.

Harriet Pullen, *Soapy Smith, Bandit of Skagway*

Harriet Pullen had come to Skagway in September 1898, two months too late to be present when Soapy Smith was killed, despite all of her stories to the contrary. In later life, she told the story that she arrived a year earlier so that she could put herself with the first arrivals. In that account, she rode to shore in a small boat, "as no wharf had yet been built." Of course, to do that, she would have had to land in the winter of 1895–96, as Moore's Wharf was built in the spring of 1896.[4]

In 1902, Harriet Pullen opened her magnificent Pullen House in the two-story, "show-boat"-style mansion built by William Moore. Unlike her competitors, who catered to the traveling businessmen and Yukon residents waiting for a southbound ship, Pullen openly courted tourists. A natural showman, she dressed up in buckskins and wore long braids, and she regaled her guests on the hotel's long porch with tales of the gold rush days. Of course, her stories of the wild, chaotic, and lawless days of '97 and '98 reflected her version of those events.[5]

While the Skagway Chamber of Commerce had long eschewed negative images of Skagway, and said only good things about the town, Harriet Pullen believed otherwise. She gloried in the rough and ready image of its pioneer days of the town, and loved to portray herself as a hardy woman who had struggled with the best of them in a muddy, ramshackle, lawless place. She found that tourists loved that image. She had a wealth of stories to tell, and among them was the killing of that evil villain who had ruled the city, uncontrolled: Soapy Smith. In order to bring intimacy to her stories, she placed herself in them. Harriet told her eager listeners that she came a year earlier than she actually did; that she had "lost" her husband, Daniel; that she baked pies and cooked for the A&NNT Company mill; that she lived in a one-room cabin at the edge of tidewater until she could make enough money to bring her "babies" to her; that she competed with Captain William Moore and his luxurious hotel during the days that Soapy Smith ruled Skagway.[6]

In reality, Pullen had left her four teenaged children with her carpenter husband, Daniel, and her middle-aged sister-in-law, Sarah Pullen, in La Push, Washington, and come to Skagway in September 1898. All of the family joined her in Skagway three to five months later. It was probably Daniel who drove the team of six horses up the Brackett Wagon Road, not Harriet, in the years that followed. By the time the 1900 census was taken, Harriet was listed as having no occupation, simply "at home," with Daniel providing for the entire family, including sister Sarah.[7]

A regularly scheduled tour loop termed the "Inside Passage Tour" had begun in southeastern Alaska in the 1880s. It started in San Francisco or Portland, wended its way through British Columbia to Wrangell, Juneau, and Douglas and on to Glacier Bay. Skagway was added in 1898, and by 1900 five thousand tourists a year were taking the tour. When the WP&YR added Whitehorse and Dawson to the excursion by rail, Skagway became an overnight stop, and the economy of the community benefited.[8] With World War I closing Europe, the "See America First" boosters continued to attract travelers to the North during the teens and twenties.

Harriet loved to tell the stories of the gold rush days to the tourists, but other old-timers were not allowed to listen in. She would shoo them away, mostly because they would interrupt her stories with their own versions, saying she told it wrong or did not have all the facts right. She appropriated the story of Skagway's first white woman resident, Annie Leonard, and made it her own in order to put herself in Skagway during the first days of the rush. It was really Leonard who cooked for the A&TNN Company, and who staked lot 2, block 1, almost at tidewater. Annie Leonard, not Harriet Pullen, was the woman who testified in April 1898 that she saw claim jumpers haul the remains of one of William Moore's first sheds down to the beach and leave it there; it was Leonard who was Skagway's first female landowner, whose testimony at the townsite lawsuits became so critical in curbing the size of the final award to Moore's Wharf and the railroad.[9]

By taking the persona of Skagway's woman pioneer, Harriet Pullen put herself into a place she really did not know except through hearsay, and developed her own version of the Soapy Smith legend.

Chris Shea may have beaten her to the publishers, but Harriet kept the legend alive until her death in 1947. When she published her version in the late 1920s, it was far more exciting, and far more serious. She reinforced her "accuracy" by mentioning the use of "authorities" such as magazine, newspaper, and "other" articles, but did not name them (could she have meant pieces by Don Steffa and Barkalow Barnacle?). We must suppose they included the firsthand *Skaguay News* and *Daily Alaskan* accounts, and perhaps Rev. Sinclair's, Harry Suydam's, and Shea and Patten's versions, and probably the books by

Samuel Graves and Samuel Steele, all of which had been published by this time.[10] And of course, she needed to rebuff the fanciful incidents that Guy Forsney had invented in his 1927 articles for the *St. Louis Post-Dispatch* and the *Rocky Mountain News* (see discussion of Forsney's article in chapter 6).

So it is from Harriet Pullen that we learn that Smith was brave and fearless, "the prize bunco steerer of the west, and his games of chance were masterpieces of their kind. He could draw a gun as handily as he could deal four aces from the bottom of the deck. . . . Money did not mean much to him."[11]

According to Pullen, the organization of the town began with a committee of two hundred (not 101), which came ashore during the first days of the gold rush, decided "it would be good business to jump Capt. Moore's claim [she meant Bernard's] and establish a city in order to take care of the thousands of prospectors who would soon be coming in."[12] The townsite was then laid out by Frank Reid, and when Captain Moore protested, she continued fabricating, this committee took his cabin and dumped it on the tidal flats. Thus she established that the city founders, whom she called "Skinners," were as evil and greedy—if not more so—as the bunco men and villains who followed in their wake, stealing land from the good, hard-working Captain Moore. The late Marshal Tanner would have been irate at her version (perhaps that is why she awaited his death to publish it).

It was in this atmosphere of "Skinners" and "Skinned" that Harriet Pullen's version of the legendary Soapy Smith arrived, and there he thrived among his own kind in a sort of Sodom of the North. He immediately set himself up as a leader of the rougher element, and to oppose him meant death. The respectable citizens of town would either be victims of claim jumpers or of Soapy's men. It was not a nice place to be.[13] In keeping with the emerging myth, the town of Skagway was riddled with graft, and was as irredeemable as Smith and his con men.

It was such a lawless place that Smith kept the vigilance committee from lynching a bartender who had killed a miner robbed in a saloon and the marshal who had come to investigate the complaint. Although a jury found a verdict of self-defense, the vigilance committee was set on a hanging, and only Soapy, with his Law and Order

Society of Three Hundred and Three (a fit number for a parable) was able to overcome the vigilantes, thus saving the bartender from a hanging.[14] In order to make Smith redeemable, he had to have some good qualities. Whereas no contemporary evidence exists of Smith interfering with either the trial or the hanging, the repeated legend that he tried to stop Fay's hanging becomes the first testimony to Smith's innate goodness in Skagway, placing him morally above the vigilantes. Pullen, with her publication of *Bandit*, solidified the legend into fact.

According to Pullen, with that victory behind him, Smith's popularity became so great that he went on to lead the Fourth of July parade. He came to Pullen's house and persuasively asked her to be in his parade, telling her it would be a failure without her participation. He galloped up and down the length of the parade on his white charger, and thanked her for agreeing to take part. It was the height of his fame.[15]

In this way, Pullen was able to include herself in the story, making herself one of the "old-timers" of Skagway, without being one of the "Skinners," the founding citizens. She admits to becoming a dupe of the charmer, the man who ruled Skagway. Indeed, it was his charm, his handsome manner, his gentlemanly ways that fooled the "good" people of Skagway. Only in that way could he be the sinner in need of redemption, and have so tricked honest folks like the good Mrs. Pullen.

Pullen understood the entertainment principle that the truth is often limiting, and she did not let it stand in the way of a good story. She echoed the newspaper accounts of the shooting itself, adding only that she was down at the wharf that night with her "small" son Royal—who was ten years old—looking for her oldest son, Dan, who was twelve at the time. Inserting herself into the story gave it immediacy and added "authenticity" to the tale; her listeners would never be able to pick out the legend from the facts.[16] Indeed, they had no reason to, as only the legend had been told in every vehicle beginning with Shea and Patton's *"Soapy" Smith Tragedy*.

And then, in typical romantic, early-twentieth-century fashion, Pullen ended the legend with a poem that she claimed was found in multiple copies in Smith's trunk, an ode to friendship between him and a

man named Joe, in Creede, Colorado. To reiterate Smith's potential
for redemption, "Joe" emphasized his faithfulness to his friends:

> And as for Jeff, well, I can say,
> No better man exists today.
> I don't mean good the way you do,
> No not religious, only true;
> True to himself, true to his friend,
> Don't quit nor weaken to the end;
> And I can say, if any can,
> That Jeff will help his fellow man.[17]

So it was that Harriet Pullen, instead of honoring the real hero,
Frank Reid, bolstered the legend of a faithful, kindly, generous Robin
Hood. In leavening Smith's villainy, his worst crimes became petty
indiscretions, and his greatest virtues grew to loyalty to friends and
kindness to strangers. It was assuredly Harriet Pullen who most force-
fully introduced the concept that Jefferson Randolph Smith was a
basically good man gone astray in order that she, the narrator, might
not be viewed as one of those evil Skagwayans for whom Frank Reid
gave his life.

Thirty years after Smith and Reid died, Pullen inserted herself into
the story and put her own twist on it. Instead of a redemption tale, it
became a character study of a charming misanthrope pitted against a
community full of evildoers.

Harriet Pullen could not entirely abandon the legend. Too much
of it worked to her advantage. Her elaboration of it, *Soapy Smith, Bandit of Skagway*, became the sixteenth published depiction of Smith's
death (see the chronological bibliography at the end of this book)
and one of the most referenced in following years. After this point,
the Legend would become Myth.

Montana writer William Kittredge best explained the interconnection between legend and myth when he wrote, "A mythology can
be understood as a story [or legend] that contains a set of implicit
instructions from a society to its members, telling them what is valuable and how to conduct themselves if they are to preserve the things
they value."[18] By this time, Harriet Pullen, bound to the legend, could
not deny that she had been a part of the story. The best she could do

was put herself in the best possible light. She made herself one of the good people of Skagway taken in by the lovable rascal.

———

> Right here you see "Soapy" Smith riding a horse at the head
> of a parade on the 4th of July, 1898. He was elected Marshal of
> the day, which shows you that he was well liked by the people.
> Four days later he was shot and then got bad. He was a good
> fellow up to that time but when he died his reputation was bad.
>
> Martin Itjen, *The Story of the Tour on the Skagway,*
> *Alaska Street Car*

Myth notwithstanding, not everyone would bow gracefully to the inevitable. In 1935, Martin Itjen, supplementing his Skagway "Street Car" tour, bought the small building that Jeff Smith had once used as his saloon from gambler Lee Guthrie. He turned it into the Soapy Smith Museum, complete with a mannequin made up to look like the villain, holding a glass of beer in one hand and a revolver in the other. When a sightseer walked through the door, the life-sized doll was rigged to lift his glass in salute before firing at "Dangerous Dan" McGrew, a character in the Robert Service poem "The Malemute Saloon," located in Dawson. The tourists, after perusing the items in the museum, would climb back on board the Street Car and ride out to the cemetery, where they could compare Soapy's plain wooden marker falling into a nearby ravine with Frank Reid's carefully tended, imposing stone monument. The visual contrast reminded them who was hero and who was villain.[19]

The previous year, 1934, Itjen printed the first edition of *The Story of the Tour on the Skagway, Alaska Street Car*, a description of the tour he conducted in the buslike vehicle he had constructed from the body of Ford truck. Bouncing around town, he treated his customers to a great many anecdotes about Skagway, only a few of which involved Soapy Smith and the days of 1897–98. Surprisingly, in his book Itjen refused to embroider the legend or contribute to the myth. The caption under the photograph of Soapy on the trotting gray horse, taken by Rev. Sinclair on July 4, 1898, and quoted at the beginning of this section, is a prominent exception. Although he inserted Smith's mug into photographs that clearly could not have been taken until long after the con man's death—creating amusing anachronisms for those in the know—he never came out and said that Smith was the uncrowned king of Skagway. He did repeat the legend that Smith donated to the construction of the Union Church, a fact later denied vehemently by Rev. Dickey.[20]

Significantly, Itjen hinted several times in his narrative that Frank Reid was not the only person to shoot Soapy Smith on the day that he died. He stated:

> Reid went down mortally wounded. Another shot was heard, and "Soapy" went down, shot through the heart. Some say that a bystander slipped this bullet into "Soapy's" side. . . . This bullet did not correspond with Reid's gun, but that did not matter. Reid got the credit for killing "Soapy" just the same. Now, you will note that the bullet went in on the left side. Reid and "Soapy" must have faced each other and in order for Reid to get a bullet into "Soapy's" left side and have it come out to the front would be a pretty hard thing to do. However, they said that Reid did it and that was all there was to it.[21]

Did Itjen and the boys in the saloons, working the railroads and the docks, know that Jesse Murphy killed Smith? Probably. But Itjen's caption for the photograph of Reid's cemetery monument notes only that Reid was shot by Jefferson R. Smith, not the other way around.[22] To the point, at the end of his 1938 edition, Itjen added a poem, which read in part:

> You'll listen to the tricks of Smith
> And how he won the duel
> With Reid, his greatest enemy,
> Then died from wound more cruel.
>
> For as Reid's bullet missed Jeff Smith
> Someone fired a shot
> Which found its way to "Soapy's" Heart—
> The killer they knew naught.[23]

In addition to not consuming the legend that hero Reid killed sinner Smith, Itjen would not condone the notion that Skagway had been lawless before July 8, 1898. In telling the story of the theft of J. D. Stewart's poke of gold, Itjen wrote: "He got his gold back with the exception of a few hundred dollars that they had spent for him. This shows you we had law and order those days."[24]

And Itjen, alone of all the early chroniclers after the *Skaguay News* and the *Daily Alaskan*, pictures and names Si Tanner as one of the members of the posse who arrested members of Smith's gang in the days that followed Smith's death.[25] For Tanner had never had a part in the Smith legend. As a hero in his own right, he did not fit into the evil vigilante scenario. His role as a member of the Committee of One Hundred and One and head of the Safety Committee made it too difficult to account for him in the days before July 8. In later years, others would mention him in passing for his post–July 8 role, but they could not reconcile his—and his compatriots'—actions and continue to promulgate the redemption story. So Tanner, as well as Charles Sperry, Tom Ward, Tom Whitten, and other members of the "vigilantes," continued to be vilified as nameless men in order to perpetuate the legend.

And Martin Itjen's nonconforming account was largely ignored.

Martin Itjen died in 1942. He mentored George Rapuzzi, who was born in Skagway on December 18, 1899, as the Soapy Smith gang was being tried for their assault on Si Tanner and their robbery of J. D. Stewart's bag of gold. As a boy, Rapuzzi delivered newspapers to the saloons, including the Pack Train and the Mascot, where he heard the stories of Soapy's life and death. He loved Skagway's lore, and purchased the Soapy Smith museum and streetcar from Martin Itjen in 1942. Rapuzzi lived to a ripe eighty-seven years old, continuing to tell the stories of Skagway—a wide variety, not just those about Soapy—to as many people as would listen. Among them numbered people like Steve Hites, who bought the streetcar company from George's scions and continues to tell his stories to tourists today. Listeners also included Robert Spude, historian with Klondike Gold Rush National Historical Park from 1977 through 1979, who later shared them with his wife, the author of this book. Not all tales of the gold rush days start with the discovery of primary documents in historic archives. Some continue to be ferreted out the good old-fashioned way, by simple word of mouth.

Besides collecting the stories of the gold rush, George Rapuzzi gathered as much paraphernalia of the old days as he could stuff into the old buildings that he also collected. When he died in 1995, his niece, Phyllis Brown, sold the Soapy Smith Museum and Martin Itjen Street Car to the Rasmussen Foundation, which in turn donated the building to the National Park Service.[26]

The National Park Service has conducted a study on how best to rehabilitate and interpret the building once used as Jeff Smith's Parlor. It is the agency's decision to use it as a museum to interpret the history of tourism in Skagway, as begun with the story of Soapy Smith. The museum is as much a tribute to Martin Itjen, Harriet Pullen, and George Rapuzzi as it is to Smith and the characters of the gold rush days.[27]

Tourism has and always will be a vital part of Skagway's economy. That renovated historic building is a visible reminder of the Soapy legend. It is a classic story, which cannot be changed back into its original version, despite the efforts of people who have interviewed all of the "old-timers," talked to those who were there, and who have reason to know better. They cannot fight a firmly established myth. Soapy as the redeemable sinner who refused to do what was right has become a part of Skagway's glorified days of '98. Those hellion days would stay that way forever. The legend has become myth.

––––––––

The step from printed page to stage takes no more than the climb of four or five stairs, especially in Skagway, Alaska, and especially if it is for tourists from out of town. What plays is a good story like the Legend of Soapy Smith and Frank Reid. In 1926, Martin Itjen and his compatriots at the YMCA took that step from the cool shadows of their gymnasium on Fifth Avenue to the limelight. They needed money for their yearly round of sports: hockey, basketball, and bowling in the winter; baseball in the summer. The distance between rival teams in Alaska and the Yukon meant travel, and travel took money.

Logically, with the tourists coming to town, the high-spirited lads should put on a show. The cost of admission would go to buy uniforms, equipment, and round-trip tickets for team members.[28]

"The Days of '98 Show" premiered in 1926 and has not missed a season since, arguably, it is the longest running theatrical production in Alaska. A street gunfight—not always the killing of Soapy Smith—has often been featured in this musical pageant. Today, the show starts with the Smith story and ends with the creation of the state song and statehood. One of the show's greatest admirers, the man who took over the Skagway Street Car Company from the scions of Martin Itjen, said that the "Days of '98 Show" took on the "selling" of the Soapy legend in 1978.[29]

Steve Hites, who had a hand in penning the first outline of today's script, said he learned the Soapy story when he first came to Skagway in the early 1970s. It was a version of the morality play as taught by the White Pass vice president of public relations, Roy Minter, in the late 1950s and early '60s. He told a simple parable of good vs. evil—"the way of the transgressor is hard"; Frank Reid redeemed Skagway.[30] At the same time, Westours, a cruise-tour company founded by Alaska entrepreneur Chuck West, had added the Soapy Smith tale to its Skagway City Tour and to the sales brochure printed up for its customers.[31]

In the summer of 1973, aspiring businessman and young actor Tom Biss from Anchorage came to town and set up his one-man show, in the log cabin American Legion Hall at Seventh and Broadway. Judy Irving, who ran the hall's single follow spotlight, wrote Tom a script for a play entitled "Soapy Lives," based on a paperback novel, *Soapy* (1970) by Mike Miller. The book, told in the first person from the perspective of Smith, is a sympathetic look at the last days of a man reexamining the mistakes of his youth, simply another take on the redeemable sinner. Miller, a Juneau resident, legislator, and journalist for *The Alaska Sportsman*, probably got most of his material from the articles published in that magazine in the 1950s and 1960s (see appendix A).[32]

In 1975, Biss sold his show (which had acquired a piano player and a narrator) to Jim Richards. They did not do nighttime shows, so as not to compete directly with the Eagles' community-run "Days of '98

Show." "Soapy" played to the day business off the cruise ships, which was minimal in those early years. Skagway in 1975 had only about forty thousand cruise ship day visitors. So it was a hand-to-mouth summer stock production that supported Richards, one actress, and one musician.[33]

During the winter of 1977–78, the Eagles Hall pipes froze up, as there were not enough old-timers left to pay the oil bill. Neither the property taxes nor the club dues had been paid. The "Days of '98 Show" had not netted any profits in 1977, and it was the only source of the Eagles' revenue. Seeing the writing on the wall, two of the last six remaining club members, George Flemming and J. D. True, invited six young entertainers to join the Eagles, hoping they could save the building, keep it from going back to the Grand Aerie, and keep the "Days of '98 Show" going. The six young men all became club members at an initiation ceremony held at Flemming's kitchen table. They included Jim Richards and Steve Hites. As a result, the "Soapy Lives" play and the "Days of '98 Show" merged.[34]

The inspiration came to Jim Richards one night in December 1977, the night the White House—once Lee Guthrie's house—burned. Steve Hites had spent hours helping put out the fire. He trudged to the house he shared with Jim, sat down in a chair, and fell asleep fully clothed. He continues the story this way:

> I woke up to Jim wild-eyed, shaking me. "Wake up, Steve, wake up, you've gotta write this down!" And he pushed a pen and a legal pad into my hands, his eyes getting really wide and he kept yelling, "Quick! Write this down! This is it! It's the new show!"
>
> And he paced back and forth, waving his arms, smoking a cigarette, and laid out his vision of Captain Moore coming on stage telling about his discovery of White Pass, of a crowd suddenly running in yelling "stampede!," of new songs, of putting whole sections of the old Soapy Show into a new show, a show that had the '98 Show can-can girls and the garter auction and the whole Skagway story right up through Soapy's demise and on up through the Depression and the War to Statehood, ending with the Alaska Flag Song. He suddenly went silent, slumped down on the sofa, and passed out again.

There in my hands was the first draft of what became the "new" Days of '98 Show with Soapy Smith. I took it to Tom Healy, who flushed out the scenes and dialogue, and together Tom, Jim, and I wrote the new script. The new show had a cast of 26 people . . . but it was headed in a brand new direction.

There is one major difference between how we portrayed the gunfight in the new '98 show, and how it was done in the old Soapy show. It used to be that Soapy and Frank approached each other in the dim red lighting, yelling their lines taken from eyewitness accounts, and then both men blazed away at each other, the black powder blanks spewing flames across the stage. The surprised audience jumped, screamed, and laughed self-consciously. As the clouds of gunpowder wafted through the theater, there was no question about who shot Jeff Smith.

In the new show, Smith yells "They can't take this town from me! I run this town!" He cocks his Winchester rifle and stomps off the stage into the darkness. The narrator steps into the tiny spotlight downstage, and softly intones,

"Soapy's headed for the Juneau Company Wharf.

"The Vigilantes are meetin' over him, and Lord knows they're mighty sore.

"Well, I've seen Jeff face mobs like this before, but never so quite alone.

"A man like Reid did his deed . . ."

At this moment, a blank is fired off stage, and a loud report of the gunshot in the closed space of the theater sounds like a cannon going off. People jump, scream and yell in surprise, then laugh self-consciously: it's perfect theater. The Narrator smiles knowingly at the audience and continues.

". . . And sent poor Soapy home."

"The intention is, of course, to leave it up to the audience to decide who shot Soapy Smith, with the implication, of course, that Reid did the deed."[35]

————

Whoa. That means that Jim and Steve *knew*, clear back in 1977, that it was not just one bad guy and just one good guy, redeeming a town full of evil vigilantes. They were not confused about who was who. They really knew the difference between the history and the legend.

Well, maybe. Maybe just as much as Chris Shea and Harriet Pullen and Martin Itjen did. But the story has always been just a little bit hard to tell that way. Plus, the purpose might get missed in all of that confusing detail.

And what would be the point, anyway? Back in 1898, was a showman like Jim Richards trying to save one-quarter of the value of the lots of five hundred merchants from a land-grabbing British corporation, in the same way that the Committee of One Hundred and One did?

Or through the years was his kind—Chris Shea, Martin Itjen, Harriet Pullen, George Rapuzzi, and recently Steve Hites—trying to keep a town alive by publicizing a legend? A legend that is so much bigger and better than the sum of its parts.

It is, of course, much better to tell it as a legend, the Soapy Smith Legend become Myth. It is as western and as American as the legends of Wyatt Earp, Billy the Kid, and Jesse James, and cannot be changed.

For Skagway must prosper, and it cannot do so on the reputations of William Moore, Si Tanner, Harriet Pullen, and Martin Itjen. It can only do so on the legend of Soapy Smith. Just as Tombstone, Arizona, or Dodge City, Kansas, would not thrive as tourist attractions today without Wyatt Earp; Deadwood, South Dakota, without Wild Bill Hickok; or Lincoln, New Mexico, without Billy the Kid. Heritage and economy depend on legend as much as history.

Chris Shea, the jokester politician *(center)*. Detail of
photo SCL 1-677, Seward Hunting Club, ca. 1912. Seward
Community Library, Seward, Alaska.

Political cartoon of Mayor Chris Shea. From the
Skagway Interloper, May 19, 1908.

Lieutenant Colonel
Samuel B. Steele,
Northwest Mounted
Police, ca. 1900. Glenbow
Archives, Glenbow
Museum, Calgary,
Alberta, NA-3755-9.

Richard Harding Davis.
Courtesy Library of
Congress, Burr MacIntosh
Studio, LC-USZ62-103860.

The rock formation above Moore's Wharf painted to look like a skull, ca. 1930. Klondike Gold Rush National Historical Park, George and Edna Rapuzzi Collection, Rasmuson Foundation, #000630.

Harriet Pullen in front of the Moore House refurbished as her hotel in about 1902. She later expanded the hotel and renamed it the Pullen House. Alaska State Library, Robert Dumond Collection, P258-III-085-793.

Martin Itjen, seated in a studio in Oregon, ca. 1900. Klondike Gold Rush National Historical Park, George and Edna Rapuzzi Collection, Rasmuson Foundation, #000578-K/C-A.

George Rapuzzi in the "Soapy Smith" Museum. Klondike Gold Rush National Historic Park, George and Edna Rapuzzi Collection, Rasmuson Foundation, #00076.

Photograph of the cast of the "Days of '98 Show," about 1976. Dedman's Photo, courtesy Skagway Museum.

CHAPTER EIGHT

A Literary Legacy

The King of the Thimbleriggers was only thirty-eight years old when he met his death on July 8, 1898, only four days after his greatest triumph. His nimble fingers, glib tongue, and audaciousness had brought him more than a million dollars. Most of his winnings had been spent or given away almost as fast as the money rolled in, and he died virtually penniless.

Forbes Parkhill, *Wildest of the West*

In Skagway, he was in his element. As in the early days in Creede, the boom was on: crowds had come to seek their fortunes; life was rough and ready. Soapy even boasted that he'd be the dictator of Skagway as he had of Creede. All the charm he had, he used—and Soapy had plenty. He had hardly arrived before he was recognized as a leader by the sporting group. When he stopped a lynching, the more substantial group respected him, too. . . . Indeed, Soapy has emerged as a modern Robin Hood.

Amanda Ellis, *Pioneers*

It is hard to read anything about Soapy Smith without running across mention of someone trying to impress by name dropping. Whether or not Soapy associated himself with the notorious and well-known, his acquaintances seemed to believe he was close with them.

Cy Warman, a famous Colorado and Canada journalist, humorist, and poet, had written a paragraph or two about Smith's Creede days in *Frontier Stories*, published the year of Soapy's death, 1898. Counting on his notoriety as a journalist for *McClure's*, a national magazine, Warman no doubt thought Smith could win him an introduction to the notorious "Black Bart," a California stage robber in the 1870s and 1880s. The following dated February 16, 1987, was found among Smith's belongings after his death. From the context, it appears that Smith claimed to have known "Black Bart," and Warman, capitalizing on his acquaintance with Soapy, wanted an introduction.

> Friend Smith:
>
> So you know Black Bart, do you? Well, I want to know him. What sort of Rooster is he? Will he talk to me and tell me some good stories? Will he be—or is he likely to be in Los. A. for any length of time? What are his relations to the Wells Fargo people now? I don't quite make out from your letter. I hope to go to Los. A. the coming fall—'97. I know the Fargo people all right and can get all his inside history, but I want to know him. Can't we get him out in the hills somewhere and make some wild pictures to make the thing interesting? I go to Canada, London, Ont., next month to stay six months—will you be down that way?
>
> Your Respectable Friend,
>
> CY WARMAN[1]

Cy Warman was born on June 22, 1855, in Greenup, Illinois, to Nancy Askew and John Warman, descendents of early settlers of Kentucky. Educated in the public schools, Cy had an inveterate interest in writing from an early age. Although he tried farming and wheat-brokering, he eventually gave those up and moved to Denver in the 1880s, beginning to write and edit for the *Western Railway* in 1888. Early on, a Denver newspaper noted that Warman considered giving up writing biographies of railroad officials after receiving two black eyes from one of his subjects, who did not take kindly to his sense of humor.[2]

In 1892, Warman moved to the new mining camp of Creede, Colorado, where he took over as the editor of the *Creede Chronicle* and earned both praise and criticism from rival newspapers. There, Warman came to know the irascible Soapy Smith.[3] He spent only a couple of years in Creede before returning to Denver, where he went to work for the *Rocky Mountain News*. In Denver, he kept up his acquaintance with Smith and may have authored several of the newspaper's pieces on the con man between 1893 and 1896. By 1896, Warman had moved to Washington, D.C., where he wrote for such popular magazines as *McClure's, Frank Leslie's Popular Magazine, Harper's*, and *The Century*, and for any newspaper that would print his short stories. Although the vast majority of these pieces were about railroads, Warman loved to write about colorful characters. And he had a decided soft spot for the romantic sort of poetry that claimed the day. What people remembered most when he died in 1914 was a love poem he wrote in 1893 to his fiancée, which he titled "Sweet Marie." It became the lyrics to one of the best-loved songs of the time.[4]

It was in February 1896, while Warman was in Washington, that he first wrote Soapy Smith begging for an introduction to "Black Bart." The stage robber's real name was either Charles E. Boles or Charles E. Bolten. He was credited with the robberies of twenty-eight Wells Fargo stages between 1875 and 1883 in California before he was confined to San Quentin Prison for his last theft. He served his term and was released in 1888, after which he committed no more crimes.[5]

It is easy to understand why Smith would have admired Black Bart and broadcast his regard. Bolten, when not disguised as a bandit, deported himself as an older gentleman who wore fine clothes, ate good food, and drank fine wines. He spoke well, wrote poetry, and fooled everyone with his cultivated ways.[6] He was the sort of criminal that Smith emulated, and that interested a scribe like Warman.

When Soapy didn't respond to Warman's letter—he either didn't know Black Bart, didn't know where he was, or was afraid to give up his location—Warman wrote a second time, on September 22, 1897, from London, Ontario, where he'd joined his Canadian wife: "Where is Black Bart? I want to write a story of his life. It would be a calker. . . . Write me some of the real thing and I'll immortalize you some more. Faithfully yours, Cy Warman."[7]

The third and last time Warman wrote to Smith, there was no more mention of Black Bart. Soapy was not cooperating, at least not in giving out Bart's location or making an introduction. Although Warman said he received a letter from Smith in "the Klondike," that doesn't mean Soapy was in Skagway. He also said he'd heard from "the old Soak" in "Fayattesville," New Orleans, and "Juno." There was not much time for Soapy to spend in Skagway with all of this traveling around. This third letter, dated November 16, 1897, also from London, Ontario, gives Soapy facetious advice to stay out of the bad parts of town in New York City, which Smith was planning to visit on his way to or from Washington. Warman also asked Soapy not to make him out to be a liar if he saw the editor of the *Philadelphia Press* on his visit back east, referencing that the two of them took opposite stances on morality when they lived in Creede. Warman signed this letter "Guardedly Yours."[8]

The point is that Smith and Warman knew each other, but did not exactly trust one another. While they enjoyed the notoriety of their acquaintance, it could hardly be called a friendship, or a relationship that worked to each other's benefit. Warman, who ended up writing countless short stories during his twenty-five-year career and publishing eleven books, only mentioned Smith twice, and both times merely as a way of setting a scene. Soapy was used as a "prop" to build a picture of the rough town of Creede in the story of the assassination of Bob Ford, and in a nostalgic poem about the rise and fall of the Colorado mining town. [9] If Warman had been after a "calking good story" and Smith's story had not been mostly legend, why then did he not write it all down before he died in 1914?

Despite the fact that Cy Warman would become a long-standing officer of the American Humorist Association, a nationally known journalist, and a beloved American poet in demand by national magazines, he never used his influence to write about Smith's life. It appears that he did not treasure the friendship the way Smith did in safeguarding the three letters kept in the trunk behind his parlor. Perhaps they were not "old friends." Certainly during Warman's lifetime, Smith's story was not yet the legend it would become.

––––––

The legend would grow, though, just not in the first couple of decades after events, and not enough to capture Cy Warman's imagination. At first it was the story of a town redeemed by the blood shed when a martyr died killing a villain; later it would become the story of the villain himself. It would not be until after most of the people who had actually known Soapy Smith had died that the legend of his character would begin to evolve as well. After three decades, the few remaining people who had once known him began to remember Soapy Smith as a legend in the second sense of the word: "an extremely famous or notorious person."

In 1927, William Francis Hynes wrote the following:

> Some 30-odd years ago, in the city of Washington, four of us sat at dinner in the Raleigh hotel; Richard Harding Davis, Soapy Smith, the well-known sporting character of Denver, and his cousin, who looked more like his twin, a reporter on the Washington Post, whose name was also Smith, and myself.
>
> An interview with Soapy, published in the New York World, a few days prior, was so attractive to Davis in its many peculiar sidelights, that in discussing it with the reporter cousin, he expressed a desire that should Soapy come to Washington he would like to meet him.[10]

Hynes, enchanted with the company, could hardly contain his enthusiasm for the witty mealtime conversation.

> Soapy, during the meal, was highly entertaining: he was full of humor and interesting anecdotes; he bubbled and sparkled like champagne; he was without restraint, outspoken and unaffected; but was absolutely silent on anything that went to his credit, altho some of us knew much of it. He acted like one who was enjoying a rare and unexpected treat; when in truth it was the other way around. His talk and opinions were like the frank expressions of an individual who was weary of watching his step, but now free to speak his mind without fear of suspicion. He certainly let himself go. Davis, by shrewd, discreet questions, brought out many phases of his character which I doubt that even Soapy with all his depth had suspect.[11]

Hynes quoted Soapy as blurting out the following gem: "Oh, I like the contest, the matching of wits, the study of the other fellow, the courage of the bluff—if he's got the nerve to stand pat; and I like the thrill of putting up your last chip on your judgment of the play!"

Then, later, Soapy remarked with a sigh, "And yet, when all is said and done, I often wonder if the fame is worth the candle."

Hynes showered glowing praises on Smith for 120 paragraphs, as he recounted the legend of Soapy's days in Denver and the Colorado mining towns. Who was Hynes, and what was his authority?

———

William Francis Hynes was born in Ireland in March 1858 and immigrated to the United States in 1873. He married his wife, Helena, in 1882, and they settled down in Denver. In 1890, Hynes was listed in the Denver City Directory as a reporter living at 935 11th Street. By 1900, he had become the secretary of the Board of Arbitration, which oversaw complaints about taxes in Arapaho County. He was appointed a justice of the peace in 1904 and, by 1910, had his own law practice, which he continued well into the 1920s.[12]

It takes no imagination to figure out where Soapy Smith and W. F. Hynes first ran into one another. As a reporter working for one of the Denver newspapers, probably the *Rocky Mountain News*, Hynes probably drew the job of reporting on con man Smith's shenanigans in Denver's lower downtown, then a tenderloin area. At that time, the area attracted those seeking gambling dens, brothels, saloons, and other tawdry businesses, and this was where Smith thrived. His gambling house, the Tivoli, was located at Seventeenth and Larimer, the heart of the tenderloin, where he learned and perfected all of his usual con games, and met most of his loyal followers.[13] Hynes, whose career reporting on vice evolved into a legal one, may well have been a crime reporter, so he had plenty of opportunity to bump into a man who spent a good portion of time in the city jail.

There can be no denying that Smith had a charming way about him, and Hynes must have liked the man personally, not for disobeying the law but for his charisma. Hynes also, as he betrays in his 1927 article, enjoyed pairing himself with famous characters. He could not resist drawing attention to the fact that he dined with Richard Harding Davis, who had written columns in the *New York World*, had been a foreign correspondent for decades, and who, by the late 1920s was also a nationally known playwright and book author. It would be like a modern-day journalist tossing off the fact that he had shared a meal with Walter Cronkite or Bob Woodward; the association elevated the journalist to a position of some authority.

To say that someone of Davis's prestige had been captivated by Soapy, well, that would give any legend a great boost. The readers of the *Rocky Mountain News*, even if they did not know who Hynes was, were set up to believe his authority by association with the famous journalist and with Smith's cousin—who, Hynes said, worked as a reporter for the *Washington Post*.

But what about Richard Harding Davis's interest in Smith?

In 1897, the globe-trotting journalist had just returned from Venezuela, and was spending his time critiquing New York theater, giving book readings across the country for his best-selling *Soldiers of Fortune*, crossing the Atlantic on the steamer *Paris* to speak in London, and similar activities. His movements were followed daily by the national press. Only once was his name mentioned in the same breath with that of Soapy Smith: Skagway's *Daily Alaskan* noted that Davis had mentioned Smith in his book *West from a Car Window*, written about a trip to Creede, Colorado, in 1892. A perusal of that story indicates that Harding thought little of Smith and saw him only as a minor curiosity during his railroad car tour of the West.[14] Somehow this passing mention grew into the idea that Davis had written a glowing article about Smith in an eastern newspaper.

A search of the *New York World Sunday Magazine* between January 1, 1896, and February 1, 1898, turned up no pieces about Jefferson Randolph Smith, contrary to claims by W. F. Hynes. Smith came to Skagway from Washington, D.C., on January 21, 1898; the article was reputed to have appeared before that time.[15] The *World Sunday Magazine* featured articles on odd personalities of the type that appear in modern supermarket tabloids: "The Oldest Man in America," "The Snake with Two Heads," "Mme. Diss DeBarr, The Spook Priestess Tells the Story of Her Life," "Talking Cat," and "George E. Smith, 'Pittsburg Phil,' King of the Turf Gamblers, Keeps $200,000 in Cash on Hand at All Times." After the gold rush began in late July 1897, the *World*'s magazine routinely devoted a page to the northern rush, but between July 25 of that year and January 9, 1898, no articles appeared featuring Smith. The *World* did publish a piece on "A Klondike Poker Game," featuring huge odds in Dawson; one on the tortuous journey over the trails; and a double about "A Modern Robin Hood" ("Black Jack" Howard McDonald, a train robber of New Mexico) as well as "A Woman Jesse James" (Cora Hubbard, who committed crimes in Missouri).[16]

And surely Smith, who narcissistically kept clippings of himself in a scrapbook, would have saved a *World* article, and flaunted it before friends in his parlor in Skagway, had one existed. The more important articles in the scrapbook were supposedly published by the *Alaska-Yukon Magazine* in December 1907 and January 1908, but there was no *World* reprint among them. A diligent search of all Sunday issues in 1896 and 1897 failed to find such a piece. Hynes could only be remembering Davis's brief 1892 mention of Smith in *West from a Car Window.*

The only article about Soapy that had appeared in a nationally known newspaper about this time was an interview that the con man had done for his cousin Edwin "Bobo" Smith at the *Washington Post.* Published on November 11, 1897, it was a promotion piece designed to get people interested in traveling to the Klondike through Skagway. Soapy's name was mentioned only as the source of information, not as a famous (or infamous) person.

Did the meeting with Richard Harding Davis at the Raleigh Hotel really take place some thirty-odd years before 1927? This author finds it difficult to believe. It seems more likely that Hynes remembers a dinner with Soapy Smith, his cousin "Bobo," and Cy Warman, who would have been almost as famous in 1897 as Richard Harding Davis, but whose name would not have had the same impact in 1927. Both Davis and Warman had passed on by the latter date, so neither could have questioned Hynes's memory of the event: indeed, only Hynes was still alive, for even Edwin "Bobo" Smith had died in early 1927. In late 1897, Warman, as related in the beginning of this chapter, was still trying to arrange a meeting with "Black Bart," and had promised Soapy that he would write up Soapy's story as well, if he could get an introduction. What better way to woo the con man than to treat him to a meal at the Raleigh Hotel and "by shrewd, discreet questions, [bring] out many phases of his character which [Hynes doubted] that even Soapy with all his depth had suspect."[17]

Ironically, Hynes's article about Soapy Smith in the August 28,

1927, issue of the *Rocky Mountain News* did not cover any of the time that the con man was in Alaska. That portion of Smith's life was published the following Sunday, in the previously discussed and highly inventive article authored by Guy Forsney, who worked for the *St. Louis Dispatch*.[18]

And so three decades after Smith's death, the legend was embellished, not because of the facts involved but because each contributor to the legend wished to bolster his own image, not by association with Smith but by association with men who had fame and prestige. No one ever called them on the obvious invention of details because the spirit in which the invention occurred bolstered the legend that had become mythology.

Significantly, each writer would attempt to explain Smith's character in a new or slightly different way. Hynes, for instance, in emphasizing his bubbling charm, also showed some moments of regret, echoing Reverend Sinclair's initial theme of the sinner, who could have been redeemed. Those familiar with the mythology knew that Smith's fatal mistake was in refusing to return the gold—refusing to seek redemption—and therefore the sinful town as a whole could only be redeemed by shedding the blood of both the sinner Smith and the martyr Reid.

In the process, however, Soapy's character was evolving, becoming something it had not been before.

———

Soapy's story was too big, too legendary, yes, too mythic to stay in Skagway. While it had ventured south and east several times before, now Soapy had become national. Even Frank Reid began to get lost in its telling.

On the national level, the funding provided by the Works Progress Administration (WPA) in the 1930s played an important role in fleshing out the Smith legend become myth. One of the WPA projects included indexing the newspapers, magazines, and books of the Denver Public Library, home of one of the premier historical collections in the country. By 1935, this gargantuan project had been completed, and today the 22,000-card subject file is one of the more important resources of the library's Western History Collection. To date, most of that card file is being digitized for eventual online access. Thirty-seven of those cards, each with two to four entries, are devoted to Jefferson Randolph Smith. When a pair of novelists named William Ross Collier and Edwin Victor Westrate decided to try their hands at writing nonfiction in the early 1930s, they found the subject index of the Denver Public Library invaluable to their research.

In 1935, Collier and Westrate issued what is considered the first full-length biography of Smith, at 299 pages, appropriately entitled *The Reign of Soapy Smith*, published by the prestigious New York house of Doubleday, Doran and Company. Although it contains no footnotes or bibliography, the authors obviously owe their sources to the Denver Public Library, which was one of the first public libraries in the West to create a notable Western History Department. The book describes Smith's "rescue" of Ed Fay, his parade on "Memorial Day," his role as "Grand Master" of the Fourth of July parade, an incorrectly "crowded" church at Soapy's funeral, and the "carving" of Soapy's skull on the cliff above Skagway Harbor—all of it portrayed as faithfully as Denver's newspapers of 1898 and after had told the story. The Denver Public Library index, at the time, did not have copies of the Shea and Patton booklet, Harriet Pullen's account, or Itjen's account. The library did possess Barkalow Barnacle's 1920 article from *The Trail*, and Don Steffa's 1908 version from the *Pacific Monthly*. The last two relied heavily on the redemption theme.[19]

A plethora of articles and reminiscences followed the biography of Collier and Westrate, mostly in Alaska publications, by people who had been witnesses to the shootings, and who may have wished to correct the inaccuracies in the biography. Over the next twenty years, these articles would prove most informative, not about the events of 1898, but in changing the view of the Klondike gold rush and its favorite con man. However, because of their Alaska venue, they would not, for the most part, end up in the possession of the Denver Public Library or in its subject index.

The next major publication of the Smith story appeared in Pierre Berton's first edition of *Klondike Fever*, published in the United States in 1958. Berton wrote that his sources were so numerous for his section on Smith that "it would be impractical to detail them all." He states that he interviewed four men who had *witnessed* the shooting, but names only R. J. Dick of Vancouver.[20] No information about Dick or his connection to the events is available, so the reliability of the witnesses cannot be assessed. Unfortunately, like many Canadians, Berton had consumed the legend whole and never questioned the concept of a lawless Skagway, a con man as uncrowned king, or the need for a vigilante committee to wrestle back law and order south of the Canadian border. Berton later admitted his Canadian nationalism grabbed hold of him as he told this story. Starting with such good material, he only had to use his unquestionable gift for writing to further embellish the tale and reaffirm it as an irreplaceable part of the Klondike saga.[21]

Published by a New York house, *Klondike Fever* made its way into the stacks and subject index of the Denver Public Library, and of course, the bibliography of the next major biography of J. R. Smith, *Soapy Smith, King of the Frontier Con Men* (1962), by Frank G. Robertson and Beth Kay Harris. Well-known writers of western fiction and nonfiction, these journalists do include a two-page bibliography at the back of their book, indicating that they made ample use of the Denver Public Library's resources. Unfortunately, they also referred to a number of other dubious sources, including some downright fiction, such as Richard O'Connor's *High Jinks on the Klondike* and Kathryn Winslow's *The Big Pan-Out*. In the latter, the legend includes such inaccuracies as this exaggeration:

> Leaving Smith's body where it lay, the Vigilantes fell upon the town, raiding one place after the other, slugging, shooting, wounding, and killing. Forty prisoners were taken to an improvised jail but a mob stormed that shack and was about to conduct a mass lynching when the marines arrived from Dyea. Martial law had to be threatened before the prisoners could be put safely back in jail.[22]

Interestingly, Robertson and Harris do try to correct minor details of the legend, but for the most part they perpetuate the myth that had taken deep root. They indicate the primary cause for the formation of the Committee of One Hundred and One was the McGrath and Rowan murders, and that Smith organized the Law and Order Society of Three Hundred and Three (!); they call Smith "the silent

master of Skagway"; and they state the now universally accepted
"fact" that Soapy led the Fourth of July parade.[23] They do not mention the early instability over the townsite and land claims or conflict
over transportation routes, facts long since forgotten and never mentioned in any account. But to their credit, they do discuss the pos-
sibility that someone else might have killed Smith, although they do
not discuss whom it might have been. Unlike previous biographers,
they do have Tanner turning Reid over and asking him about his gun;
Reid saying he was hurt bad, rolling off his gun; and Tanner taking it
to find one misfired cartridge and two empty shells. They downplay
the hero Tanner in the story by not introducing him until July 8.[24]

Although filled with a lot of the mythology that had evolved
to this point in time, Robertson and Harris's version indicates that
they had also read the Alaska accounts and included those particulars as well. They obviously wanted to incorporate all the details, and
they brought everything together, making it bigger—and certainly
better—than life.

Robertson and Harris's book debuted in 1961. In the almost fifty
years since its publication, forty new accounts have been published,
most of them variations on the themes established by Rev. Sinclair on
July 22, 1898, Harry Suydam in 1901, Chris Shea in 1907, Don Steffa
in 1908, Sam Graves in 1908, Harriet Pullen in 1929, and Collier and
Westrate in 1935. Because journalists like Robertson and Harris used
Pierre Berton and Collier and Westrate, and because those sources
used the sources listed above, the legend created as a morality story,
tweaked by political satire, then crafted into myth for tourists was
evolving into a dubious sort of history.

––––––

Among these copycat biographers were two romanticists who claimed
to have written their stories of Smith in the absence of previous
knowledge about this little-known crook. Amanda Ellis was associate
professor of English at Colorado College in Colorado Springs. She
included a chapter entitled "A Modern Robin Hood" in her 1955
book *Pioneers*. Ellis made much of the Robin Hood comparison. She
did not question Soapy's generosity in giving his riches to the poor
widows and churches and helping out the starving miners, and she

almost ignored his predation on miners and those who came to play his con games. She repeats the inaccurate stories of how respected Smith became after saving Fay from the hangman's noose, and how the deaths of Smith and Reid led to the deaths of many others of Smith's gang as the vigilantes formed lynch mobs and hung the gang in retribution before martial law was installed.[25] Ellis's book lacks a bibliography, but her association with Colorado College, and the fact that ten of the eleven pages in her account cover Smith's Colorado days, makes it probable that she relied almost exclusively on the resources at the Denver Public Library for her research.

Another example of a legend-maker with very little knowledge but apparent credentials was Forbes Parkhill, who wrote *The Wildest of the West* in 1951. The promotional material at the beginning of the book states that Parkhill "writes about the West with fresh new material . . . his writing 'is not a retold tale.'" This claim "a completely fresh approach"[26] is clearly exaggeration, as at least thirty-four versions of the Soapy Smith story had been written by this time, not counting the newspaper reports, and Parkhill adds very little except embellishments to the tale.

Parkhill called Smith "The King of the Thimbleriggers," but he introduced no new material to the story or to the obvious legend. In fact, he got his facts downright wrong. According to this nationally known journalist, the killing of Andy McGrath and Deputy Rowan by John E. Fay occurred in March 1898. Soapy intervened. He persuaded the mob to turn the killer over to the authorities. Smith took up a collection for Rowan's wife and then proclaimed himself boss of Skagway; the Committee of Three Hundred and Three (!) took up a collection of six hundred dollars to build a church (an incident that occurs in November 1897 in most legendary accounts, long before the formation of the Committee of 317). He mentions this fictional generosity in one sentence with the formation of the Committee of One Hundred and One. Six-foot-tall Diamond Lil' (who was never in Skagway, by the way) was supposed to have been the principal madam of Skagway and queen of the red light district. (Parkhill never explains what she has to do with Soapy.) Smith was grand marshal of the Fourth of July parade; Stewart went straight to Reid, who called a meeting of the Committee of One Hundred and One. Only

Smith and Reid were on the wharf. The two fired simultaneously. The Committee of One Hundred and One jailed forty people afterwards. The U.S. Army had to take over the town, and forty people were sent south.[27]

And why were these books by Ellis and Parkhill important? Frank G. Robertson and Beth Kay Harris use them as sources for their biography of Smith. And practically every biographer of Smith since 1961 has done so. Incredibly, Parkhill's and Ellis's books are among only five that are listed in the Denver Public Library's subject card index as authoritative on Smith.

––––––

It is unfortunate that Alaska libraries have never quite caught up to the Denver Public Library in the way they have done their indexing of newspapers and magazines. Yes, some indexing has occurred in some institutions, but in fits and starts, and only for some journals, not all.[28]

In the meantime, the biographers who happened to read the articles printed in the *Alaskan Sportsman* between 1935 and the time it ceased publication in 1969 were treated to versions of the Smith story that corrected many of the details of the legend. These versions were authored by eyewitnesses or descendents of eyewitnesses who had facts not presented in the original newspaper accounts or those told by Harry Suydam, Samuel Graves, or Dr. F. B. Whiting. It was from these accounts—in particular that of Calvin Barkdull, who was in J. M. Tanner's posse and who helped J. D. Stewart find the members of the Safety Committee, and that of Clarence Andrews, the Skagway customs agent, who kept detailed records of his many interviews with eyewitnesses—that we learn some of the best corrections to the legend.[29]

Frank Clancy, John Clancy's son, recalled the Fourth of July parade and the eagle that was kept in a cage behind Smith's saloon; Hazel Stewart Clark, the niece of J. D. Stewart, explained why her uncle never told his version of the story after his testimony at his trial. It was because a San Francisco newspaper bought exclusive rights to his story, and then never used it. She then purports to give his version of the story, one that fits well with the records from the trial.[30] As a body, these Alaska accounts, not included in the otherwise thorough

Denver Public Library index, tend to be more accurate and moderate than the legend promulgated by the biased versions in certain of the Denver newspapers. It is unfortunate that very good writers like William Ross Collier, Edwin Victor Westrate, Frank G. Robertson, Beth Kay Harris, Forbes Parkhill, and Amanda Ellis did not use these sources.

That Pierre Berton did use the Alaska resources is abundantly evident when studying his version. Not only did Berton tell us that he used them, but he took many of these eyewitnesses' words, and used them as his own. Examples from Berton's quotes and those of others appear elsewhere in this book, as indicated in endnotes.

The next biography of any note was self-published by Howard Clifford, a retired Seattle journalist who had long been interested in collecting and reprinting the early versions of Soapy's legend.[31] Thanks to Clifford, reprints are now available of Shea and Patton's 1907 *Soapy Smith Tragedy*, Harriet Pullen's 1929 account, some correspondence by Soapy found in a shed behind his saloon and published in 1907 and 1908 issues of *Alaska-Yukon Magazine*, and Don Steffa's article in the 1908 *Pacific Monthly*. Clifford's 1995 popularly written, slim and highly affordable volume has no footnotes, but does include a comprehensive ten-page bibliography, which indicates he supplemented his reading of the full span of published literature with visits to archives in Alaska, British Columbia, Yukon, Washington, and Colorado.

Clifford's decades-long study completed the transformation of the rogue con man into a charming Robin Hood, a concept introduced by Harriet Pullen and elaborated on by Amanda Ellis. His prologue refers to Smith as a brigand, a philanthropist, a scoundrel, and one of the most respected men of the community. "He hobnobbed with presidents, his articulate speech left politicians mesmerized, he swayed unruly mobs with his oratory and fleeced the gullible with his gentle, soft spoken southern accent. . . . A kind and generous family man, he was a loyal friend in his personal relationships and took pride in viewing himself as a public benefactor. He was an impostor unparalleled, master of every 'con,' ruler of rogues and vagabonds, friend of the friendless, protector of criminals, builder of churches, and benefactor of the godly and needy."[32]

In an acknowledgment that reads like a dedication, Clifford thanks Smith's grandsons and his great-grandson, Jeff Smith, for their assistance. After decades of collecting bits and pieces of a legend's history, who would not be thrilled to meet and talk to the descendents? Living family members with a biased viewpoint obviously influenced the tone of the biography, either consciously or unconsciously pressuring the author to speak well of the dead Soapy.

Where Berton's book brought the legend to full flower, Clifford's made it accessible to the Skagway tourist wanting more detail specifically about Soapy. For a ten dollar bill, the average tourist could purchase the entire Soapy-in-Alaska story, complete with photographs on most pages, and expect to be able to read it all in two or three sittings. While, for the most part, the details and facts are correct in the book, interpretations mirror the legend. For instance, Clifford does reveal that Jesse Murphy may have been responsible for Smith's death and that Soapy did not lead the Fourth of July parade. However, he mistakenly places Smith on the podium next to the governor at that parade, and repeats the story of Smith's church donations, revealing that he did not look at Reverend Sinclair's papers. These changes enhance the evolution in the legend from Smith as villain to Smith as Robin Hood.

The next biographer published almost a decade later: Jane Haigh, a historian teaching at Kenai Peninsula College in Anchorage, one of the University of Alaska's community colleges. In the wake of the success of three popular Alaska histories,[33] a Yukon publisher asked her to write a history of Soapy Smith in Alaska. Haigh accomplished something never done with the previous Smith biographies: endnotes, bibliography, and an index.[34]

To her credit, Haigh relied heavily on original newspaper accounts and early publications instead of the later secondary accounts. Due to an increasing interest in political corruption in Denver, she researched primarily the Denver newspapers instead of Alaskan and West Coast newspapers, and made heavy use of the Denver Public Library's card catalogue. As a result, her research was biased toward the legend as filtered through Soapy's friends and colleagues in Denver and the later sifting of accounts that occurred due to the way the Denver Public Library accumulated its collection. Although she did a very good job of sifting the secondary literature for facts and using the primary literature, she admitted in a personal conversation that she was not able to use archives in Alaska to the extent she would have liked.

Therefore, Haigh's account, while introducing a scholarly tone and format to a 105-year-long history of Soapy tales, did not add to the facts behind or change the interpretation of the legend.

The next, and one of the most important developments in the presentation of the Soapy Smith story, was the publication of a 628-page biography by Smith's great grandson Jeff Smith in 2010.[35] *Alias Soapy Smith: The Life and Death of a Scoundrel*, was brought out by a small historical press in Juneau, Alaska, which had previously published the almost-forgotten manuscript of the Reverend Robert M. Dickey[36] in 1997. While descendent Jeff Smith claims no academic credentials, either in the fields of journalism, English literature, or any of the social sciences, his credentials as a skilled genealogist cannot be questioned. His life-long family association has given him unprecedented access to a wealth of both archival and secondary literature about his subject, and his family possesses a wealth of photographs and other artifacts associated with Soapy, all of which have carefully curated family provenience and histories. *Alias Soapy* presents a great deal of this material.

Jeff Smith's grandfather, Jefferson Randolph Smith III, and his father, John Randolph (Randy) Smith, were the source of much of the oral history Jeff absorbed during his childhood. His grandfather remembered Soapy and was raised by Soapy's widow, Mary. In the wake of Soapy's death, Mary invited his friends to her St. Louis home, where the tales of Skagway were often repeated.[37] The stories and exaggerations developed in Skagway to fit Soapy's self-styled image consoled a grieving widow and her children. As is evident from Jeff Smith's biography, these stories no doubt emphasized Soapy's good works and were soft on the more cruel or iniquitous aspects of the gambler's behavior. Jeff Smith also relied heavily on a large collection of personal letters (many of which he published in *Alias Soapy*) and the large newspaper collections in the Denver Public Library, where he read all issues of many Colorado newspapers for the periods when Soapy was in residence.[38] Smith lists 113 newspapers in his bibliography, many of which can be obtained through online sources and which were probably accessed through word searches for "Soapy Smith." His use of Alaskan and other West Coast newspapers, such as the *Skaguay News* and *Dyea Trail*, which do not have complete collections for the period in which Soapy was alive, probably represents selected articles from clippings collections or online searches. As discussed elsewhere, it is suspected that the few surviving issues of the *Skaguay News* and the *Daily Alaskan* from November 1897 to October 1898 were archived by Clarence Andrews, who preserved selected issues from March, July, and August 1898 specifically because they dealt with Soapy Smith. These selected issues made it appear that Smith was in the news more often than he really was. This slanted news coverage specifically of Soapy Smith in Alaska does not provide the wider political context that Jeff Smith would have been able to obtain by reading all of the issues of Denver, Leadville, and other mining camp newspapers in Colorado.

Although Jeff Smith acknowledges the help of individuals at archives such as the Skagway City Museum and Klondike Gold Rush National Historical Park in Skagway, the Alaska State Archives in Juneau, Alaska, and the National Archives in Anchorage, Alaska, none of their collections are cited by name or number in the bibliography. Of the two dozen footnotes to Alaskan archival documents in the Alaskan portion of *Alias Soapy*, all cite particularistic material, such as trial records of known gang members, Soapy's probate, and the letters written by Sam Steele. None appeared to have been researched for a broad understanding of context.[39]

Throughout his book, it is obvious that Smith emphasized correcting factual details, without increasing his understanding or interpretation of them. For instance, in his effort to convince his readers that Jesse Murphy "murdered" Soapy, he cites as one of several pieces of evidence an article in the *Portland Morning Oregonian* of July 19, 1898. The article contains the sentence "A man named Murphy claimed after the first autopsy that it was his bullet that killed the gambler." What Jeff Smith fails to mention is that the sentence continues "and it was necessary to perform a second to determine that Reed's [*sic*] did the work." In other words, he fails to point out that that very article dismissed Murphy as Smith's killer, specifically stating that the coroner's jury had questioned Murphy and found that it was Reid's bullet that killed Smith, not Murphy's.[40] Without a doubt, Jeff Smith's intent was to show that Murphy admitted being Smith's killer; he used the article to justify his interpretation that Soapy was murdered rather than killed in a shoot-out in self-defense.[41] However, Jeff Smith then went on to conclude that the vigilante Citizens' Committee (which he confuses with the Committee of One Hundred and One, the Merchant's Committee, and the group of townspeople who gathered on the evening of July 8, 1898) tried to "hush-up" the "murder" of Soapy Smith for fear of "vigilante rampage, and more violence and death."[42] He failed to understand the political relationships among the players as members of the Committee of One Hundred and One and city council. In particular, he did not take into consideration their recent negotiations with the railroad over the rights-of-way, and the ongoing suit over the townsite.

That lack of understanding is particularly betrayed when Smith speculates that "John Clancy made some kind of deal with the Citizens' Committee" that gave him "full exoneration."[43] John's brother, Frank Clancy, owned the building that Smith leased as Jeff Smith's Parlor, and that the business died with its owner. Frank was in Dawson at the time of the robbery and shoot-out, and ended up retaining ownership of Smith's Parlors. Jeff Smith is apparently unaware of the fact that Clancy was a member of the city council, which was nominated and voted into office by the Committee of One Hundred and One in December 1897. He was also the only member to retain a seat in July 1898, and again in December 1898. As stated earlier, this author believes it was Clancy and his brothers of the Clancy Syndicate who controlled Smith, not the other way around. Viewed from that perspective, there was no "deal" for the Clancys to make. The Clancy brothers were extremely powerful in Skagway and would remain so for several more years. They owned a great deal of real estate and most of the businessmen in town who were making the decisions on both the outgoing and soon-to-be-incoming city councils knew about their influence. One did not mess with the Clancys.

This lack of understanding of historic context betrays the major weakness of this otherwise bulging treasure house of Soapy facts. Jeff Smith gives equal weight to the fact that Soapy wrote a letter to his wife from Skagway on August 28, 1897, and the newspaper item that a J. Smith attended a masked ball in Skagway on Thanksgiving, 1897, speculating that both pieces indicated Soapy was in town as early as August and returned in November.[44] While the strength of the first piece of evidence is strong, the second is much weaker. Without corroborating evidence, a professional historian would assume that the newspaper's J. Smith was U.S. Commissioner John U. Smith, as other data indicate that Soapy was on the East Coast in November 1897. Jeff Smith informs his readers that Soapy owned Jeff Smith's Parlor despite the fact that Frank Clancy's name is on the deed records and the *Skagway Alaskan* reported that Smith and Clancy had reached a lease agreement on May 11, 1898, for the opening of Jeff Smith's Parlor.[45] Jeff Smith, the great-grandson, like many of his predecessors, has assumed that Jeff Smith's Parlor existed as early as March 15, 1898, because it fit so well with the legend of the King of Skagway.[46]

Throughout the biography by his descendent, Soapy is portrayed as a complex personality of strong character, misguided morals, and ultimately as the victim of a gross injustice. While factual details of the legend have been corrected and embellished, the legend of the gifted con man and gang leader who became the king of Skagway in the spring of 1898 only to fall to an assassin's bullet on July 8, 1898, thus purging Skagway of crime, is brought to its full flower. The fond treatment by a namesake clothing all of his interpretations in the guise of "history" nudges the legend from that of community redemption to that of a rascally, Americanized Robin Hood.

Such a fascinating American legend cannot be summarized and put to bed by a final word from his great-grandson. A mere year passed before award-winning journalist and *New York Times* best-selling author Howard Blum published, in 2011, *The Floor of Heaven*,[47] ostensibly a nonfiction retelling of the discovery of gold in the Klondike. For his version, he intertwines three true-life stories, those of the gold discoverer, George Carmacks, the famous Pinkerton detective, Charlie Siringo, and the legendary Soapy Smith. Blum does not let it bother him that there is no solid evidence that the three ever met.

Like the many journalists before him who have written Soapy's story, Blum has not let the facts get in the way of a good story. Despite praising Jeff Smith's *Alias Soapy* as the "only [source] the interested reader needs to make his way through,"[48] an examination of his note on sources indicates that his flamboyant accounts of the killing of Andy McGrath and Deputy Marshal Rowan, Soapy's rise to power, the Fourth of July parade, and the duel on the Juneau Wharf come from a myriad of secondary sources, none of which include Berton's, Haigh's, or Smith's, the ones most likely to have used primary source material.[49]

Without the burden of Smith's recent corrections, Blum tells the legend in its greatest glory. Ed Fay, the bartender who shot McGrath and Rowan in February 1898, appeals directly to Soapy for help, and it is Soapy's bravado that keeps Fay from swinging at the end of a vigilantes' necktie party. Soapy intimidates the Committee of One Hundred and One to the point that they will no longer meet. He becomes king of Skagway, commanding his own private military force in the form of the Skagway Militia. He heads the Fourth of July parade and the crowds cheer him. The gunfight on July 8 happens as it was always told until only recently, with no mention of Jesse Murphy. Si Tanner, curiously renamed "John," makes a cameo appearance to calm the crowds and inspire an accolade about his remarkable courage. The Soapy portion of the story ends with Rev. Sinclair's admonition that "the way of the transgressors is hard," and a note that all of the Soapy gang was shipped out of town: redux the redemption theme.[50]

———

So the legend lives on, promulgated by the friends and cohorts of Soapy from the days he lived in Denver and as recorded in the Denver newspapers that are indexed at the Denver Public Library and that passed down through to his great-grandson. So imbedded is the legend-become-myth that only the details can be corrected as aging eyewitnesses set their memories to paper. After Martin Itjen's failure to turn the legend on its head, those who had seen Smith die satisfied themselves with publishing corrections of detail in Alaskan venues. They fell victim to Canadian nationalism, which gloried in a belief that frontier Americans were lawless and immoral. They embraced the mythology that taught that lawlessness and disorder must inevitably give way to social order. Crime does not pay. Redemption will be made with the blood of sinners and martyrs. The Robin Hood theme played counterpoint to that of Redemption. Mixed with the image of the villain who corrupted Skagway was one of a charming scalawag capable of salvation, but who chose the path of the transgressor, an incipient Robin Hood. Which image would Americans ultimately favor?

CHAPTER NINE

Legend, Heroes, and Myth

Like all heroes, the Buddha doesn't show you the truth itself, he shows you the way to the truth.

Bill Moyers in Joseph Campbell, *The Power of Myth with Bill Moyer*

The hero is never power-mongering, sanctimonious or self-righteous, although he is prey to arrogance, abuse and flawed judgment. He confronts situations, he does not embrace causes. If he takes sides at all, it is for challenge of the occasion, not for ideological reasons. His code of power, rooted in moral independence and dignified acceptance of the suffering it entails, continues to sustain us when other creeds, especially the transcendent ideologies of sin and obligations, fail to square against the brute facts of life.

John Lash, *The Hero: Manhood and Power*

Every legend has a hero. Despite the efforts of "Stroller" White, Rev. Sinclair, Chris Shea, and later writers to make Frank Reid the hero of the Soapy Smith legend, it was not to be. Inevitably, in the end, Smith himself became the hero. Like the outlaws Jesse James and Billy the Kid, he overcame his rascally, thieving reputation to become the tragic hero of his own legend. How did that happen?

In 1963, Dixon Wector published *The Hero in America*. While not addressing legendary or mythic heroes, he defined the American hero as follows. He (Wector's heroes were male) must be popular, and of the people's choice. He is a man of goodwill, one who provides unselfish service, and a servant of his age; he is a man of peace, who serves only long enough to beat authority at its own game. Despite his outstanding characteristics, no man is really a hero until he is dead. The hero "has sympathy for handicap, struggle and failure," and tales about the hero indicate that he has personally suffered these faults, making him accessible and identifiable to the masses. The populace will bestow upon him a nickname, to indicate the American informality of hero-worship.[1]

John Lash, in his lavishly illustrated 1995 book called, simply, *The Hero*, wrote that the legendary hero displays "a consistent capacity for action that surpasses the norm. . . . In excelling and exceeding himself, the hero becomes a model of higher potential for his clan, his race or nation, even for humanity at large. . . . His career is turbulent and controversial because virility is close kin to violence. . . . The hero is uniquely charged with the responsibility to use violent forces, as the situation requires, without being consumed by it."[2] Once again, Lash's hero was unmistakably masculine.

Kent Steckmesser listed the qualities of the legendary hero, as applied to the American frontier myth, in the following way: gentility, prowess, clever traits, and epic significance. In legend, the historic figures are made more refined than their historic counterparts, they are given better manners, they speak in a purified language, have philosophical depth, and understand their historical roles. Their gentility often takes the form of chivalry to women or generosity to the downtrodden. In western legend, physical prowess usually involves fisticuffs and/or gun-fighting abilities. Tales of their exploits abound with examples of the clever ways they outmaneuver their enemies, such as the way Wild Bill Hickok leaped off a sixty-foot cliff to escape Blackfeet Indians (a tale borrowed from a Daniel Boone episode), or the way Billy the Kid broke out from the Lincoln County jail (described with horror by contemporary press). Fifty years after it happened, Walter Noble Burns turned Billy the Kid's horrific escape into an ingenious act of heroism.[3]

Of particular interest to this discussion is Steckmesser's fourth characteristic of the legendary hero: the assignment of epic significance to the hero's career. Biographers compare the American hero to accepted heroes of previous ages. Custer's biographer Frederick Whittaker in 1876 put him on a par with Napoleon, Cromwell, Caesar, and Hannibal; Hickok was said by his biographer, J. W. Buell, in

1880 to have "played his part in the reformation of pioneer society more effectively than any character in the annals of American history." Stuart Lake called Wyatt Earp "this most famous marshal of the old frontier." The earliest biographers of Billy the Kid named him "the peer of any fabled brigand on record." Novelist Will Henry, in attempting to kill the Jesse James legend, only perpetuated it by reiterating the stories of "The Robin Hood of the Blue." These accolades led biographers to neglect or gloss over events or episodes that failed to contribute to the epic significance of their subjects.[4]

Richard Slatta's extremely useful discussion of the myth of the American frontier splits the myth into three categories: American exceptionalism, individualism, and frontier violence. These qualities of the American myth can be directly translated into characteristics of the legendary hero. He is exceptional in his capabilities. Despite the American historical necessity to use cooperation to solve myriad problems (wagon trains, posses, barn-raisings, communal harvests, quilting bees, granges, co-ops, unions, vigilantes), the hero's ability to strike out on his own and use his individual ingenuity places him a cut above his peers. And like so many others, especially Richard Slotkin, Slatta cannot escape the observation that heroes in American frontier myth must use violence to solve their problems.[5]

While these four writers—Wector, Lash, Steckmesser, and Slatta—conceptualize the hero differently, there is some overlap in the qualities of their heroes. Steckmesser emphasizes the aristocratic or genteel nature of the hero, and Wector states that the hero must have goodwill, provide unselfish service, and certainly be genteel, aristocratic, or knightly. Lash emphasizes that a hero excels and exceeds himself, while Steckmesser indicates that a hero is clever and exhibits prowess, both qualities of excellence. In a way, Wector's "man of peace" could be interpreted as a figure of gentility by some; Lash's responsibility to use violent force without being consumed by it could be seen also as a form of gentility, prowess, or epic significance by others. These two themes interrelate with Slatta's theme of violence, while emphasizing the role of violence in the hero narrative differently. Slatta's concept of myth helps us categorize the heroes in yet another way, as men who are exceptional, individualistic, or violent, or men who are all three. It's all in the interpretation.

Another folklore specialist to discuss the legendary hero is Orrin Klapp in his seminal discussion on the folk hero. He speculates that there might be such a thing as a universal hero that takes one of several forms, such as Monster-Slayer, Avenger, or Martyr. The universal hero tends to exhibit many of the qualities discussed by those authors above. American folk heroes or villains can be analyzed with reference to his thesis.[6]

Throughout the discussion to this point, other legends and legendary heroes have been evoked. Is Soapy Smith the hero of his own legend? And does he compare on the scale with the heroes of other American legends, such as Wild Bill Hickok, Wyatt Earp, Billy the Kid, and Jesse James? In all four cases, their legends hardly need to be told, so well known are they to the American public.

————

James Butler "Wild Bill" Hickok was born on May 27, 1837, in Troy, Illinois. In the thirty-nine years until his death in Deadwood, South Dakota, on August 2, 1876, he became a legend, thanks to his reputed prowess with a gun and exaggerated counts of the number of men he had killed. One of his first biographers, J. W. Buel, wrote of Hickok in 1880: "He was essentially a civilizer, in the sense of a vigilante posse. . . . When Bill drew his pistol there was always one less desperado to harass the law-abiding, and his presence served to allay the hunger of cut throats and rapacious plunderers."[7] Likewise, in 1926, when theatrical manager Frank Wilstach published one of Hickok's next biographies, *Wild Bill Hickok, The Prince of Pistoleers*, the same themes were evoked. Wilstach wrote of Hickok that he "brought order out of chaos and made life endurable for the rightly disposed who lived in his jurisdiction."[8] In 1933, William E. Connelly, the secretary of the Kansas Historical Society, published a biography of Hickok that once again viewed Hickok as "the harbinger of civilization."[9]

All three biographers, in creating Hickok's legend, built upon the gunslinger's prowess with pistols. They regarded Hickok in the light of a selfless servant of the people (the civilizer) and presaged Lash's criterion of the responsibility to use violent forces without being consumed by them. This was shown by how little Hickok liked killing each time he did it. In each telling of Hickok's death (note that Wector believes the best heroes are dead ones), the true tragedy is that he was killed for no good cause or reason, having been a man of true peace. The tales related in all of Hickok's early biographies are ones of cleverness, skill, and prowess at physical feats and marksmanship, until all of his acts take on epic proportions. Even down to the minor point of his being better known by his nickname, "Wild Bill," than by his true first name, James, Hickok meets all of the definitions of the western hero advanced by Wector, Lash, and Steckmesser.

Orrin Klapp uses Wild Bill as an example of the American hero of the "Feat" and the "Contest," much like Ajax, Hercules, Beowulf, and Lancelot. His prowess with his guns is his overriding characteristic, and the stories in his legends recount, over and over, the deeds and acts he committed to demonstrate that skill.[10]

Wyatt Stapp Earp was born in Monmouth, Illinois, on March 19, 1848. The fact that he lived to be eighty years old, dying on January 13, 1929, allowed him to contribute to his own legacy, and in refusing to be killed or even wounded, he became the exception that proved that rule that a hero must die to become a true hero. While innumerable tales have been told of his days as a lawman in Kansas cow towns, his real fame came from his participation in a gunfight on the streets of Tombstone, Arizona, on October 26, 1881, the subsequent wounding of his brother Virgil, death of his brother Morgan, and his vendetta ride to find and kill the suspected perpetrators of those deeds.

Allen Barra, one of the latest and more rigorous biographers of Earp, wrote that Earp is one of the two or three dozen most famous Americans, that an Earp historian and connoisseur of Hollywood westerns can connect Earp and any western film, and that the two great parallel legends of the mythic West are Wyatt Earp and Billy the Kid.[11] For those reading this book, a summary of Earp's exploits would be both unnecessary and superfluous. Such is the epic significance of Earp's legend.

Earp's legendary exploits took place in the 1870s and 1880s. He wrote stories about himself in the 1890s for the *San Francisco Chronicle* in an attempt to clear his sullied reputation after being accused of throwing the judgment of a prize fight. But his legendary status did not really become apparent until his friends took up his cause in the twentieth century. The legend of Wyatt Earp probably started with tales promulgated by Bat Masterson, who wrote an article for *Human Life* in 1907, which emphasized Earp's cool-headed bravery. "Wyatt Earp is one of the few men . . . whom I regarded as absolutely destitute of physical fear. . . . Personal bravery is largely made up of self-respect, egotism, and an apprehension of the opinions of others. Wyatt Earp's daring and apparent recklessness in time of danger is wholly characteristic; personal fear doesn't enter into the equation, and when everything is said and done, I believe he values his own opinion of himself more than that of others."[12]

The first—and without a doubt, most flattering—published biography is that by Stuart Lake, *Wyatt Earp, Frontier Marshal.* (Earp was never a marshal.) Casey Tefertiller states that "*Frontier Marshal* emerged as the story of a white knight on horseback, defending the populace against corrupt officials and vile desperados. Lake erased the many shades of gray from Tombstone to create a conflict of good versus evil, rather than exploring the complex questions that actually existed."[13]

In producing the 1955 television series *The Life and Legend of Wyatt Earp*, Robert Sisk and Lew Edelman wanted to make an adult western that "told the truth," but by that time, the truth had been overwhelmed by myth. According to Tefertiller, they wanted to portray the West's greatest gunfighter, the lawman who had tamed three of the frontier's toughest towns, and they used Lake's best-selling book as the source of their material on Earp. They also hired Lake as a consultant on the show. As a result, they filmed the legend, and not the truth. As in Lake's biography, the show portrayed no wives, no secret love affairs, no bunco arrests in Los Angeles, no conflicts of opinion in Tombstone, and no Arizona war.[14]

By that time, however, Earp had become the model, the very archetype of the western gunfighter hero. During the filming of *The Life and Legend of Wyatt Earp*, John Wayne told Hugh O'Brian, who played Earp, that he admired Earp above all real-life heroes. "I often think of Wyatt Earp when I play a film character. There's a guy who actually did what I'm trying to do [in the movies]." Earp was John Wayne's—the western character actor's—prototype.[15]

As Earp's legend grew through the romantic biographies, television series, and movies, detractors inevitably came forward to "correct the record." Allen Barra points out, "The greatest irony of Wyatt Earp's life is that it was his [writing] enemies who kept him famous." One-time Tombstone deputy sheriff William Breckenridge's *Helldorado* and Walter Noble Burns's *Tombstone—An Iliad of the Southwest* both simply added fuel to the raging fire of the controversy surrounding him. In attempting to expose the "lie" of Earp's mythology, Frank Waters instead put him at the center of it, and exposed the complexity of the man. Early detractors such as Ed Bartholomew and Ramon Adams painted Earp as "bully, sadist, hypocrite, stage robber, bigamist, pimp, homosexual, predator and killer." In Barra's words, "Since no hero can ever live up to his legend, to many the reputed image will always be truer than the original. As the years passed, of course, it became increasingly difficult to say what the original image was."[16]

If those were the qualities painted by his detractors, and if his legend-maker, Stuart Lake, saw Earp as a white knight defending the populace, how do modern biographers portray him? Allen Barra sees the Earp qualities as centering on family loyalty, innocence, ambition, pride, blood feuds and revenge, courage, loyalty, and nerve. As hero, he is constantly being reinvented as enforcer of the law or avenger.[17] Casey Tefertiller adds, "He killed only when he believed he had no other choice, and his victims had been criminals who deserved bullets, not sympathy."[18]

Wyatt Earp, a Legendary Hero? A review of the preceding shows an amazing amount of concordance. Earp's goodwill to his fellow man; his unselfish service as an officer of the law; his sympathy for those who were handicapped, who struggled and failed (for example, Johnny-Behind-the-Deuce); his career as a man of peace (as a law enforcement officer); his excelling and exceeding himself; his becoming a role model, however turbulent and controversial; his responsible use of violence without being consumed by it; his cleverness; his prowess in using a six-shooter and in buffaloing miscreants—all add up to his epic significance. His fame after his death reinforces his rising legendary status before his death. All of the novels, films, and so-called biographies of Earp (including Lake's, which is written as a first-person narrative) portray him as well-spoken and literate despite recent evidence that shows he was more as John Wayne depicts the "strong, silent type," given to few words and liable to speak seldom and roughly. The legend made him more genteel than he was.

Only the lack of a nickname sets him apart from the archetype, and with a name like Wyatt, who needs a nickname? His continuing popularity can best be measured by the monthly publication of his story in such popular magazines as *True West*, *Real West*, and *Wild West*.

In examining Klapp's typology of hero roles, Earp's place leaps out. His role as "Avenger" during the vendetta ride is unequivocal and he has become the archetype for such in the American vocabulary. While his legend embraces other heroic types, those requiring great prowess, and overcoming "Feats" and "Contests," his acts of vengeance puts him on a par with Achilles, Ulysses, Charlemagne, and Samson.[19]

———

William "Billy the Kid" Bonney (he had other names, but Bonney was one of the more common) was born, it is believed, in the fall of 1859: no one is sure which day. Late in 1877, Billy was hired by John Tunstall, an English rancher in Lincoln County, New Mexico, as a cowhand. As a devoted employee, the young man became embroiled in a range war typical of the violent feuds being fought across the West at the time. When members of the feuding factions took to hazing, robbery, besieging a town, and even murdering, Billy's youthfulness, likeable personality, and boldness—some would call it bravery—earned him a place in American legend.

In his biography of the Kid, Robert Utley indicates that it was Ash Upson, writing for Pat Garrett, who penned the first biography of Billy the Kid, publishing it less than a year after Bonney's death. He portrayed the Kid as a "happy, likable youth who was also a merciless killer."[20] Paul Hutton credits Charlie Siringo with turning Billy the Kid into a Robin Hood-like figure when he published *A Texas Cowboy* in 1885. This book about Siringo's life stayed in print for more than forty years, and included stories of Pat Garrett's hunts for Billy. Siringo portrayed Billy as even more charming than Garrett and Upson had dared.[21]

According to Kent Steckmesser, Billy the Kid emerged as a hero instead of a villain in a play by Walter Woods in 1901, in which he was treated as a victim of circumstances. This theme was taken up by Walter Noble Burns in *The Saga of Billy the Kid* in 1926. Steckmesser calls his treatment "a magnificent classic of American folklore and mythology. Burns was a superlative writer rather than an objective reporter and the virtues of the book are those of novelistic fiction."[22] That, combined with the fact that Burns talked almost exclusively to people sympathetic to Billy, resulted in a one-sided view of the Lincoln County War. Billy's friends made much of his technical skill with arms and his generous and selfless characteristics. Naturally, Billy's friends espoused his belief in the retribution for the death of Tunstall.[23]

Burns expanded on the theme of vengeance and generosity to the downtrodden to make Billy into a "social bandit," a sort of "saintly figure" adored by Mexican peasants. It was Burns who first called him an American Robin Hood. As in the case of Jesse James, it did not matter whether he did, in fact, rob from the rich and give to the poor, but whether people believed he did. Through Burns's depiction, Billy became an avenger for the Tunstall cause, and a hero of the Hispanic people in the region.[24]

Steckmesser points out that Burns's tales of Billy built on the outlaw's sense of humor, his popularity with women and Hispanics, and his loyalty to his friends. These are all traits of the outlaw-hero in folklore of all times and places.[25] Utley described Billy's characteristics thus: strength and endurance, lithe and swift movement, quick mind. He was resourceful, ingenious, cunning, possessing an acuteness that lifted him above his peers. He was "happy-go-lucky all the time." He drank little, but frequented dance halls and *bailes.* He had a steely steadiness that never faltered and he excelled at gunmanship. Although he was credited with killing twenty-one men, he probably killed only four. "In the flesh and in legend, Billy the Kid embodies the frontier's affinity for violence."[26]

Orrin Klapp, in categorizing the folk hero, called Billy the Kid a "Clever Hero," one who outwitted his enemies in much the same way that Ulysses, Robin Hood, and El Cid did. He also saw the Kid as a hero of the "Defense and Deliverance" type, in the vein of Achilles, Lancelot, and once again, Robin Hood, having "Human Enemies" instead of monsters.[27] Although Klapp does not go so far, he might also have mentioned the Kid's death by betrayal at the hand of Pat Garrett as another case for hero status.

Billy's popularity in the late nineteenth and early twentieth century, through to the present day, marks him as a hero in Dixon Wector's definition, as well as other characteristics: his nickname; his apparent goodwill and reputation for unselfish service; and his sympathy for the unfortunate and down-trodden. He lived a career that was turbulent and controversial, without a doubt, exhibiting a prowess with his guns and a cleverness excelling that of others and often himself, in the definitions of John Lash and Kent Steckmesser. All of his early biographers, especially Burns, gave him a more genteel and refined way of speaking and behaving, one of Steckmesser's characteristics of the hero, which also accounts for his attraction to women and Hispanics.

And there can be no denying that Billy the Kid's life was defined by violence, a characteristic of Wector's, Lash's, and Steckmesser's heroes. Whether the Kid was consumed by his life of violence will probably be argued by his followers *ad infinitum*. The epic significance of his life, however, can scarcely be debated.

————

Jesse Woodson James was born September 5, 1847, and died at the hand of Bob Ford, one of his own gang members, on April 3, 1882. Between the ages of sixteen and thirty-five, James became a living legend. Less than a decade from his death, he was known as "The American Robin Hood," long before Walter Noble Burns so christened Billy the Kid.

Jesse and his brother Frank were part of the larger James and Younger gang that lived in the contentious borderland between the North and South before, during, and after the Civil War. During Reconstruction, the raids and depredations this gang made on agents of restoration struck a popular chord with the local press and the region's antebellum leadership.[28] Jesse, in particular, eventually developed a reputation for generous good works combined with steel-hearted bravery.

John N. Edwards, in a piece written in 1877, five years before James's death, was one of the first to describe the outlaw. The writer described him as having "a face as smooth and innocent as a school girl's" and a form "tall and finely moulded," thus imbuing the bandit with aristocratic qualities.[29] Edwards also portrayed James as having great skill with a gun, being a great horseman, and being partial to a particular horse. These traits would become hallmarks of the western folk hero.[30] An 1882 biography of the James brothers edited by R. T. Bradley depicted Jesse as brave, devoted to friends, and devoted to principle. In his chronicle, the brothers were not cruel by nature, but when roused they would show no mercy.[31]

Frank Tripplet, the next biographer of James and writing immediately after the outlaw's death, portrayed Jesse as an aristocratic Anglo-Norman, "the born ruler of the world," superior to mere Anglo-Saxons. In his outlawry, James separated himself from those who were inferior by taking to the wilderness where he could remain true to his racial and aristocratic gifts. He refused to abandon Clay County after the war, which in Triplett's mind was a genetic virtue, as was his chivalrous treatment of all women.[32]

A long series of dime novels about the James brothers followed James's death in the 1880s and continued through the early 1900s. In this sensational medium, the brothers were depicted as having unusual shooting ability, courage in the face of danger, pity for the unfortunate, deference to women, and ability to surmount all obstacles. These qualities carried through to the later legends seen in biographies and movies.[33] When the James and Younger gang took to robbing trains, they entered the national mythology, taking on national corporations in the form of banks and railroads. Dime novelists followed the positive press that the James and Younger gang had received on the local scene to cast them as Robin Hoods victimized by Pinkertons and big corporations. Laborers, union members, and anarchists—the down-trodden—saw them as heroes.[34]

In 1891, James biographer Welche Gordon took a cue from the dime novels, when he wrote that Jesse is "superior in audacity and rashness, courage and hellishness to all other romantic scoundrels."[35]

Twenty-six years later, Carl Sandburg would write that "Jesse James is the only American bandit who is classical, who is to this country what Robin Hood or Dick Turpin is to England, whose exploits are so close to the mythical and apocryphal."[36] Sandburg cannot be blamed for repeating the legend. By this time, James had so often been compared to Robin Hood that the legend had become fact.

Biographer William Settle believes James became a legend and a hero because so many Americans identified with his "outlaw spirit and their suppressed rebellion against the restrictions of modern society."[37] Living and working in a border state during the Civil War, the James and Younger gang engaged in banditry that easily garnered adherents from factions viewing their depredations as political statements rather than simple outlawry or greed. That laid the foundations for the legend. Dime novels, exploitation of the sensational, contempt for corporations such as the banks and railroads that were robbed by the James and Younger gang—all conspired to turn the outlaw's histories into legend.[38]

Was Jesse James a legendary hero? Without a doubt. Orrin Klapp classified him as a "Benefactor Hero" in the vein of Robin Hood and Christ, and viewed his death at the hand of the assassin Bob Ford as a hero-maker in terms of "Death by Treachery." Wector's, Lash's, and Steckmesser's definitions applied to the James legend yield positive correlations in most categories. The lack of a nickname, like that of Wyatt Earp can easily be dismissed with the alliterative sound of Jesse James. Who needs a nickname with a real name like that?[39]

————

So that brings us back to Jefferson Randolph "Soapy" Smith. Does he, in any way, deserve to share the same legendary stage as Hickok, Earp, Billy the Kid, and James? Does he fit the definition of a legendary hero?

In Dixon Wector's definition, Soapy Smith did indeed enjoy a certain popularity, especially among his cohorts in the sporting communities of the mining towns like Creede, Denver, and Skagway, where he was said to be a ruler. His acceptance of a nickname demonstrates that popularity. Tales of his goodwill and unselfish service, likewise, are a defining characteristic of his legend. His real donation of fifty dollars to the widow Rowan fund, for example, became exaggerated in legend to his starting a fund of seven hundred dollars. Smith's legend holds that he donated hundreds of dollars to the construction of the Union Church in Skagway, despite the fact that Reverend Dickey later denied that Smith had anything to do with the building of the church.[40]

Smith's reputation for cleverness and prowess as a con man cannot be denied. He was constantly excelling and exceeding even himself at the craft of stealing money from those foolish enough to enter into his schemes. Lash, Steckmesser, and Slatta all state that prowess of some sort is important to a popular hero. While they cite skill with weapons is preferable—in the case of the American hero, guns—other types of skills can be accepted by a populace, especially if it chooses the hero. According to the Soapy legend, he was no amateur with a six-shooter, but his skill with a gun was never touted as one of his great capabilities.[41] The men who chose to lionize Soapy, the gambling and sporting crowd, were obviously much more impressed by his ability to dupe the naïve than to outdraw the gunfighter.

Steckmesser's criterion of gentility is amply demonstrated by the legend of Georgia-born Smith, whose biographers almost universally point to his southern manners, refined speech, and cultured bearing. None of them mentioned the *Seattle Post Intelligencer*'s posthumous depiction of him as "slouchy in appearance" with "no pretentions to dress,"[43] it being easier to ignore a deviation from the legend than to try to explain it.

That Smith's career was turbulent and controversial can hardly be denied. Although not discussed in this study, his days in Denver ended in a large part because he was considered persona non grata by the Progressives gaining political office in the mid-1890s. Smith had left the capital of Colorado due to continued conflict with politicians seeking to curb corruption associated with the gambling, sporting, and saloon world, where Smith had some influence.[43] Wisely, he left for places where his activities were better tolerated, and, perhaps, more admired. Indeed, a place like Alaska, where the American frontier myth lived on, with its lawlessness, social chaos, and opportunities for men with individual initiative.

There again, Soapy's story captures the American imagination, for his entrepreneurialism, his climb from store clerk in Round Rock, Texas, to legendary uncrowned king of Skagway proves once again the value of American individualism, ingenuity, and exceptionalism. A man who can take a five-cent cake of soap and exploit other men's gullibility by turning it into countless dollars (five dollars or twenty dollars, depending on the version of the story) cannot be taken lightly, indeed might be admired. Arguably, the person to be held in contempt is the fool who gambled dollars for a cake of soap.

The theme of violence in Smith's legend appears only at the end, and at its inception the legend began. With the death of Smith, the legend came to full form, turning the "Clever Trickster" into a "Martyr," a hero betrayed by a man he feared and respected as no other. He died for a cause—the loyalty of his friends. It is this final act, the death of Soapy Smith on the Juneau Wharf in Skagway, that made him a legend, and set all other facets of the story in place. It was the tragic death of Soapy that gave his story the epic significance that turned him from an ordinary con man into a legend.

———

Daniel Justin Hermann, in discussing modern American values, noted that loyalty to one's word, one's friends, and one's family, is a matter of honor. As such, it has been reenacted time and time again in legendary feuds, quarrels, and social wars. In Hermann's thesis, *Hell on the Range*, honor was disputed in the Pleasant Valley Range War in Arizona of 1892. As a literary example, he cited the Grangerford–Sheperdson feud of Mark Twain's *Huckleberry Finn*, but he might also have cited Louis L'Amour's Sackett–Higgins feud that sends the Sackett brothers west. Hermann summarized writer Bertram Wyatt-Brown as describing the nineteenth-century old southern concept of honor as "epitomized by physical courage, loyalty to kin, fierce defense of family and personal reputation, conspicuous display of wealth, eager hospitality, gambling, drinking, ritualized braggadocio, and communal shaming."[44] After reviewing the traits of Soapy Smith, these characteristics sound familiar.

Hermann hypothesizes that pride of honor's antagonist was conscience: that physical courage or violence found its nemesis in moral courage; that a family reputation's bugaboo was individual piety; that instead of public display of wealth, frugality became of value; and drinking and gambling met its match with temperance.[45] At the end of the nineteenth century, the Progressive movement, spurred on by temperance advocates and leaders of the social gospel conscience movement, advocated a different set of values than those praised in the earlier Old South and on the western frontier.

So, too, could the Soapy Smith legend be framed. Smith, his loyalty to his family and his friends, and his dedication to his world of gambling, drinking, and prostitution were a part of the Old South's value system of honor. When the members of the Committee of One Hundred and One questioned his honor, he stood by it, to the death. The new order—the Progressives from the Midwest and North, opposing the sporting world, social chaos, and anarchism—"civilized" Skagway violently, with the gun.

————

In conclusion, legends are the stories we tell ourselves to reinforce our myths, which articulate our value systems. One builds upon the other, feeding back and forth. History becomes shaped by legend. Myth shapes how we express our perception of history. Legend becomes historic fact.

The myth of the American frontier holds that we Americans civilized the wilderness and brought social order to lawlessness. More often than not, we did this by violent means. Our heroic legends, ranging from the civilizer, Wild Bill Hickok, to the American Robin Hood, Jesse James, reinforce that myth. Somewhere in between is Soapy Smith, whose violent death, in terms of legend, saw an end to the lawlessness of the North and its code of individualistic honor and brought about the rebirth of a town and its moral conscience.

But, of course, it was much more complicated than that, just as the history behind our other legends is much more complex than at first seems. The Earp–Cowboy feud has been characterized as a classic urban–agrarian conflict played out as mining corporations became more powerful in territorial Arizona. Stephen Tatum believes that Billy the Kid's popularity shortly after his death and well into the twenties had a great deal to do with the conflict between agrarianism and industrialism after the Civil War when stories of simpler, pastoral times held great appeal. This theme became articulated by the Lincoln County War, in which Billy the Kid was seen as folk hero, just as Jesse James would be seen as a folk hero of the border war after the Civil War during Reconstruction.[46] Slotkin interprets the legendary James brothers in the context of railroad labor wars in Kansas and Missouri in the 1870s and the portrayals of the James gang's train robberies by dime novelists and editorialists. Jesse James's story is a tale of fanatical opposition to progress, which becomes a myth of justified resistance.[47] In the James and Kid legends, the populace eagerly accepted the simple "hero" who took on the complex "evil" that represented progress.

In just such a way is Soapy Smith seen as Klapp's "Clever Trickster," with an Old Southern-style sense of honor thwarting the plans of the "stuffed shirt" Teetotalers (in the form of the Committee of One Hundred and One) who wanted to shut down the saloons, gambling halls, and brothels, places where itinerant men just wanted to relax and have a little fun. At the turn of the century, the Progressives, with their political agendas to impose moral reforms in the arenas of political corruption, temperance, prostitution, and gambling definitely posed a threat to Smith's way of making a living. There is every reason why he would use his considerable talents for leadership to oppose those movements. From later perspectives, those stuffy Progressives, more often than not visualized as stiff-necked older women in corsets, Carrie Nations, or teetotal preachers, would find few advocates. It is no wonder that the Smith biographies would become so popular in the years after Prohibition.

Daniel Hermann hypothesizes that Zane Grey, in his writings about the West, introduced a new equilibrium between honor and conscience with his western ethic. Grey's hero did not smoke, drink, gamble, or patronize prostitutes. He solved his problems with his gun or fist. He embraced honor and behavioral conscience simultaneously. He "represented a new blend of honor and conscience that prescribed assertive manliness—and submissive womanliness—for the twentieth century."[48]

As Americans, through people like Zane Grey, reinvented their western legends, they also reimagined their western heroes. Lee Clark Mitchell does a masterful job of showing how Americans continually revisualized their Western heroes in popular literature and movies—from novelist James Fenimore Cooper's Natty Bumppo to writer Jack Schafer's *Shane* to movie director Sergio Leone's *Fistful of Dollars* to comedian Mel Brooks's *Blazing Saddles*.[49] So, too, was Soapy Smith's story reconfigured.

Throughout this book I have stressed the redemption theme, or that of the morality play. In order to bring civilization to the wilderness, law and order to the social chaos of Skagway, the early narratives made Smith a worse villain than he was (the uncrowned king or, in Frank Reid's words, "that fiend in Hell") in order to make Reid a martyr. But by now, the early twenty-first century, he has taken on the identity of Orrin Klapp's "Clever Trickster," Robin Hood, and "Betrayed Martyr."

Where did that start? Although it was Amanda Ellis in 1955 who first named Soapy "a modern Robin Hood," his national reputation as a generous donor to the friendless and poor was established as early as George Buffin's short tale of him in Creede, Colorado. Actually, it was in a Portland, Oregon, newspaper editorial soon after his death that the inevitable comparison to Robin Hood first appeared. "The mischief of such careers lies not in their overt acts of lawlessness, but in the false impressions of heroism uninformed minds are apt to receive from their contemplation. It is a pernicious fallacy that Robin Hood's benefactions to the poor palliated his dastardly assaults upon the well-to-do traveler. Not only life, but literature and the drama are full of these grievous refractions and discolorations of truth."[50] The well-educated editor of this important newspaper, the *Morning Oregonian*, which had published since 1850 (and is still alive and well today), warned his readers not to fall under the con man's spell. This editor may not have immediately grasped the lure of the redemption myth, the symbolism of the Robin Hood icon being all too obvious to one who was well-read.

————

One of the functions of myth, as long expressed by anthropologists and sociologists, is to help society deal with the conflict between social beliefs and articulations. To explain events in the context of myth helps individuals deal with the conflict.[51] In other words, casting the confrontation between Smith and Reid in the form of a "Martyr" willing to sacrifice himself in order to resurrect a community by killing the "Villain" who had caused its downfall helped Skagwayans categorize and explain to themselves the much more complex issues of the town claim lawsuit, the railroad right-of-way through town, and emerging class wars between businessmen and laborers.

An important aspect of the American western myth, or myth in general, is that it is not cognitive. Those who created it, did not intend to do so. Will Wright best expressed this concept in *Sixguns and Society* when he wrote, "The theoretical relationship between specific social tensions and unconscious cultural expressions is no longer seen as direct and emotional but as indirect and cognitive."[52] When E. J. "Stroller" White sat down to write his July 9, 1898, coverage of the shooting of Soapy Smith, when Rev. Sinclair penned his July 22, 1898, article on the same subject for the *Toronto Globe*, or when Chris Shea wrote his *Tragedy of "Soapy" Smith*, these classically educated men were not consciously evoking an image of a hero sacrificing himself for the redemption of community taken over by one of the devil's minions. It is simply that the mythology had become so much a part of their subconscious that, for them and the members of their culture, the myth explained the event, and gave it structure. Any details that did not fit the myth—Jesse Murphy, the town lots suit, the railroad right-of-way, the existence of the Committee of One Hundred and One before the killing of McGrath and Rowan, even Smith's relatively innocuous position in Skagway—would be ignored to make a legend that fit the myth.

Yet as time went on, the redemption legend began to be replaced by something else. Writers began to focus more and more on Smith's character instead of his deeds, and he took on the characteristics of the legendary hero. Without a doubt, he possessed many of these qualities in some form already, but the legend emphasized his charm, his cleverness, and his generosity to widows and the destitute. His villainy, once crucial to the redemption legend and the sole reason he was promoted from "wants to be boss of Skagway" to "uncrowned king," became secondary to the Robin Hood persona. The charming scoundrel became the stuff of legend, and, to read some biographies, the very truth of the man.

"And either must die at the hand of the other for neither can
live while the other survives."

J. K. Rowling, *Harry Potter and the Order of the Phoenix*

In the early 1960s, John Ford and Willis Goldbeck adapted Dorothy
M. Johnson's 1949 short story, "The Man Who Shot Liberty Valance,"
into an award-winning film starring such luminaries as Jimmy Stewart playing Senator Ransom Stoddard, John Wayne as gunfighter
Tom Doniphon, and Lee Marvin in the title role. Stoddard, a down-
and-out tenderfoot, is beaten by the bully Liberty Valance. Stoddard
lures the villain into the street for a gunfight where he appears to
shoot Valance dead; Doniphon, unbeknownst to anyone but the
audience, was the one who killed Valance from an alleyway; Stoddard gets credit for killing the town badman and goes on to become
a U.S. senator. Years later, when Doniphon dies, penniless and almost
without mourners, the famous Senator Stoddard tells a newspaper
reporter the true story, that Doniphon was the man who shot Liberty
Valance. The shocked newspaper editor throws away his notes, says
he can't tell the story, and declares the memorable line: "When the
legend becomes fact, print the legend."[53]

There are indeed a few parallels between the movie story and the
one about Smith: a bad man wants to take over the town; an ineffective lawman cannot control him; in a climatic gunfight, the wrong
man gets credit for killing the badman; and the true hero dies without ever getting recognized for the feat. Ultimately, law and order
prevail. But expositors and critiquers of both the original short story
and the film agree that the themes are lost youth, a spiritless present,
and nostalgia for the past, not a town's redemption through violence.
Most seem to agree that the point was the loss of the frontier and its
mythology with the death of the wilder elements and the triumph
of the "civilized" easterner.[54] If Johnston drew upon the Jefferson R.
"Soapy" Smith story for her inspiration, it could only have been in
part. The killings of dozens of other badmen in the late nineteenth
century could have served as adequate models, but none fit the tale
exactly. Who shot Soapy? Who shot Liberty?

It is, perhaps, the universality of the western myth that makes Alaskans feel that Liberty Valance is their own, and that makes it such a

classic "close of the frontier" tale. After all, social chaos—the outlaws and gunmen—could run the town only so long before law and order in whatever form caught up with them. Billy the Kid, Jesse James, the Cowboy gangs of Tombstone, and Soapy Smith all eventually found their nemeses—Pat Garrett, Bob Ford, Earp Brothers, and Frank Reid. Willis Goldbeck, Dorothy Johnson, and John Ford wrapped it all up neatly for us in a morality play in the form of Liberty Valance meets Ransom Stoddard and Tom Doniphon. Skagway's Soapy Smith is just another act in the morality play of nostalgia, and the loss of the American frontier, and, as Richard Slotkin would have it, of "regeneration through violence."

Just so does the simpler story always become fact. Politician Chris Shea printed the legend, and The "Soapy" Smith Tragedy became history. It is a good story, and so much easier to tell than the complex one of petty in-fighting between merchants and homesteaders, supporters of a wagon road, and those who knew a British-owned railroad would ultimately ensure the survival of their town. It should be recognized for what it is. Legend.

Despite recent efforts of some writers to make him so, Soapy was not, in reality, the hero of Skagway in the spring and summer of 1898. And, as much as he did for his town, neither was Frank Reid. Not entirely by himself. It is telling that in October 1916 Elmer J. "Stroller" White, who had been editor of the Skaguay News on July 8, 1898, recognized that the Soapy Smith story had lost much in the telling. As owner and editor of the Douglas Island News, he wrote the following, paying tribute to the one hero he thought had been gone unrecognized through the years:

> Away back in the pioneer days, Senator [J. M.] Tanner and the editor of this paper were both residents of Skagway, days when that now placid town was accounted the "toughest place on earth." It was "Si" Tanner who redeemed it. When the people mutinied and refused to further be rode over rough-shod by "Soapy" Smith and his band of assassins, when the then deputy U.S. marshal was deposed by a citizen's meeting, it was to Tanner that the people of Skagway turned and asked him to guide them out of the wilderness. . . . Today but few people realize what Skagway was in those early days nor do they realize

what would have happened that summer of 1898 in the way of murder and robbery of people coming from the interior with gold dust had not J. M. Tanner proved himself the fearless, brave and cool-headed man that he is. He was Skagway's savior then as he has been scores of times since.[55]

And, according to the *Seattle Post Intelligencer*, Smith wanted to add "Boss of Skagway" to his list of accolades,[56] but was never able to succeed in doing so. That title instead went to Josias M. Tanner, given him in 1914, after he had served five terms as city councilman and four terms as the town's mayor.

"For the past ten years, 'Old Si' has had control of the affairs of the town as absolutely as though he owned it in fee simple," wrote Republican Louis B. Keller, editor of the *Daily Alaskan*, a man who had never cared much for Tanner's Democratic politics. "But thanks to the women voters of Skagway, who yesterday for the first time were accorded the privilege of the ballot in a municipal election, the burden of oppressive bossism has been lifted with every prospect of vast improvement in the conducting of civic affairs from an economic as well as a moral standpoint."[57]

Flattering? No. But his point was made. The only man who was officially given the title of "boss" of Skagway, and for over a decade at that, was Si Tanner. With the loss of his mayorship, he left for bigger responsibilities, and became a territorial senator, then a U.S. marshal.

———

Regeneration through violence: it is a powerful theme that Americans have loved throughout their history, dating from the war of independence and supported by scripture. It is no wonder we are so quick to grasp the fundamentals of the tale when laid out so simply and to reject the more complex portions of the story when they get in the way of the legend, the myth come to life. Who wants to "explain" the confusing ethics of land claims squabbles, rights-of-ways, and vigilantism when presented with a straightforward story of Uncrowned King, Martyred Hero, and Redeemed Town?

It is the strength of the morality play that has kept the Smith legend-turned-to myth alive, not the greatness of its characters. The redemption story conceived by Rev. John A. Sinclair was a classic, retold from tales as old as the battle between the dragon and Beowulf, as that of Hector and Paris in liberating Troy, as the final battle between King Arthur and Mordred to save the ideals of Camelot. It is a theme that would stand the test of time well into the twentieth century, where it would take the form of Frodo and the fellowship marching into Mordor and certain death to kill the evil Sauron in J. R. R. Tolkien's *The Lord of the Rings*. Stephen King's small troupe of plague survivors confronts the personification of all evil, Randall Flagg, the Dark Man, as their deaths redeem a post-apocalyptic world in *The Stand*. Anti-hero Darth Vader saves the Jedi as he kills the evil Emperor. In the twenty-first century, Harry Potter walks at last into the clutches of Voldemort in order that the Death Eaters not conquer the Wizarding World. The story continues to have appeal. Frank Reid was one of those evil "vigilantes," just as Vader had been a member of The Federation. Emphasizing Smith's charm only explains the hold he had over "good" people; exaggerating his generosity points out that he was redeemable and therefore could have chosen to return the stolen gold, but did not do so; through his sacrifice, the fallible but heroic Reid redeemed not only himself, but his entire community.

––––––––

It is frustrating for the academics when their own work goes unnoticed while the Kid, just as he challenged the establishment a hundred years ago, mocks them by his hold on the public's imagination. They take their potshots, but always miss.

Paul Hutton, "Dreamscape Desperado"

Casting Smith's story into the realm of myth and allegory does not do it an injustice, but it does raise questions that allow the rest of the story to be told. Contrasting the legend to Skagway's real history—the settling of the townsite, the formation of city government, the conflict between transportation companies—allows the outsider to understand that not all city pioneers were greedy crooks of a different stripe as portrayed by Harriet Pullen. Skagway's early history varied little from the chaotic social history of any early mining community of the time.

That her citizens were able to organize a city government, provide for property rights, light, water, safety, and most other amenities in the complete absence of constituted authority to do so is remarkable, and has not yet been documented outside of this publication. Instead of being recognized for their achievements, those same citizens have been vilified in an effort to perpetuate a legend that Skagway was evil until July 8, 1898, when Frank Reid shot and killed Soapy Smith—the lies agreed upon—in an effort to cleanse the town of its sins.

In the end, of course, it is important to understand the discrete places of mythology, legend, and history in a community's heritage, whether that community is Skagway, Alaska; Tombstone Arizona; Dodge City, Kansas; Deadwood, South Dakota; or Frontier Town, U.S.A. Recognizing the difference between legend and historic fact is important in comprehending the social process and interpretation of events.

From time to time, incidents occur that exceed the sum of the facts. Because the circumstances mirror mythology so very well, the event is interpreted within the structure of the myth, and all details that belie the myth are cast aside. The history of the event is told in the form of a legend that supports the myth. And so the heroes of the legend become historical figures.

Thus it is that Jefferson Randolph "Soapy" Smith became a significant historical personage—after his death—and the longtime lawman, councilman, mayor, senator and marshal, J. M. Tanner, faded into obscurity. For sometimes myth interprets history that molds legend that shapes myth.

Appendix A

A Chronological List of Soapy Smith Accounts

The following listing of the accounts of the Soapy Smith story in Alaska is offered because no bibliography of the story is found in any publication until Clarence Andrews's 1944 book, *The Story of Alaska*. Before that time, it is instructive to see what sources each writer had available to him or her, and the biases inherent in their perspectives. The author has examined all versions of the story recounted in these sources.

Primary sources—firsthand accounts—are indicated with an asterisk (*). Newspapers marked with an asterisk contain first-hand accounts of Smith in Alaska. While Denver newspapers often reported Smith's doings in Alaska, they were usually accounts taken from second-hand witnesses, or witnesses biased by their close relationship to Smith. I have marked those sources I consider suspect with a dagger (†). I cannot speak for their authority on Colorado matters, where Denver editors were able to check facts.

Newspapers

1898	*The Denver (Colorado) Post,* June 19.
1898	*The Dyea (Alaska) Trail,* February 25–July 30.
1898	*The (Portland Morning Oregonian,* July 18–23.
1898	*The San Francisco (California) Chronicle,* Feb. 8–March 16.
1898	*The Seattle (Washington) Post-Intelligencer,* February 6–15.
1898–99	*The (Skagway) Daily Alaskan,* July 2–September 10.
1898–99	†*The Denver (Colorado) Times,* January 6–January 6.
1898–99	†*The Rocky Mountain News (Denver),* February 6–April 14.
1898–99	*The Skaguay Alaska) News,* June 16–February 3.
1899	*The Denver (Colorado) Republican,* March 16.
1916	*The Douglas (Alaska) Island News,* October 13.

The five most important newspaper accounts of the killing of Jefferson Randolph Smith are as follows, and all are considered primary sources:

1898   White, E. J., "Stroller," ed. and au., *The Skaguay News, Skagway, Alaska, July 8, 1898.

1898   de Succa, George W., ed., *The Daily Alaskan, Skagway, Alaska, July 15.

1898   Letter by Dr. C. W. Cornelius, *The Morning Oregonian, Portland, Oregon, July 19.

1898   Rev. John A. Sinclair, *The Globe, Toronto, Ontario, July 22.

1898   Testimony by J. D. Stewart, *The Tacoma Daily News, Tacoma, Washington, December 27.

Magazine Articles and Books

1899   Anonymous, "Odds and Ends." *Wide World Magazine* (July): 331.

1900   *Jackson v. United States, Circuit Court of Appeals, Ninth Circuit, May 14, 1900, No. 570. In *The Federal Reporter: Cases Argued and Determined in the Circuit Courts of Appeals and Circuit and District Courts of the United States, July–September 1900.* St. Paul: West Publishing.

1901   *Suydam, Harry. "The Reign of 'Soapy' Smith." *Frank Leslie's Popular Monthly* (January).

1907   Shea, Chris and Fred Patten, *The "Soapy" Smith Tragedy.* Skagway, Alaska: *Daily Alaskan*; repr. Seattle: Clifford Publishing, 1972.

1908   *Graves, S. [Samuel] H. *On the White Pass Payroll.* Chicago: Paladin, 15–31.

1908   Jones, R. D. "Correspondence of a Crook." *Alaska-Yukon Magazine* (January 1907 and February 1908; repr. in Seattle: Sourdough Enterprises by Howard Clifford, 1997).

1908   Steffa, Don. "Soapy Smith: Bad Man and Bluffer." *Pacific Monthly* 20, no. 4 (October 1908): 347–60.

1909   Rickard, T. A. *Through the Yukon and Alaska.* San Francisco: Mining and Scientific Press, 1909.

1909   Smith, Edward H. as told to Will Irwin. *Confessions of a Confidence Man.* New York: B. W. Huebsch, 1909.

1915   Ferrell, Ed. "Josias Martin Tanner." In *Biographies of Alaska-Yukon Pioneers 1850–1950, Volume 2.* compiled and edited by Robert DeArmond. N. P.: Heritage Books, probably 1950. 321–22.

1915   Steele, Samuel Benfield. *Forty Years in Canada: Reminiscences of the Great North-West with Some Account of His Service in South Africa.* New York: Dodd, Mead & Co., 1915.

1920   Barnacle, Barkalow. "'Characters' of the Early Day: 'Soapy' Smith, The Gambler." *The Trail,* 12, no. 8 (January 1920): 5–11.

1927   W. F. Hynes. "Soapy Smith, Old-Time Rule of Denver Underworld." *Rocky Mountain News Sunday Magazine* (August 28, 1927): 10, 11.

1927   Forsney, Guy. "Soapy Smith's Death." *Rocky Mountain News Sunday Magazine* (September 4, 1927): 9.

1927   Anonymous. "Soapy Smith's Skull: An Ironic Monument to a Two-Gun Tyrant." *Literary Digest.* (September 3, 1927): 48–52.

1928   Walden, Arthur T. A. *Dog Puncher on the Yukon.* Originally published Boston: Houghton, Mifflin, 1928. Repr. Whitehorse, Yukon Territory: Wolf Creek Books, 2001.

1929?   *Pullen, Harriet S. *Soapy Smith, Bandit of Skagway, How He Lived; How He Died.* Skagway, Alaska: Skagway Tourist Agency, about 1929, rept. Seattle: Sourdough Press, 1973.

1933   Willoughby, Florence Barrett. *Alaskans All.* Boston: Houghton Mifflin, 1933.

1933   *Whiting, F. B. *Grit, Grief and Gold: A True Narrative of a Pathfinder in Alaska.* Seattle: Peacock Publishing, 1933.

1934   Itjen, Martin. *The Story of the Tour on the Skagway, Alaska Street Car.* N.P., 1934.

1935   Collier, William Ross and Edwin Victor Westrate. "The Reign of Soapy Smith." [Portland] *Oregon Journal,* Sunday supplement, May 26, 1935, 1–15.

1935   Collier, William Ross and Edwin Victor Westrate. *The Reign of Soapy Smith: Monarch of Misrule.* New York: Doubleday, 1935.

1936   Van Clise, Philip S. *Fighting the Underworld.* Cambridge, Massachusetts: Riverside, 1936.

1938   Wickersham, James. *Old Yukon: Tales—Trails—and Trials.* Washington, D.C.: Washington Law Book, 1938.

1939   Woods, Ann. "Gold Rush Bad Town." *Alaska Sportsman* (August 1939): 10–13, 34–35.

1940   Maurer, David. *The Big Con.* New York: Bobbs-Merrell, 1940.

1941   *Mayberry, Genevieve. "The Hero of Skagway." *Alaska Sportsman* (August 1941): 18–19, 41–43.

1941   *Anonymous. "Who Shot Soapy Smith? Not Reid, Says Old Timer." *The Fairbanks Daily News Miner* (June 23, 1941): 5.

1942   Ryan, Gerald. "Little Known Facts about the Life and Death of Soapy Smith." *Alaska Life* (April 1942): 4–5, 19, 22.

1942   *Suydam, Harry. "Soapy Smith." *Alaska Sportsman* (May 1942): 14–15, 22–26.

1943   Mayberry, Genevieve. "Where in Hell Is Soapy?" *Alaska Life* (June 1943): 18–22.

1943   Anonymous. "Man of Skagway." *Alaska Sportsman* Silver Jubilee Edition (1943).

1944   Andrews, C. L. *The Story of Alaska.* Caldwell, Idaho: Caxton, 1944.

1947   Andrews, C. L. "The Real Soapy Smith." *Alaska Sportsman* (November 1947): 6–7, 36–40.

1951   Anonymous. "Caveat Emptor." In *The Brand Book* (Denver Posse, Westerners), September.

1951   Parkhill, Forbes. *The Wildest of the West.* New York: Henry Holt, 1951.

1951   Winslow, Kathryn. *The Big Pan-Out.* New York: Phoenix House, 1951.

1952   *Barkdull, Calvin H. "I Saw Soapy Killed." *Alaska Sportsman* (June 1952): 8–11, 44–50.

1954   O'Connor, Richard. *High Jinks on the Klondike.* Indianapolis, Indiana: Bobbs-Merrill, 1954.

1955   *Clancy, Frank J. "I Was Just a Kid." *Alaska Sportsman* (October 1955): 16–18, 25.

1955   Ellis, Amanda. *Pioneers.* Colorado Springs, Colorado: Denton, 1955.

1955   Lynch, John T. "Devil's Grin." *True West* 2, no. 4 (March–April, 1955): 16–17, 35–36.

1956   Davis, Clyde Brion. *Something for Nothing.* New York: Lippincott, 1956.

1958   Anonymous. "A Pioneer Gangster." *Saturday Evening Post* (March 22, 1958): 78.

1958   Berton, Pierre. *Klondike Fever: The Life and Death of the Last Great Gold Rush.* New York: Alfred A. Knopf, 1958; repr. as *Klondike: The Last Great Gold Rush,* Toronto, On.: McClelland and Stewart, 1972.

1958   Clark, Hazel Stewart. "A Man of Honor." *Alaska Sportsman* (March 1958): 40–41.

1959   Ellis, Amanda. *The Strange, Uncertain Years.* Hamden, Conn.: Shoe String: 1959.

1960 Berton, Pierre. "Dictator of Skagway." *True Western Adventures* (August 1960): 30–33, 62–64.

1960 Hunt, Inez, and Wanetta W. Draper. *To Colorado's Restless Ghosts.* Denver: Alan Swallow, 1960.

1960 Majors, George Malcom. "Soapy Smith's Greatest Hoax." *Real West* (November 1960): 14.

1962 Robertson, Frank G., and Beth Kay Harris. *Soapy Smith, King of the Frontier Con Men.* New York: Hastings, 1962: 162–219.

1963 Kalen, Barbara. "This Month in History." *Alaska Sportsman.* (November 1963): 32.

1964 O'Connor, Wilson. "Take Him to See the Eagle." *The West* (July 1964): 26–28, 62–64.

1965 Anonymous. "In Alaska's History." *Alaska Sportsman* (February 1965).

1966 Kelly, J. N. "Soapy Smith: Dirtiest Crook in Skagway." *The West* (November 1966): 25, 41–42.

1967 Anonymous. "Gamblin' Man." *Alaska Magazine* (May 1967).

1968 Martin, Cy. "He Died to Save Skagway, Part I." *Real West* (January 1968): 16–17, 49–51.

1968 Martin, Cy. "He Died to Save Skagway, Part II." *Real West* (April 1968): 38–41.

1969 DeArmond, R. N. *"Stroller White," Klondike Newsman.* Vancouver: Mitchell, 1969, 34–37.

1969 Christian, Bill. "The One-Man Cowboy Mafia." *Pioneer West* (September 1969): 48–52.

1969 Green, Kenneth J. "First Christmas in Skaguay." *Alaska Sportsman* (December 1969): 3, 48–53.

1969 Martin, Cy. *Gold Rush Narrow Gauge.* Corona del Mar, Calif.: Trans-Anglo Books, 1969, 27– 36.

1970 Bearss, Edwin C. *Proposed Klondike Gold Rush National Historical Park Historic Resource Study.* Washington, D.C: U.S. Department of the Interior, 1970.

1970 Miller, Mike. *Soapy, The Saga of Jefferson R. "Soapy" Smith of Skagway—Alaska's Most Notorious Outlaw and Con-Man.* Juneau: Alaskabooks, 1970.

1973 Martin, Cy. *Hell at White Pass.* New York: Tower Books, 1973.

1974 Reid, Bert. "In Search of a Frontier Hero." *Jacksonville* (Florida) *Times Journal Magazine* (December 8, 1974): 3–4, 6.

1975 Clifford, Howard. *The Skagway Story.* Anchorage: Alaska Northwest, 1975.

1975   Henderson, Grace G. "Soapy Smith's Least Favorite Cheechakos."
        Frontier Times (March 1975): 29.

1975   Martin, Jeannie. "The Slickest of the Bad Men." *Real West,* (July
        1975): 20.

1978   Sinclair, James M. *Mission: Klondike.* Vancouver: Mitchell, 1978.

1983   Howard, G. S. "Badman of Skagway Meets Insp. Wood." *RCMP
        Quarterly* (Fall 1983): 21–47.

1985   Weller, Michael. *The Ballad of Soapy Smith.* London: Samuel
        French, 1985.

1987   Hunt, William R. *Distant Justice: Policing the Alaska Frontier.* Nor-
        man, Oklahoma: University of Oklahoma, 1987.

1987   Minter, Roy. *The White Pass, Gateway to the Klondike.* Fairbanks,
        Alaska: University of Alaska, 1987.

1990   Guttman, Jon. "Con Man's Empire." *Wild West* (December 1990),
        43–48.

1993   Nickell, Phil. "'Soapy' Smith of Skagway." *NOLA Quarterly* 17, no. 3
        (July/September), 13–16.

1995   Tanner, Donald M. "Josias M. Tanner: Skagway's First Marshal of
        Law and Order." *The Skaguay Alaskan,* 12.

1997   Clifford, Howard. *Uncrowned King of Skagway.* Seattle: Sourdough,
        1997.

1997   Dickey, R. M. *Gold Fever: A Narrative of the Great Klondike Gold Rush.*
        Edited by Art Peterson. Auke Bay, Alaska: Klondike Research,
        1997; manuscript first written about 1945. *Note: Contains pri-
        mary source material.

1997   Kirchoff, Jon. "The Sins of Soapy Smith." *Old West* (Fall 1997): 26.

1998   Brady, Jeff. "Who Shot Soapy Panel: Reid Did Not Fire Fatal Blow."
        Skagway News, July 24, 1998, 1, 8.

2005   Sauerwein, Stan. *Soapy Smith, Skagway's Scourge of the Klondike.* Can-
        more, A.: Altitude Publishing, 2005.

2006   Atwood, Evangeline, and Lew Williams, Jr. *Bent Pins to Chains:
        Alaska and Its Newspapers.* (Xlibris, 2006), 72–74, 83.

2006   Jane G. Haigh. *King Con: The Story of Soapy Smith.* Whitehorse,
        Yukon Territory: Friday 501, 2006.

2006   Spude, Catherine Holder. "Josiah M. 'Si' Tanner: Southeast Alas-
        ka's Favorite Lawman." *Quarterly of the National Association for
        Outlaw and Lawman History, Inc.* (January–March): 29–37.

2007   Spude, Catherine Holder. "Con Man's Curse." *True West* (July
        2007): 50–53.

2008   Smith, Jeff. "July 8, 1898: Who Shot Soapy? Who Knew What? Sinner Soapy Smith Murdered." *Skaguay Alaskan* 31, no. 1908 (Summer 2008): 8, 10.

2008   Spude, Catherine Holder. "Saint J.D. Stewart Conned and Robbed." *Skaguay Alaskan* 31, no. 1908 (Summer 2008): 8, 24–25.

2009   Mike Coppock. *Terror in the Klondike: The Reign and Killing of Soapy Smith.* Agoura Hills, Calif.: Graphic Images, 2009.

2009   Smith, Jeff. *Alias Soapy Smith: The Life and Death of a Scoundrel. The Biography of Jefferson Randolph Smith II.* Juneau: Klondike Research, 2009.

2011   Blum, Howard. *The Floor of Heaven: A True Tale of the Last Frontier and the Yukon Gold Rush.* New York: Crown, 2011.

Appendix B

"Soapy Smith's Last Bluff and Its Fatal Ending"

The *Skaguay News* Extra Edition of July 8, 1898 (actually printed on July 9, 1898), was the first story written and published about the shooting and killing of Jefferson Randolph "Soapy" Smith. Its main story is referred to so often in this text that it is reprinted in its entirety here. The *Skaguay News*'s competitor, the *Daily Alaskan*, did not print the story about the shooting until July 11 because its editor was Allan Hornsby, who had been jailed as a possible accomplice. When the *Alaskan* finally published its account, it mirrored the story told by the *News*. Stories that appeared in Victoria, Seattle, San Francisco, and Denver beginning on July 16 cited the *Skaguay News* article on July 8. The *News* repeated its July 8 story in its July 15 edition, adding several columns and stories dealing with the round-up of Soapy's gang. As discussed throughout this book, the *Skaguay News* article of July 8, 1898, was used as the basis of other accounts so often that it is taken to be the standard source of most versions.

"Soapy Smith's Last Bluff And Its Fatal Ending"

By E. J. White

The Skaguay News, July 8, 1898

Armed With a Winchester He Endeavors to Intimidate a Large Meeting of Indignant Citizens on the Juneau Wharf

SHOT THROUGH THE HEART BY FRANK REID.

THE JAIL NEARLY FULL OF MEMBERS OF "SOAPY'S" GANG, AND CITIZENS ARMED WITH WINCHESTERS

STILL ROUNDING THEM UP:
BRAVE FRANK REID WILL PROBABLY RECOVER.
THE INQUEST.

"Soapy" Smith is dead. Shot through the heart, his cold body lies on a slab at People's undertaking parlors, and the confidence men and bunco steerers which have had their headquarters here for some time have suddenly taken their departure, the tragic death of their leader having completely unnerved them.

It was at 9:30 last night that the checkered career of "Soapy" Smith was brought to a sudden end by a 38 calibre [*sic*] bullet from a revolver in the unerring right hand of City Surveyor Frank H. Reid, while the latter lies at the hospital dangerously wounded by a bullet from Smith's rifle.

The cause which lead up to the trouble which ended Smith's life, had its origin in the morning shortly before 10 o'clock when J. D. Stewart, a young man just out from Dawson, was robbed of a sack containing from 12 to 15 pounds of gold. There are conflicting stories as to how the robbery was committed, the accepted version being that Stewart desired to sell his gold, and that one Bowers, a well known member of Smith's gang, represented to Stewart that he was here for the purpose of buying gold for some big assaying company below. The unsuspecting stranger accompanied Bowers to a point in the rear of Smith's place on Holly ave., and near the Mondamin hotel, where, it is alleged, two of Bowers' pals were in waiting, where the three men overpowered Stewart, wrested the sack of gold, containing $2670, from his hands, and disappeared from sight around adjoining buildings, leaving the returned Klondiker as poor as when he started for the land of gold and hardships nearly a year before.

As soon as the news of the bold and daring broad daylight robbery became circulated about the city, there was fire of indignation. People were inexpressibly surprised and shocked that such a flagrant outrage should have been committed in the city. Business men quietly discussed the situation, and, feeling assured that it was Smith's men who did the job, many of the best and most influential of our citizens went quietly to the leader and informed him that the gold must be returned, and that he and his gang must shake the dust of Skaguay from their feet. During the earlier part of the excitement, Smith partially promised several men, including the writer, that, in case there was no "roar" made in the papers, the gold would be returned by 4 o'clock last evening, and that his influence would be used to prevent his men from in any way interfering with returning Klondikers in the future.

The promise was not kept, however, nor was the gold returned. On the contrary, Smith began to drink heavily and talk in a rash, defiant manner. When told by a News representative that unless the gold was returned there would be trouble last night, Smith replied: "By ——, trouble is what I am looking for." He got it in a way he least expected.

The gold not being returned, public indignation continued to increase until at eight o'clock it had reached fever heat. Cool heads prevailed, however, and no outward demonstrations were made, although there was an ominous look worn by several hundred of men, including the best of Skaguay's citizens, which plainly said: "Sure thing men must go." At nine o'clock last night a meeting was started in Sylvester's hall, but the space being inadequate to accommodate the crowd, an adjournment was taken to the Juneau dock, where, at a point half way to the ware house, a meeting was called to devise ways and means for ridding the city of the lawless element, which for some time has infested it. The meeting was called to order by J. T. Hayne, foreman of the News Office, who suggested the election of a chairman, Thomas Whitten of the Golden North hotel, being chosen. Frank H. Reid, Jesse Murphy, J. M. Tanner and Mr. Landers, to guard the approach to the dock, in order that no objectionable characters might be admitted to disturb the deliberations of the meeting.

It was while this committee of four was stationed at the end of the dock that Jeff Smith appeared carrying a Winchester rifle in his hands. He walked straight up to Reid and with an oath, asked what he was doing there, at the same time striking at him with the barrel of the gun. Reid grabbed the gun in his left hand as it descended, pushing it down towards the ground, and drawing his revolver with his right hand at the same time. When the point of the rifle was close against Ried's [*sic*] right groin, Smith pulled the trigger. The ball passed clear through and came out through the lower part of the right hip. At about the same time Reid fired two of three shots in rapid succession, one of which pierced Smith's heart, another striking one of his legs.

Smith also fired a second shot, striking Ried [*sic*] in the leg. Both men fell at about the same time, "Soapy" Smith stone dead and City Engineer Reid dangerously, perhaps mortally, wounded.

Needless to say, the meeting which was in session down the dock speedily adjourned. The dead and wounded were picked up and brought to town, Smith's remains being taken to the undertakers and Mr. Reid being carefully carried to Dr. Moore's office where a number of physicians made a careful examination of his wounds. At first it was thought the wounded man could live but a few hours, but he has since rallied materially and his chances for recovery are now considered very fair, and strong hopes are entertained.

Later in the evening the citizens again convened in meeting, with the result that a thorough organization was effected. It appearing to the citizens that Deputy Marshall [*sic*] Taylor, by his affiliations with the Smith crowd was not the proper man to head an armed body of men, Captain J. M. Tanner was sworn in as deputy marshall [*sic*] by U.S. Commissioner Sehlbrede, about twenty five others were deputized to assist Captain Tanner. Captain Sperry was placed at the head of the deputies, each of whom carried a Winchester rifle.

All last night the measured tread of the guards could be heard as they patrolled the streets. All the haunts where any of those supposed to be in any way connected with "Soapy's gang" was liable to be found were visited. But in most cases, the birds had taken warning and fled. However, quite a number were placed under arrest, and are now confined in the city jail, which is closely guarded. It is feared that the three men who robbed Stewart of his sack of fold have escaped to the hills, as did several others of the gang last night, on learning of the death of their leader. All the avenues of escape from the city have been closely guarded, and unless the bold highwaymen got out by small boats yesterday, their chances for escape are very small. Every wharf is closely guarded, and detachments of deputies have been sent to Dyea, as well as to Lake Bennett. The entire trail from Skaguay to Bennett is closely watched. Business is practically suspended today. Hundreds of men, the majority of them armed with Winchesters, are congregated on the streets, but the best of order prevails.

Four deputy Marshals, Caswell, Joy, Barney, and another, were sent over the trail to Lake Bennett this morning in search of the notorious three who stole the bag of fold. Joy is an ex-detective, from New York and smart as a whip. Caswell is equally as brave, and when they return it is safe to say that they will render a good account of themselves.

THE DEAD MAN'S FAMILY.

Although there was not a single person in Skaguay who appeared to do honor to the man who yesterday was a popular hero and is to day [*sic*] but a dead "highwayman", yet there are those who will deeply mourn his untimely end. Smith received on the last mail photographs of his wife and 6 children, who are living at St. Louis, also loving letters from them. Smith was born at Camilla, Ga., 48 [*sic*] years ago, and has a brother who is one of editors of the Evening Star, Washington, D.C. He had a large correspondence with leading politicians, and by the last mail received a letter from the Secretary of War declining the tender of the volunteer company which he had organized on account of the cost of transportation, but the secretary accompanied his declination with warm expressions of the government's appreciation of Mr. Smith's patriotism.

REID MAY RECOVER.

City Surveyor Reid was taken after the shooting in Dr. Moore's office, where all the leading medical men of the town called later and tendered their services. These formed a medical council for his treatment and at three o'clock this morning decided to remove the sufferer to the Bishop Rowe Hospital. Three hours later, when Mr. Reid had recovered from the shock incident to his removal, the council made an examination of his wounds.

The sufferer was found to have been shot by a Winchester, 45 caliber, the ball entering two inches above the groin on the right side and making its exit an inch to the right of the point of the spinal column. The ball made a compound comminuted fracture of the pelvic bone, and several fragments of this were removed at the time of the examination.

It needs no words to tell of the agonizing pain of the operation, yet Mr. Reid showed the same Spartan coolness and endurance which he has exhibited since first struck by the rifle of "Soapy" Smith. Before the doctors begun the examination and operation he asked for a cigar, and this he calmly smoked while the shattered fragment of his anatomy were being removed. The opinion of the medical council is the chances of Mr. Ried's [*sic*] recovery are fairly good.

As we go to press Mr. Reid is resting easily, and talking over the stirring events of yesterday with philosophic calmness that excite wonder and admiration.

Notes

Newspaper Abbreviations Used in Notes

AMD *Albuquerque Morning Democrat*, Albuquerque, New Mexico
AMR *Alaska Mining Record*, Juneau, Alaska
AS *Anaconda Standard*, Anaconda, Montana
ASJ *Alaska Searchlight*, Juneau, Alaska
AJ *Albuquerque Journal*, Albuquerque, New Mexico
BJ *Boston Journal*, Boston, Massachusetts
BWM *Butte Weekly Miner*, Butte, Montana
CDT *Chicago Daily Tribune*, Chicago, Illinois
DA *The Daily Alaskan*, Skagway, Alaska
DAD *The Daily Alaska Dispatch*, Juneau, Alaska
DIN *The Douglas Island News*, Douglas, Alaska
DMN *Dallas Morning News*, Dallas, Texas
DO *The Daily Oklahoman*, Oklahoma City, Oklahoma
DP *The Denver Post*, Denver, Colorado
DR *The Denver Republican*, Denver, Colorado
DT *The Denver Times*, Denver, Colorado
DyT *The Dyea Trail*, Dyea, Alaska
FDNM *Fairbanks Daily Miner News*, Fairbanks, Alaska
GT *Gazette-Telegraph*, Colorado Springs, Colorado
HI *The Independent*, Helena, Montana
LAT *Los Angeles Times*, Los Angeles, California
LDC *Leadville Daily Chronicle*, Leadville, Colorado
MO *Morning Oregonian*, Portland, Oregon
NM *New Mexican*, Santa Fe, New Mexico
NYT *The New York Times*, New York City, New York
NYW *The New York World*, New York City, New York
RMN *The Rocky Mountain News*, Denver, Colorado
SFC *The San Francisco Chronicle*, San Francisco, California
SFE *The San Francisco Examiner*, San Francisco, California
SJMN *San Jose Mercury News*, San Jose, California
SLT *Salt Lake Telegram*, Salt Lake City, Utah
SN *The Skaguay News*, Skagway, Alaska
SPI *The Seattle Post-Intelligencer*, Seattle, Washington
TDN *The Tacoma Daily News*, Tacoma, Washington
WP *The Washington Post*, Washington, D.C.

Introduction

1. Kittredge, *Owning It All*, 62.

2. Campbell, *The Power of Myth*, 5, 11.

3. See in particular Slotkin, *Regeneration through Violence; Fatal Environment; Gunfighter Nation*. For other discussions of the American frontier myth, see also Athearn, *Mythic West in Twentieth-Century America*; Bellesiles, *Arming America*; Cawelti, *Six-Gun Mystique*; Johnson, *Hunger for the Wild*; McGrath, *Gunfighters, Highwaymen and Vigilantes*; Rosa, *The Gunfighter*; Steckmesser, *Western Hero in History and Legend*; Slatta, "Making and Unmaking;" 84–85; Wright, *Sixguns and Society*.

4. Tangherlini, "It Happened," 385.

5. Slotkin, *Gunfighter Nation*, 5.

6. Ibid., 11–12. Emphasis in original.

7. The most widely used sources for the legend as summarized above are: Berton, *Klondike Fever*, 333–65; Collier and Westrate, *Reign of Soapy Smith*; Robertson and Harris, *Frontier Con Men*, 162–219; Clifford, *Uncrowned King of Skagway*; Haigh, *King Con*, 67–104.

8. Tefertiller, *Wyatt Earp;* Utley, *Billy the Kid*; Nolan, *Billy the Kid Reader*.

9. Berton, *Klondike Fever*, 333–65.

10. Catherine Holder Spude, "Josiah M. 'Si' Tanner," 29–37; "Con Man's Curse," 50–53; "Christopher C. Shea," 16–29; "Saint J.D. Stewart," *Skaguay Alaskan*, 8, 24–25.

11. Jeff Smith, *Alias Soapy Smith*.

12. For instance, see Bancroft, *Denver's Lively Past*; Max Miller and Fred Mazzulla, *Holladay Street*; Feitz, *Soapy Smith's Creed*; Blair, *Leadville*.

13. Haigh, "Political Power" (PhD Diss. University of Arizona, 2009).

14. Jeff Smith, *Alias Soapy*, 104, 107–108.

15. Tangherlini, "It Happened," 385.

16. Andrews, *Story of Alaska*.

17. Berton, *Klondike Fever*; Robertson and Harris, *Frontier Con Men*.

18. Bearss, *Historic Resource Study*, 181–97.

19. Hunt, *Distant Justice*, 52–67.

20. Haigh, *Political Power*.

1. Conceived in Lawlessness

1. Thornton, *Ethnographic Overview*, 53–54.

2. Robert L. S. Spude, *Skagway*, 6.

3. National Archives, Record Group 49, *Valentine v. Moore* (henceforth referred to as NARA, RG-49), Brief for Moore, April 17, 1899, 2–3.

4. *SPI*, July 11, 1897; *SFE*, July 15, 1897.

5. Mayberry, "Hero of Skagway," 18–19; NARA-RG 49, Frank Reid Testimony, April 4, 1898.

6. NARA, RG-49, Frank Reid Testimony, April 4; Brief for Moore, 4–11.

7. *ASJ*, July 17, 1897.

8. NARA, RG 49, *Valentine v. Moore*, Brief for Moore, April 17, 1899, 2–3.

9. Ibid., 5–6; Alaska State Archives, RG 202, Skagway Historical Records, Volume 19, Lot Locations, 1897–1898, 1–73.

10. NARA, RG 49, Testimony by E. Valentine, April 1898, 74–75.

11. NARA, RG 49, *Valentine v. Moore*, Brief for Moore, Exhibit "A," 3–4.

12. McGrath, *Gunfighters, Highwaymen & Vigilantes*, 241, 244.

13. NARA, RG 49, Adverse Claim, October 27, 1897.

14. Ibid.

15. NARA, RG 49, Brief for Moore.

16. Quote in *SN*, December 31, 1897, 8; NARA, RG 49, Brief for Moore, 11.

17. *DA*, January 1, 1901, 3.

18. *SN*, December 31, 1897, 8; T. H. Breen, *American Insurgents*.

19. *SPI*, March 15, 1898, 8.

20. U.S. Marshal's Office, Register of Marshals and Deputy Marshals in Alaska.

21. *SN*, October 15, 22, November 5, 12, 19, December 31, 1897; National Archives, RG-21, Sitka Criminal Files, Boxes 11–13, cases #733–800, Skagway Liquor License Violations, December 1897.

22. *SN*, December 31, 1898, 2.

23. Jeff Smith, *Alias Soapy*, 446–49; *DP*, September 23, 1897.

24. Haigh, *Political Power*. Tammany hall was a New York City Democratic party political machine run by "bosses" and supported by the Irish immigrant population. It was a large corrupt organization that enriched its leaders through political graft for more than two centuries, from the late eighteenth century into the 1950s.

25. NARA, RG 21, Box No. 13 01/01/04(5), District of Alaska, Sitka, Criminal Cases, 1884–1900, Case #'s 799–849, Folder "820 & 821 U.S.

vs. Edward Fay, " Affidavit and Order, November 25, 1898; Excepts to Instructions Filed by Defendant, Filed December 22, 1898; Motion for a new trial, filed December 23, 1898; *MI*, February 6, 1898, after a *Skaguay News* article; *SPI*, March 5, 1898; Suydam, "Reign," 215.

26. NARA-RG 21, "U.S. vs. Edward Fay," Motion for a new trial, filed December 23, 1898; Suydam, "Reign," 215; Andrews, "Real Soapy Smith," 37.

27. NARA-RG 21, "U.S. vs. Edward Fay," November 25, 1898. Affidavit and Order. Signed by Edward F. Fay.

28. Jake was in direct competition with his brother, George, who opened the Board of Trade across the street. Whereas George would go on to operate a syndicate of saloons and gambling places in Skagway, Whitehorse, Dawson, Nome, and other mining camps in the Far North, Jake concentrated on personally operating dance halls and gambling houses with a wider venue of entertainment. After he left Skagway in June 1898, Jake Rice went to Nome for a while, where he tried his hand at mining. Shortly thereafter, he returned to running a saloon, and then made his way through the mining camps of Council City, Eagle City, and Fort Egbert, Alaska, where he opened general merchandise stores. Eventually, he would hie himself off to Juneau to take over the Louvre Saloon and Opera House in 1905 as stage manager. *SN*, November 5, 1897; February 11, 1898; Polk Directory, 1901, 585 and 613; 1902, 468 and 471; 1905, 221; 1909–10, 300; 1880 U.S. Federal Census, New Madrid, Missouri, Roll T9_705, Enumeration District 77, 317; 1900 U.S. Federal Census, Nome, Northern Supervisors District, Alaska, Roll T623, 23A.

29. NARA-RG 21, *U.S. v. Edward Fay*, December 22, 1898. Instructions to Jury Asked by Plaintiff.

30. NARA-RG 49, J. G. Price testimony, October 18, 1897; Adverse Claim October 27, 1897; Brief for Moore, April 1899; *SPI*, Feb. 6, 1898, 2; Skagway Lot Location files, City of Skagway Historical Records, Alaska State Archives, Record Group 202, Volume 19, 1897–1898.

31. *SPI*, February 6, 1898; Suydam, "Reign," 215; *SN*, February 11, 1898; *Directory and Guide*, 141.

32. Ibid.; *HI*, February 6, 1898.

33. Ibid.

34. Ibid.

35. *HI*, February 6, 1898.

36. *SPI*, February 6, 1898; Suydam, "Reign," 215.

37. Ibid.; *SN*, November 5, 1897.

38. *SN*, December 31, 1897; NARA, RG 49, Brief for Moore, 4.

39. NARA, RG 21, *U.S. v. Edward Fay*, U.S. Commissioner's Log, 35; John Sinclair Papers, newspaper notes, transcription of *Skaguay News* article, undated, presumably early February 1898.

40. Suydam, "Reign," 216–17.

41. Ibid., Hunt, *Distant Justice*, 56–57; NARA-RG 21, *U.S. vs. Edward Fay,* (5); U.S. Commissioner's Journal, Dyea, Alaska, dated February 1, 1898, 35.

42. The A&TTNCo. was subsumed by the Close Bros. Company in 1899 and became the White Pass and Yukon Route, which had a railroad division. The railroad division operated out of Skagway and, as far as I know, never had capital letters attached to it.

43. NARA-RG49, Brief for Moore, April 17, 1899, 11.

44. Suydam, "Reign," 216–17.

45. Andrews, "Real Soapy Smith," 37.

46. Alaska State Archives, RG 202, Lot Locations, 2; Letter from Lynn Tanner to Catherine Spude dated September 25, 2006; Ed Ferrell, "Josias Martin Tanner," 321.

47. Sinclair, *Mission Klondike*, 44.

48. Barkdull, "Soapy Killed," 9.

49. *SPI*, March 6, 1898; *DT*, August 7, 1898, and January 6, 1901; Suydam, "Reign," 211–12; *RMN*, August 28, 1927.

50. *SPI*, 19 July 1898.

51. Jeff Smith, *Alias Soapy*, 75–93. Smith lists fifty-six members on these pages. I disagree that all of these people should be considered members of Soapy's gang. Men like Bat Masterson, Ed Chase, Wolfe Londoner, Allan Hornsby, and William Saportes had their own agendas and their own power bases. They may have cooperated with Soapy Smith from time to time, but could not be said to be controlled by Soapy in any way, shape, or form. In fact, Ed Burns's association with Smith may have been one of mutual advantage, and not one in which Smith was a leader and Burns a followed.

52. Quote in *SPI*, July 16, 1898; *MO*, February 11, 1898; Suydam, "Reign," 215.

53. *RMN*, February 8, 1898; *MO*, February 8, 1898; Collier and Westrate, *Monarch*, 221–23.

54. John Sinclair Papers, Newspaper Notes, undated transcription, probably February 4, 1898; *MO*, February 11, 1898; Suydam, "Reign," 215; Fowler, *Timberline: Denver*, 29, 34–36.

55. *RMN*, February 26, 1898; *SPI*, March 5, 1898.

56. Suydam, "Reign," 218; Berton, *Klondike Fever*, 341; NARA, RG 21, *U.S. vs. Edward Fay*, Sentence: January 6, 1899; October 5, 1905, Certification of Release from Prison.

57. U.S. Marshal's Office Roll Call of Honor, http://www.justice.gov/marshals/history/roll_call.htm, access June 14, 2011.

2. The Committee of One Hundred and One

1. Collier and Westrate, *Reign of Soapy Smith*, 225; Robertson and Harris, *King of Frontier*, 182–84; Berton, *Klondike Fever*, 344; Clifford, *Uncrowned King*, 69.

2. *DO*, April 13, 1898; *SPI*, February 6, 1898; *HI*, February 6, 1898; *BWM*, February 10, 1898; Catherine Holder Spude, "Con Man's Curse," 50–53.

3. *SPI*, February 15, 1898; Bearss, *Historic Resource Study*, 187.

4. Haigh, *King Con*, 75; *DyT*, March 11, 1898.

5. *SN*, December 31, 1897.

6. *SN*, November 5, 1897; August 26, 1898; November 5, 1897; December 31, 1897.

7. *SN*, November 25, 1897; February 11, 1898; June 17, 1898; *DA*, September 7, 1899; September 9, 1899; March 24, 1900; March 28, 1900; April 20, 1901; March 9, 1902; NARA RG 21, U.S. Commissioner's Records, Vol. I (OS569), April 22, 1898.

8. Jeff Smith, *Alias*, 456, 457.

9. *SN*, May 11, 1898, *SN*, May 14, 1898.

10. Mathews, *Dictionary of Americanisms on Historical Principles*, 220, 375–376, 1682.

11. Berton, *Klondike Fever*, 321. Berton quotes the Sinclair papers, but does not say where this quote can be found therein.

12. Haigh, *King Con*, 75; *SPI*, March 16, 1898; *DyT*, March 11, 1898.

13. *SN*, May 13, 1898; Alaska State Archives, RG 202, Lot Locations, 1897–1898; Deeds, Volume 1, 1897–1898; National Park Service, *Jeff. Smiths Parlor Museum*, 3.

14. *RMN*, February 19, 1898; *SPI*, March 5, 1898. See Haigh, *Politi-*

cal Power, for a more in-depth discussion of the interconnection of the "gang" and Denver city hall.

15. *DT*, August 7, 1898.

16. *SPI*, February 12, 1898; *DT*, February 25, 1898; *SFE*, March 16, 1898.

17. NARA, RG 49, Brief for Moore, 11.

18. Ibid., 1–4.

19. Ibid., 6, 24.

20. Ibid., 19–22. The initial ruling of August 1899 favored the Skagway businessmen, but the case went on through appeal to Washington, D.C. While Close lawyers geared up for a long-drawn-out litigation, Skagway's business boomed in part because the White Pass and Yukon Route railroad, funded by the Close Bros. was under construction by June 1898. It would take almost ten years of litigation to resolve most of the issues. Starting in 1901 and ending in 1908, property owners in a fourth of the town south of Sixth Avenue and east of Main—40 acres instead of the original 160—would end up paying Moore's Wharf and what would become the White Pass and Yukon Route (WP&YR) a fourth of the value of their property. Because this was the main business part of town, payments to the two biggest businesses in Skagway were substantial.

21. Alaska State Archives, Record Group 202, City of Skagway Historical Records, Volume 19, Lot Locations, Books 1–3, 1897–98. Note: Book 2 includes Deed transactions as well as Lot Locations. Book 1 has the index for all three Books.

22. Bearss, *Historic Resource Study*, 226–227.

23. Minter, *Gateway*, 186–188.

24. Ibid.; *SN*, June 17, 1898; Minter, *Gateway*, 182–83.

25. Jeff Smith, *Alias*, 518, 519.

26. *SN*, June 17, 1898.

27. Ibid.; Howard Clifford, *Rails North*, 18.

28. NARA, RG 49, Brief for Moore, 11; Alaska State Archives, RG-21, U.S. Commissioner's Records, Sitka, Vol. 1 (OS. 569) 238–284, 299, 346–357, 368–369.

29. *DT*, June 12, 1898; *LDC*, October 31, 1890; October 14, 1891; February 23, 1892; March 3, 1892; March 17, 1892; May 12, 1892; June 8, 1892; February 22, 1893; September 3, 1894; *AMR*, May 10, 1899.

30. *DA*, April 27, 1898; Jones, *Correspondence*, 10–14.

31. Sinclair Papers, "Transcribed Newspapers Articles," *SN*, May 2, 1898. "Tanner" was probably John (or William) Tener.

32. Willoughby, *Alaskans All*, 201–234; Atwood and Williams, *Bent Pins*, 82–83; Atwood and DeArmond, *Who's Who*, 104.

33. DeArmond, *Stroller*, 15–21.

34. DeArmond, *Klondike Newsman*, 17–18.

35. *DP*, May 24, 1898.

36. *DT*, June 12, 1898; *Denver Post*, June 19, 1898.

37. Jeff Smith, *Alias Soapy*, 494–495; Clifford, *Uncrowned King*, 79 and 83; Jones, *Correspondence*, 10–14.

38. U.S. National Guard, *Report on Mobilization*, 9–10.

39. *DA*, January 10, 1900, 1.

40. *DA*, May 2, 1898; *SN*, May 2, 1898.

41. *SN*, May 13, 1898; *DA*, May 16, 1898.

42. John Sinclair Papers, Diary, July 4, 1898.

43. Sinclair, *Mission: Klondike*, 131.

44. Ibid., 261.

45. *SN*, July 1, 1898; *DA*, July 2, 1898.

46. Ibid.; *SN*, Nov. 5, 1897.

47. Sinclair, *Diary*, July 4, 1898; Hinkley, *Alaskan John G. Brady*, 175–76.

3. A Con Gone Wrong

1. Atwood and Williams, *Bent Pins*, 83–85; *SN*, July 8, 1898; Suydam, "Reign."

2. *TDN*, December 27, 1898; Clark, "Man of Honor," 41; Barkdull, "Soapy Killed," 8, 9, 11.

3. Ibid.

4. Ibid. There was also an entrance to the Burkhard Hotel on Fifth Avenue.

5. *TDN*, 27 December 1898.

6. Ibid.

7. Ibid. Some punctuation and paragraph styling was changed from the original to make the text more readable.

8. *SN*, July 8, 1898.

9. Bearss, *Historic Resource Study*, 181, 182, 188; Hunt, *Distant Justice*, 57–58.

10. *DA*, July 11, 1898; *SN*, July 8, 15, and December 9, 1898; *TDN*, December 27, 1898; Clark, "Man of Honor," 41; Bardull, "Soapy Killed," 45.

11. Ibid., 11.

12. Barkdull, "Soapy Killed," 46.

13. S. [Samuel] H. Graves, *White Pass Payroll*, 19–20; Roy Minter, *Gateway*, 211.

14. Ibid.

15. Ibid.

16. Ibid.

17. Ibid.

18. *DA*, July 11, 1898.

19. *DT*, 20 July 20, 1898.

20. *GT*, December 9, 10, 11, 1908.

21. *SN*, July 8, 1898, 1; *DA*, July 11, 1898, 1; Graves, *Payroll*, 21–22.

22. Clinton, *1899 Directory*, 136; *SN*, July 8, 15, 1898.

23. *TG*, July 22, 1898.

24. *SN*, July 8, 1898; July 15, 1898; *DA*, July 11, 1898; Graves, *Payroll*, 19–21; Suydam, "Reign," 220–221; U.S. Department of Justice, *Jackson v. United States*.

25. *Jackson v. United States*, 475–76.

26. *SN*, July 8, 1898; *DA*, July 11, 1898, 1; Testimony by Frank H. Reid, April 1–4, 6, 1898.

27. *SN*, July 8, 1898; *DA*, July 11, 1898, 1; Suydam, "Reign," 220–21; *Jackson v. United States*.

28. *Jackson v. United States*.

29. Graves, *Payroll*, 23–24.

30. Ibid., 24.

31. Sinclair, *Diary*, July 8, 1898.

32. Smith, *Alias Soapy*, 534–42.

33. Library and Archives of Canada, Ottawa, Ontario, RG 18-A, Samuel B. Steele, Collection, Letter dated July 11, 1898, Vol. 154, File 447–98.

34. *MO*, July 17, 1898; Graves, *Payroll*, 24.

35. Itjen, *Alaska Street Car*, 41; *FDNM*, June 23, 1941.

36. Robertson and Harris, *King of the Frontier*, 210; Clifford, *Uncrowned King*, 113.

37. *MO,* July 19, 1898. There are two articles on page 8 of this edition, one detailing a letter sent by Dr. Cornelius to his partner, Dr. Littlefield, and another quoting a Dawson merchant who had been in Skagway during the shooting. Both stories state that Murphy was involved in the shooting, but refuse to label him as the killer.

38. Tanner, "First Marshal"; Barkdull, "Soapy Killed," 47.

39. Tanner, ibid.

40. NARA-RG49, Brief for Moore, April 17, 1899, 11; Testimony by Frank H. Reid, April 1–4, 6, 1898; *FDNM,* June 23, 1941, 5.

41. Tanner, "First Marshal."

42. Ibid.; *FDNM,* June 23, 1941, 5.

43. Barkdull, "Soapy Killed," 47; Andrews, "Real Soapy," 40; *SN* Nov 5, 1897, 5; July 8, 1898, 1; July 15, 1898; *DA,* July 11, 1898, 1; *TG,* July 22, 1898, 1. Note: Clayson's Hardware Store was probably the building that became the Pantheon Saloon, now owned by the National Park Service. Clayson was a clothier and a hardware store owner. By July 1898, he had moved his building from the northwest corner of Fourth and State to the southwest corner of the same intersection and rented it to D. C. Brownwell as a hardware store (Karl Gurcke, personal communication, July 2009).

4. A Lie Agreed Upon

Epigraph. Alaska State Archives, RG 202, Skagway Historical Records, Office of the Magistrate, Inquests, 1897–1916.

1. Slotkin, *Gunfighter Nation,* 23, 157, 160–61.

2. Ibid., 161.

3. Sinclair, *Mission: Klondike,* 70–71; John Sinclair Papers, *Diary,* July 11, 1898; June 16–July 28, 1898; Letters, July 11–August 22, 1898; Ms. "Tragic End"; Smith Funeral Sermon.

4. John A. Sinclair Papers, in entirety.

5. Sinclair, *Mission: Klondike,* 131–35.

6. The editor of the *Toronto Globe* removed the quotation marks and substituted the word *curs.* Sinclair, Papers, "Tragic End"; TG, July 22, 1898, 1.

7. *SN,* July 15, 1898; John A. Sinclair Papers, *Diary,* July 9; Skagway Historical Records, Inquests, July 9, 1897; Letter to Laura Sinclair, July 11, 1898.

8. Ibid.; *SN*, November 5, 1897; *1901 Business Directory*, 848.

9. John A. Sinclair Papers, *Diary*, July 8, 1898; *MO*, July 19, 1898; Steele Collection, Letter dated July 11, 1898; Steele, *Forty Years*, 336.

10. Tanner, "First Marshal."

11. J. A. Sinclair Papers, "Tragic End," 23.

12. *SN*, July 15, 1898.

13. *DA*, July 11, 1898.

14. *SN*, July 15, 1898.

15. Ibid.

16. Barkdull, "Soapy Killed," 48.

17. Ibid., 47–48; *SN*, July 15, 1898.

18. Barkdull, "Soapy Killed," 49.

19. Ibid.

20. Ibid.

21. Fenton B. Whiting, letter dated July 27, 1929, Alaska State Library, Alaska Historical Collections, ms. 4, Box 13, #3.

22. Ibid.

23. Quotation in *SN*, July 15, 1898; Whiting, Letter to Georgia; F. B. Whiting, "Rounding up the 'Soapy' Smith Gang" in *Grit, Grief and Gold*, 45–54.

24. *DA*, July 11, 1898; *SN*, July 15, 1898; National Archives, Record Group 48, Letter from Captain R. T. Yeatman, Fourteenth Infantry to Adjutant General, Department of the Columbia, July 9, 1898.

25. Ibid., Letter from Captain Yeatman to Adjutant General, Department of the Columbia, dated July 11, 1898.

26. *DA*, July 11, 1898.

27. Ibid.

28. Barkdull, "Soapy Killed," 51; *DA*, July 11, 1898.

29. Ball, *United States Marshals*, 6, 10.

30. *DA*, July 11, 1898.

31. Ibid.

32. Ibid.

33. *SN*, July 15, 1898.

34. *DA*, July 12, 1898; *SN*, July 15, 1898; Because there could only be one U.S. deputy marshal in the Skagway District, Tanner was made Deputy of the Alaska Peninsula, and served as such until 1900. See *DA*, January 1, 1899–December 31, 1899.

35. *DA*, July 11, 1898; *SN*, June 17, 1898; and Sept. 16, 1898; 1899 Business Directory, 136.

36. *DA*, July 15, 1898; *SN*, July 15, 1898; 1899 Business Directory, 135,

37. *DA*, July 15, 1898.

38. *DA*, July 15, 1898, 2; NARA-RG 21, U.S. District Court, Box No. 16, District of Alaska, Sitka, Criminal Cases, File 1022, *U.S. v. Mrs. M. J. Torpey*.

39. *DA*, July 12, 1898.

40. Ibid.

41. Steele, *Forty Years*, 295–296; Berton, *Klondike Fever*, 149.

42. *DyT*, June 25, 1898, 1; Spude, "Chris Shea," 17.

43. *SPI*, July 16 and July 17, 1898; *DA*, July 25, 1898; *DyT*, July 30, 1898; *DT*, July 16, 1898; July 20, 1898; August 1, 1898.

44. *SPI*, July 19, 1898.

45. *RMN*, August 28, 1927; *DT*, August 20, 1898.

46. *DT*, August 20, 1898.

47. Ibid.

48. *DA*, July 11, 1898; August 3, 1898; *SN*, July 15, 1898, December 9, 1898; *TDN*, September 16, 1898.

49. NARA-PAR, RG-21, *U.S. v. Mrs. M. J. Torpey*; U.S. District Courts, Box No. 16, District of Alaska, Sitka, Criminal Cases, 1884–1900, *U.S. v Harry Bronson, Al White and Charles Butler*.

50. NARA-PAR, RG-21, U. S. District Courts, Box No. 16, District of Alaska, Sitka, Criminal Cases, 1884–1900, case no. 1014, *U.S. v. Turner Jackson and George Wilder*. Indictment for murder of Frank Reid; Indictment for assault on J. M. Tanner.

51. *U.S. v. W. E Foster, John Bowers, and Van Triplett*, indictment.

52. *U.S. v. W. E Foster and John Bowers*, Instructions to jury; *U.S. vs. Turner Jackson*, June 9, 1899, Amendments to Assignment of Errors.

53. *U.S. v. Foster, Bowers and Van Triplett*, Instructions to jury; verdicts.

54. *U.S. v. George Wilder and Turner Jackson*, sentence and release from prison; Letter from Warden, United States Penitentiary, McNeil Island, Washington, Dated November 16, 1911, to Clerk U.S. District Court, Juneau, Alaska in NARA, RG-21, *U.S. v. Turner Jackson*; *SN*, December 23, 1898; *DA*, September 14, 1905.

55. *Jackson v. United States*, 473–75; *U.S. v. Turner Jackson*; *DA*, September 14, 1905.

56. Alaska State Archives, Record Group 202, Skagway Historical Records, Skagway Coroner's inquests, 3, 4, 8–10. Hunt, *Distant Justice*, 65–66; *Tacoma Daily News*, March 21, 1898. One other murder was reported, that of "Noscitur" (unknown), a man shot in the back of the head near Dyea; the story was detailed in the *Dyea Trail*, May 7, 1898. Due to the fact that the Gregg murder happened at the same time and that the "unknown" murder was reported in a Tacoma newspaper, it cannot be credited as a separate homicide.

57. Steele, *Forty Years*, 309, 312, 327; Canadian Archives, Ottawa, Ontario, RG-18, Series A-1, Volume 165–99, George Bowman; Series 155, File: 501–98, Jacques Voler and Eugene Vogler; Volume 149, File: 167–98, C. W. Thompson; RG-10, Volume 3990, Reel C-1020, File:177044, Correspondence regarding the payment of fees to H. C. Lisle for defending Jim and Joe Dawson and Frank Mantusk for murder in the Yukon Territory.

58. McKanna, *Homicide*, 40–44.

59. McGrath, *Gunfighters*, 254.

60. McKanna, *Homicide*. See pp. 7–8 for a discussion of why Robert Dykstra's statistics on homicides in the Kansas cow towns are not useful for comparison to McKanna's studies (and the discussion here). Cf. Dykstra, *Cattle Towns*, 146.

5. The Local Legend-Makers

1. Athearn, *Mythic West*, 11–12; Johnson, *Hunger for the Wild*, 286.

2. Johnson, *Hunger*, 166–67; White, *'Its Your Misfortune.'*

3. Johnson, *Hunger for the Wild*, 168; Steckmesser, "Lawmen and Outlaws," 119, 130.

4. Sinclair, "Tragic End;" *Diary*, July 8, 1898.

5. J. A. Sinclair Papers. Microfilm Roll #544 in its entirety documents the efforts Sinclair went to in order to research and write a manuscript entitled "'Soapy' Smith, his Methods and Career in Skaguay, Alaska" for London's *Strand Magazine*.

6. Sinclair, "Jeff Smith's Funeral Sermon," manuscript notes; *SN*, July 15, 1898.

7. *SN*, July 15, 1898.

8. *The Globe*, apparently, did not feel as strongly as Rev. Sinclair that Skagway was now perfectly safe. It added "and might, almost," words not

in the original manuscript. *TG*, July 22, 1898.

9. Sinclair Papers, "Soapy's Tragic End."

10. *TG*, July 22, 1898.

11. Sinclair Papers, "Soapy's Tragic End"; *TG*, July 22, 1898.

12. Sinclair Papers, Diary, June 17–July 3, 1898; Letter from Rev. R. M. Dickey to Mrs. J. A. Sinclair, dated June 20, 1944.

13. *The Globe* omitted Rev. Sinclair's phrase "or it's Gettysburg" after "Waterloo." *TG*, July 22, 1898.

14. Willoughby, *Alaskans All*, 221.

15. *SN*, July 8, 1898.

16. Willoughby, *Alaskans All*, 201–34; Atwood and Williams, *Bent Pins*, 82–83; Atwood and DeArmand, *Who's Who*, 104.

17. *AMR*, April 5, 1899.

18. Ibid., May 10, 1899.

19. Ibid., October 10, 1901.

20. Ibid., December 6, 1899; May 22, 1901.

21. One woman was also killed in May, allegedly by members of the Smith gang. They were never charged with the crime. Ella D. Wilson was found bound and gagged, her throat slit, her body stuffed into a clothing chest and her money and jewelry stolen. Mattie Silks, a prominent Denver madam, accused the Smith gang members of the murder. Allan Hornsby and Billie Saportas were on the coroner's jury (Skagway City Historical Records, Inquest of Ella D. Wilson, dated May 28, 1898, 10; *SN*, June 3, 1898.

22. *DA*, Special Edition, January 1, 1900.

23. Atwood and Williams, *Bent Pins*, 71; Guide to Alaska Newspapers on Microfilm, http://www.library.state.ak.us/hist/hist_docs/newspapers/by_place.pdf, 337.

24. *DAD*, April 10, July 24, 1902; September 28, October 4, 1903; May 10, November 7, November 11, December 9, 1904.

25. *DAD*, July 10, 1902; May 4, 1906; J. M. Tanner's name was mentioned sixteen times by this same newspaper during this time, never once in connection with Soapy Smith. His role in the gang's round-up was so well known that it did not have to be mentioned.

26. *DAD*, April 29, 1902; September 29, 1904.

27. *DAD*, October 29, 1906.

28. *DA*, March 31, 1906, 5–6; April 4, 1906. The labor party candi-

dates that won in 1906 were also endorsed by the Citizens Party.

29. *DA*, April 3, 1907.

30. Catherine Spude, "Chris Shea," 20–21.

31. Ibid.

32. *DA*, February 6, 1902.

33. Shea and Patten, *Tragedy*, 23.

34. Ibid., 9.

35. *DA*, April 3, 1909.

36. Shea and Patton, *Tragedy*, 5.

37. *DA*, August 6, November 2, November 4, 1907. Note: Fred Patten is listed as co-author, but probably had little input. A note by Ramon F. Adams in *Six-Guns and Saddle Leather* claims that H. B. LeFevre wrote the Shea and Patton booklet, but this supposition cannot be confirmed. LeFevre served as a part-time editor of the *Daily Alaskan* in 1898 and 1899, but by 1907 he was the U.S. Commissioner in Skagway. It is unlikely he had time to be a guest editor for the newspaper, as is implied by Adams. Comparisons of LeFevre's writing style from the 1898–99 period with the *Tragedy* booklet and other items penned by Shea make it clear that Shea, and Shea alone, authored the booklet about Smith; so does the evidence in the *Daily Alaskan*. (Adams, *Six-Guns and Saddle Leather*, 575).

38. Shea and Patten, *Tragedy*, 21.

39. Ibid., 3.

40. Ibid., 5; *DT*, August 20, 1898; *SPI*, July 19, 1898.

41. Shea and Patton, *Tragedy*, 7.

42. Ibid., 13.

43. John Sinclair Papers, "Tragic End" ms.

44. Berton, *Klondike Fever*, 364.

45. Shea and Patten, *Tragedy*, 21.

46. *DAD*, August 11, 1907; *SI*, May 12, 1908.

47. *DA*, April 6–8, 1908.

48. *DA*, August 6, 1907, 1.

6. The Journalists and the Memoirs

1. Warman, *Frontier Stories*, 95.

2. Buffum, "Soapy Smith," 25–45.

3. Steffa, "Bad Man and Bluffer," 347.

4. Ibid., 355–58.

5. Ibid., 359.

6. Ibid., 360.

7. The *Oregonian* was founded in 1850 and continues to this day, being the longest-running newspaper on the Pacific Northwest Coast (Heinzkill, "Brief History," http://libweb.uoregon.edu/govdocs/indexing/newspaperhistory.html).

8. *MO*, October 4, 1908; January 10, 1909; August 7, 1910; January 17, November 7, 1911; July 13, September 28, 1913; February 12, 1914; 1910 United States Federal Census, Bend, Crook County, Oregon, Enumeration District 49, Roll T624_1279, Image 961, p. 3A; 1920 United States Federal Census, Fresno, Fresno County, California, Enumeration District 43, p. 9A, Roll 625_97, Image 405; Ancestry.com, California Voter Registrations, 1900–1968 [database on line], Provo, Utah, USA: The Generations Network, Inc., 2008; World War I Draft Registration Cards, 1917–1918, Don Steffa, Registration Location: Multnomah County, Oregon: Roll 1852143: Draft Board 5; California Death Index, 1940–1997, State of California Department of Health Services, Center of Health Statistics, Sacramento, 2000.

9. Mighetto and Montgomery, *Hard Drive,* see especially pp. 21–39 in their discussion of the competition between cities.

10. Examples include *TDN*, January 1 and 7, February 5 and 24, March 15, 1898; *MO*, January 13, 26, and March 13, 1898.

11. Irwin, *Confessions*, 166–72; Edward H. Smith, *Confessions*, 166–172; Hudson, *Writing Game*, 66.

12. Irwin, *Confessions*, 171.

13. Hynes, "Old-Time Rule," 2. Actually, Smith worked for the *Washington Evening Star.*

14. 1900 United States Census, Washington, District of Columbia, Enumeration District 118, Page 16A, Roll T623_163; 1910 U.S. Federal Census, Precinct 10, Washington, District of Columbia, Enumeration District 229, Image 962, Page IA, Roll T621_155; 1920 U.S. Federal Census, Washington, District of Columbia, Enumeration District 318, p. 2B, Image 270, Roll T625_213.

15. Hudson, *Writing Game;* World War I Draft Registration Card, 1917–18, New York County, Roll 1766251, Draft Board 128; 1880 U.S. Federal Census, Leadville, Lake County, Colorado, Roll T9_91, p. 415,

Enumeration District 80, Image O431; 1910 U.S. Federal Census, Manhattan Ward 15, New York County, New York, Roll T624_1030, p. 11B, Enumeration District 80S, Image 636; 1930 U.S. Federal Census, Manhattan, New York, New York, Roll 1558, p. 8A, Enumeration District 249, Image 364–0; http://sdrc.lib.uiowa.edu/traveling-culture/chau1/pdf/irwinw/2/brochure.pdf (last accessed May 15, 2009); *New York Times*, February 25, 26, 1948; Library of Congress list of forty-four books by Will Irwin.

16. Hudson, *Writing Game*, 66; Irwin, *Making of a Reporter*; Smith, *Confessions*.

17. Smith, *Alias*, 22–23.

18. Barnacle, "Characters," 10.

19. Smith, *Alias*, 22–23, 448–49.

20. Barnacle, "Characters," 6–9.

21. Ibid., 10–11.

22. Robertson and Harris, *Soapy Smith*, 237; Clifford, *Uncrowned King*, 136; Haigh, *King Con*, 113.

23. Forsney, "Soapy Smith's Death," 9.

24. Slotkin, *Gunfighter Nation*.

25. Graves, *Payroll*, 15–31.

26. *CDT*, November 14, 1911; *DAD*, November 13, 1911; BJ, November 14, 1911; 1910 U.S. Federal Census, Wheaton City, Milton Township, DuPage County, Illinois, Enumeration District 9, Page 2A.

27. Graves, *Payroll*, 15, 22, 24, 31.

28. Ibid., 25–26.

29. Slotkin, *Gunfighter Nation*, 157–60.

30. Steele, *Forty Years*, 296–97.

31. Hunt, *Distant Justice*, 337–41.

32. Walden, *Dog Puncher*, 132.

33. Ibid., 129.

34. Ibid.

35. Ibid., 130–31.

36. Whiting, *Grit, Grief and Gold*, 45–54.

37. Ibid., 46.

38. Ibid., 46–47.

39. Ibid., 48–49.

40. Ibid., dedication, frontispiece.

41. Ibid., 52; *SN,* July 15, 1898.

42. Fenton B. Whiting, letter dated July 27, 1929, Alaska State Library, Alaska Historical Collections, ms. 4, Box 13, #3.

7. Skagway Tourism

1. 1910 Federal Census, Skagway Town, First Judicial District, Alaska, 21st enumeration district, p. 22; 1920 Federal Census, Skagway Town, First Judicial District, Alaska, 7th enumeration district, p. 188; 1930 Federal Census, Skagway Town, First Judicial District, Alaska, 21st enumeration district, p. 163; Polk Directories, 1903, 238; 1905, 363; 1909, 449; 1923, 415; Skagway Election Registers, 1909–14.

2. Itjen, *Street Car,* 91; George Rapuzzi to Robert Spude, 1977–79.

3. *DA,* January 12, April 4, May 12, June 14, July 13, 1900, April 1, 1901, April 18, 1903, June 11, 1908. All were front-page stories, except for a second-page one on May 12, 1900.

4. U.S. Census, Skagway, 1900, 79; Willoughby, *Alaskans All,* 166; NARA RG-49, Brief for Moore, 4.

5. Willoughby, *Alaskans All,* 165–75; Howard Clifford, *Skagway Story,* 60–62; personal communications from George Rapuzzi and Oscar Selmar to Robert Spude, 1977–79.

6. Willowby, *Alaskans All,* 165–75.

7. U.S. Census, Skagway, 1900, 79.

8. Norris, "Showing Off Alaska, 1–2, 7. Contrast this to the 810,000 visitors to Skagway during the summer 2010 season (Jeff Brady, editor of the *Skagway News*).

9. Interviews with George Rapuzzi by Robert L. Spude, 1977–79; Norris, "Martin Itjen," 135; NARA RG-49, Annie Leonard testimony, April 4,1898.

10. *SN,* July 8, 1898; *DA,* July 11, 1898; *TG,* July 22, 1898; Suydam, "Reign of Soapy"; Shea and Patten, *Tragedy;* Graves, *Payroll.*

11. Pullen, *Bandit,* 2.

12. Ibid., 6.

13. Ibid., 7–8.

14. Ibid., 9–10.

15. Ibid., 10.

16. Ibid., 12; 1900 U.S. Federal Census, Skagway town, First Judicial District, Alaska, enumeration district no. 7, 128.

17. Pullen, *Bandit,* 17–18.

18. Kittredge, *Owning it All*, 62.

19. Norris, "Itjen," 133, 135.

20. Itjen, "Street Car," 1935 ed., 8, 24, 25, 27, 40; John A. Sinclair papers, letter from Robert Dickey dated June 20, 1944.

21. Ibid., 41.

22. Ibid., 70.

23. Itjen, "Street Car," 1938 ed., 95.

24. Itjen, "Street Car," 1935 ed., 40.

25. Ibid., 68.

26. National Park Service, Klondike Gold Rush National Historical Park, "Jeff Smith's Parlor Building, Determination of Eligibility to the National Register," Draft manuscript on file, 2009, 5–6; personal communication from George Rapuzzi to Robert L. Spude, 1978–79.

27. National Park Service, *Jeff. Smiths Parlor Museum.*

28. Norris, "Showing Off Alaska," 10.

29. Ibid.; e-mail from Steve Hites to Catherine Holder Spude on April 24, 2009.

30. Roy Minter went on to write a very well-researched history of the White Pass and Yukon Route, and his version of the Smith story is well told: Minter, *White Pass*, 200–17.

31. E-mail from Steve Hites to Catherine Holder Spude on April 24, 2009.

32. Ibid.; Mike Miller, *Soapy, the Saga.*

33. E-mail from Steve Hites to Catherine Holder Spude on April 24, 2009.

34. Ibid.

35. Ibid. Letter from Steve Hites to Catherine Holder Spude, dated June 23, 2009.

8. A Literary Legacy

1. Letter from Cy Warman to Soapy Smith, dated February 16, 1897, in Jones, *Correspondence*, 15.

2. Warmouth, *Notable Americans*; *DMN*, December 24, 1890.

3. Warmouth, *Notable Americans*; *NM*, March 28, 1892; *AMD*, April 16, 1892.

4. Warmouth, *Notable Americans*; *AS*, April 8, 1914; *AJ*, June 2, 1914; *SJMN*, April 7, 1914; *LAT*, April 8, 1914.

5. Jackson, *Bad Company*, 119–214.

6. Ibid.

7. Jones, "Correspondence," 16.

8. Ibid.

9. Warman, *Frontier Stories*, 95; "Rise and Fall of Creede," in *Songs*, 76.

10. Hynes, "Soapy Smith," 2

11. Ibid., 2, 10, 11.

12. Denver, Colorado City Directory, 1890 [Database on line] Provo, Utah, USA, The Generations Network, Inc., 2000; 1900 Federal Census, Denver, Arapahoe County, Colorado, Microfilm Roll T623_119, p. 4B; 1910 Federal Census, Denver Ward 10, Denver, Colorado, Microfilm Roll T624 116, p. 4B, Enumeration District 135; 1920 Federal Census, Denver, Denver County, Colorado, Microfilm Roll T625 162, p. 1A, Enumeration District 162; *CSGT*, April 17, 1904; *SLT*, May 12, 1904.

13. Goldstein, *Seamy Side*.

14. *DA*, July 25, 1898; Davis, *West from a Car Window*.

15. *SN*, January 21, 1898, according to J. A. Sinclair papers, notepad of transcriptions.

16. *NYW*, January 19, 1896; January 26, 1896; March 22, 1896; June 14, 1896; September 5, 1897; October 3, 1897; December 5, 1897.

17. Hynes, "Soapy Smith," 2.

18. Forsney, "Soapy Smith's Death," 9.

19. Collier and Westrate, *Reign of Soapy*; Denver Public Library, Western History Collection, Subject File Card Index for Jefferson Randolph Smith.

20. Berton, *Klondike Fever*, 1972 ed., 431, 437, 439.

21. Berton, *Klondike Fever*, 1958 ed., 333–65.

22. Winslow, *Big Pan-Out*, 110–11.

23. Robertson and Harris, *King*, 183–85, 200, 204.

24. Ibid., 210–11.

25. Ellis, *Pioneers*, 38, 47, 51.

26. Parkhill, *Wildest*, promotion in endplate.

27. Ibid., 94–95.

28. Although I would like to think the bibliography included with this book is complete, I know that it is not. For instance, it covers only the months Smith was in Alaska. Even then, almost monthly until May 2009, I came upon a new source; I know some have been missed. And I know somewhere out there, someone has a complete run of the *Skaguay News* and/or the *Daily Alaskan* from their starts in 1897 until the trials were

complete in January 1899, but to date they have not been found. The story and my interpretation may change dramatically the day those newspapers are discovered and published for all to read—unless, indeed, Alan Hornsby and William Saportas truly had nothing to say about an ordinary con man.

29. Barkdull, "Killed"; Andrews, "Real Soapy," 6–7, 36–40.

30. Clancy, "Just a Kid," 16–18, 25; Clark, "Man of Honor," 40–41.

31. Clifford, *Uncrowned King*.

32. Ibid., vii.

33. Murphy and Haigh, *Children of the Gold Rush, Gold Rush Dogs,* and *Gold Rush Women.*

34. Haigh, *King Con.*

35. Smith, *Alias Soapy Smith.*

36. Dickey, *Gold Fever.*

37. Smith, *Alias Soapy,* 7–8.

38. Ibid., 6.

39. Ibid., 10, 498–603.

40. *MO,* July 19, 1898.

41. Smith, *Alias Soapy,* 542, 546, 550.

42. Ibid., 550.

43. Ibid., 553.

44. Ibid., 436, 450.

45. *SN,* May 13, 1898.

46. Smith, *Alias Soapy,* 470.

47. Blum, *Heaven.*

48. Ibid., *Heaven,* 414.

49. Ibid., 418.

50. Ibid., 333–98.

9. Legend, Heroes, and Myth

1. Wector, *Hero in America,* 11–15.

2. Lash, *The Hero,* 5.

3. Steckmesser, *Western Hero,* 241–44.

4. Ibid., 244–45; Lake, *Wyatt Earp,* 375; Settle, *Jesse James,* 200.

5. Slatta, "Making and Unmaking Myths," 84–85.

6. Klapp, "Folk Hero," 17–25.

7. Steckmesser, *Western Hero,* 138.

8. Quoted in Steckmesser, *Western Hero,* 142.

9. Connelly quoted in Steckmesser, *Western Hero*, 145. See Connelly, *Wild Bill.*

10. Klapp, "Folk Hero," 18–19.

11. Barra, *Inventing Wyatt Earp*, 5–7.

12. Masterson quoted in Tefertiller, *Wyatt Earp*, 1–2. See Masterson, "Wyatt Earp," 9.

13. Lake, *Frontier Marshal;* Tefertiller, *Wyatt Earp*, 333.

14. Tefertiller, *Wyatt Earp*, 339.

15. Ibid., 340.

16. Barra, *Inventing Wyatt Earp*, 402–403; Adams, *Log of a Cowboy;* Bartholomew, *Wyatt Earp;* Breckenridge, *Helldorado;* Burns, *Tombstone;* Waters, *Earp Brothers of Tombstone.*

17. Barra, *Inventing Wyatt Earp*, 399, 404–405.

18. Tefertiller, *Wyatt Earp*, 1.

19. Klapp, "Folk Hero," 18.

20. Utley, *Billy the Kid*, 199.

21. Hutton, "Dreamscape Desperado," 360.

22. Steckmesser, *Western Hero*, 85.

23. Ibid., 85–89, 100–101.

24. Utley, *Short and Violent*, 200.

25. Steckmesser, *Western Hero*, 100–101.

26. Utley, *Billy the Kid*, 202–205. Quote on 205.

27. Klapp, "Folk Hero," 18.

28. Slotkin, *Gunfighter Nation*, 133–34.

29. Ibid., 135, after Edwards, *Noted Guerillas*, 17.

30. Slotkin, *Gunfighter Nation*, 135.

31. Ibid., 186.

32. Slotkin, *Gunfighter Nation*, 136.

33. Settle, *Jesse James*, 190.

34. Slotkin, *Gunfighter Nation*, 138.

35. Quoted in Settle, *Jesse James*, 1.

36. Quoted in Settle, *Jesse James*, 1 from Sandburg, *American Songbag*, 420.

37. Settle, *Jesse James*, 3.

38. Ibid.

39. Interestingly, two of the villains in the English-speaking version of a popular Japanese children's television animation, Pokémon, are named Jessie and James.

40. Sinclair Papers, Diary, June 17–July 3, 1898; newspaper notes, Vol. 2, F. 62, pp. C and D. Letter from Rev. R. M. Dickey to Mrs. J. A. Sinclair, dated June 20, 1944.

41. *DT*, September 5, 1901.

42. *SPI*, July 19, 1898.

43. Smith, *Alias Soapy*, 352–60.

44. Hermann, *Hell on the Range*, xiv; Wyatt-Brown, "Southern Violence," 906–25.

45. Hermann, *Hell on the Range*, xv.

46. Tatum, *Inventing Billy the Kid*, 186–87.

47. Slotkin, *Gunfighter Nation*, 128, 133–34.

48. Hermann, *Hell on the Range*, 285.

49. Mitchell, *Westerns*.

50. *MO*, July 18, 1898.

51. Wright, *Six Guns*, 9.

52. Ibid., 10.

53. *Liberty Valance*, Paramount Pictures, 1962. http://www.umt.edu/journalism/special_projects/hall_of_fame/johnson.html; http://www.lib.uiowa.edu/spec-coll/MSC/ToMsC650/MsC632/johnsond.html.

54. Lusted, *The Western*, 23–24, 182, 241.

55. *DIN*, October 13, 1916.

56. *SPI*, March 5, 1898.

57. *DA*, April 6, 1914.

Bibliography

Archival Collections

Alaska State Archives, Record Group 21, Criminal Records.

Alaska State Archives, Record Group 202, Skagway Historical Records.

Alaska State Library, Alaska Historical Collections: Fenton B. Whiting letter.

British Columbia Archives, John Sinclair Papers, MS-1061.

Canadian Archives, Toronto, Ontario: Record Group 18-A, Samuel B. Steele Collection.

Canadian Archives, Ottawa, Ontario: Record Group 10, Indian Affairs; Record Group 18, Royal Canadian Mounted Police.

Denver Public Library, Western History Collection, Subject File Card Index, Jefferson Randolph Smith.

Guide to Alaska Newspapers on Microfilm. http://www.library.state.ak.us./hist/hist_docs/nrespapers/by-place.pdf

National Archives, Pacific Northwest, Anchorage, Record Group 21, Sitka and Juneau Criminal Files.

National Archives, Pacific Northwest, Anchorage, Record Group 48, Patents and Miscellaneous Records of the Secretary of Interior, District of Alaska.

National Archives, Pacific Northwest, Anchorage, U.S. Marshal's Office, Register of Marshals and Deputy Marshals in Alaska.

National Archives, Washington, D.C., Record Group 49, Records of the General Land Office, Division K, Townsite Files, Moore Townsite Records,

Special Collections, University of Iowa Libraries, Iowa City, Iowa. Papers of Dorothy M. Johnson. Two boxes. http://www.lib.uiowa.edu/spec-coll/MSC/ToMsC650/MsC632/johnsond.html

U.S. Federal Censuses (accessed through Ancestry.com)

1880 U.S. Federal Census, New Madrid, Missouri.

1880 U.S. Federal Census, Leadville, Lake County, Colorado.

1900 U.S. Federal Census, Denver, Arapahoe County, Colorado.

1900 U.S. Federal Census, Washington, District of Columbia,

1900 U.S. Federal Census, Nome, Alaska.

1900 U. S. Federal Census, Skagway town, Alaska.

1910 U.S. Federal Census, Bend, Crook County, Oregon.
1910 U.S. Federal Census, Denver Ward 10, Denver, Colorado.
1910 U.S. Federal Census, Manhattan Ward 15, New York County, New York.
1910 U.S. Federal Census, Skagway Town, First Judicial District, Alaska.
1910 U.S. Federal Census, Precinct 10, Washington, District of Columbia.
1910 U.S. Federal Census, Wheaton City, Milton Township, DuPage County,
    Illinois.
1920 U.S. Federal Census, Denver, Denver County, Colorado.
1920 U.S. Federal Census, Fresno, Fresno County, California.
1920 U.S. Federal Census, Skagway Town, First Judicial District, Alaska.
1920 U.S. Federal Census, Washington, District of Columbia.
1930 U.S. Federal Census, Manhattan, New York, New York.
1930 U.S. Federal Census, Skagway Town, First Judicial District, Alaska.

Directories

The Alaska Club's 1905 Almanac (Seattle: The Alaska Club, 1905).
California Death Index, 1940-1997, State of California Department of
    Health Services, Center of Health Statistics, Sacramento, 2000. http://
    www.Ancestry.com
California Voter Registrations, 1900–68 [database on line], Provo, Utah,
    USA: The Generations Network, Inc., 2008. http://www.Ancestry.com
Directory and Guide, Skagway (Skagway, Alaska: C. Clinton, 1899).
Denver, Colorado City Directory, 1890 [Database on line] Provo, Utah,
    USA, The Generations Network, Inc., 2000. http://www.Ancestry.com
Ferguson, M. L., *The Only Yukon-Alaska Directory and Gazetteer for 1901*
    (Barnes and Barber: 1901).
*Polk's Alaska-Yukon Gazetteer and Business Directory, 1903, 1905–6, 1907–8,
    1909–10, 1915–16, 1917–18* and 1923 (Seattle: R. L. Polk, for years
    listed in title).
World War I Draft Registration Cards, 1917–18, Don Steffa, Registration
    Location: Multnomah County, Oregon: Roll 1852143: Draft Board 5.
    http://www.Ancestry.com
World War I Draft Registration Cards, 1917–18, New York County, Roll
    1766251, Draft Board 128. http://www.Ancestry.com

Books, Articles, Manuscripts, and Pamphlets

Adams, Ramon. *The Log of a Cowboy.* Boston: Houghton Mifflin, 1903.
———. *Six-Guns and Saddle Leather: A Bibliography of Books and Pamphlets on
    Western Outlaws and Gunmen.* Norman: University of Oklahoma, 1969.
Andrews, C. L. *The Story of Alaska.* Caldwell, Idaho: Caxton, 1944.
———. "The Real Soapy Smith." *Alaska Sportsman.* November 1947.
Anonymous. "Soapy Smith's Skull: An Ironic Monument to a Two-Gun
    Tyrant." *Literary Digest* (September 3, 1927).

Athearn, Robert G. *The Mythic West in Twentieth Century America.* Lawrence: University of Kansas, 1986.

Atwood, Evangeline, and Lew Williams, Jr. *Bent Pins to Chains: Alaska and Its Newspapers.* Xlibris: 2006.

Atwood, Evangeline, and Robert N. DeArmand. *Who's Who in Alaskan Politics.* Portland: Binford and Mort, 1977.

Ball, Larry D. *The United States Marshals of New Mexico and Arizona Territories, 1846–1912.* Albuquerque: University of New Mexico Press, 1978.

Bancroft, Caroline. *Denver's Lively Past: From a Wild and Woolly Camp to Queen City of the Plains.* Boulder Colo.: Johnson, 1959.

Barkdull, Calvin H. "I Saw Soapy Killed." *Alaska Sportsman* (June 1952): 8–11, 44–50.

Barnacle, Barkalow. "'Characters' of the Early Day: 'Soapy' Smith, The Gambler." *The Trail* 12, no.8 (January, 1920).

Barra, Allen. *Inventing Wyatt Earp: His Life and Many Legends.* New York: Carroll and Graf, 1998.

Bartholomew, Ed. *Wyatt Earp, 1848 to 1880, The Untold Story.* Toyahville, Texas: Frontier Book Co., 1963.

Bellesiles, Michael. *Arming America: The Origins of a National Gun Culture.* Brooklyn, New York: Soft Skull, 2003.

Bearss, Edwin C. *Proposed Klondike Gold Rush National Historical Park Historic Resource Study.* Washington, D.C: U. S. Department of the Interior, 1970.

Berton, Pierre. *Klondike Fever: The Life and Death of the Last Great Gold Rush.* New York: Alfred A. Knopf, 1958. Reprinted as *Klondike: The Last Great Gold Rush.* Toronto: McClelland and Stewart, 1972.

Blair, Edward. *Leadville: Colorado's Magic City.* Boulder, Colo.: Pruett, 1980.

Blum, Howard. *The Floor of Heaven: A True Tale of the Last Frontier and the Yukon Gold Rush.* New York: Crown, 2011.

Breckenridge, William M. *Helldorado: Bringing the Law to the Mesquite.* Boston: Houghton Mifflin, 1928.

Breen, T. H. *American Insurgents, American Patriots: The Revolution of the People.* New York: Hill and Wang, 2010.

Buffum, George T. "Soapy Smith," in *Smith of Bear City and Other Frontier Stories.* New York: Grafton, 1906.

Burns, Walter Noble. *Tombstone: An Iliad of the Southwest.* Albuquerque: University of New Mexico, 1999 reprint of 1927 edition by Doubleday.

Campbell, Joseph, with Bill Moyers. Betty Sue Flowers, editor. *The Power of Myth.* New York: Anchor Books, 1991.

Cawelti, John G. *The Six-Gun Mystique.* Bowling Green Ohio: Bowling Green State University, 1984.

Clancy, Frank J. "I Was Just a Kid." *Alaska Sportsman* (October 1955): 16–18, 25.

Clark, Hazel Stewart. "A Man of Honor." *Alaska Sportsman* (March 1958): 40–41.

Clifford, Howard. *The Skagway Story.* Anchorage: Alaska Northwest, 1975.
———. *Rails North: The Railroads of Alaska and the Yukon.* Seattle: Superior Publishing, 1981.
———. *Soapy Smith: Uncrowned King of Skagway.* Seattle: Sourdough, 1997.
Collier, William Ross and Edwin Victor Westrate. *The Reign of Soapy Smith: Monarch of Misrule.* New York: Doubleday, 1935.
Connelly, William E. *Wild Bill and His Era: The Life and Adventures of James Butler Hickok.* New York: Press of the Pioneers, 1933.
Davis, Richard Harding. *West from a Car Window.* New York: Harper and Brothers, 1892.
DeArmond, R. N., ed. *Klondike Newsman, "Stroller White."* Skagway, Alaska: Lynn Canal Publishing, 1990.
Dickey, R. M. *Gold Fever: A Narrative of the Great Klondike Gold Rush.* Edited by Art Peterson. Auke Bay, Alaska: Klondike Research, 1997.
"Dorothy M. Johnson, 1905–1984." University of Montana School of Journalism, 2009. http://www.jour.umt.edu/links/hall_of_fame/johnson, accessed June 25, 2009.
Dykstra, Robert R. *The Cattle Towns.* New York: Alfred A. Knopf, 1968.
Edwards, John N. *Noted Guerillas, of the Warfare of the Border.* St. Louis: Bryan, Brand and Co., 1877.
Ellis, Amanda. *Pioneers, Pioneers.* Colorado Springs, Colo.: Denton, 1955.
Feitz, Leland. *Soapy Smith's Creed.* Colorado Springs, Colo.: Little London, 1973.
Ferrell, Ed. "Josias Martin Tanner," in *Biographies of Alaska-Yukon Pioneers 1850–1950, Volume 2.* Compiled and edited by Robert DeArmond. N.p.: Heritage Books, probably 1950.
Forsney, Guy. "Soapy Smith's Death." *Rocky Mountain News Sunday Magazine.* (September 4, 1927): 9.
Fowler, Gene. *Timberline: Denver—The Rip Roaring Years.* Sausalito, Calif.: Comstock, 1933, pp. 29, 34–36.
Goldbeck, Willis, and John Ford (producers). *The Man Who Shot Liberty Valance.* Paramount Pictures: 1962.
Goldstein, Phil. *The Seamy Side of Denver.* Denver: New Social, 1993.
Graves, S. [Samuel] H. *On the White Pass Payroll.* Chicago: Paladin, 1908.
Haigh, Jane G. *King Con: The Story of Soapy Smith.* Whitehorse, Yukon: Friday 501, 2006.
———. "Political Power, Patronage, and Protection Rackets: Con Men and Political Corruption in Denver, 1889–1894." PhD Diss., University of Arizona, 2009.
Heinzkill, Richard. "A Brief History of Newspaper Publishing in Oregon." University of Oregon Libraries, August 1993. http://libweb.uoregon.edu/govdocs/indexing/newspaperhistory.html
Hermann, Daniel Justin. *Hell on the Range: A Story of Honor, Conscience, and the American West.* New Haven, Conn.: Yale University, 2010.

Hinkley, Ted C. *Alaskan John G. Brady*. Columbus: Ohio State University Press, 1982.

Hudson, Robert V. *The Writing Game: A Biography of Will Irwin*. Ames: Iowa State University Press, 1982.

Hunt, William R. *Distant Justice: Policing the Alaska Frontier*. Norman: University of Oklahoma Press, 1987.

Hynes, W. F. "Soapy Smith, Old-Time Rule of Denver Underworld." *Rocky Mountain News Sunday Magazine* (August 28, 1927): 2.

Irwin, Will. *Confessions of a Confidence Man*. New York: B.W. Huebsch, 1909.

————. *The Making of a Reporter*. New York: G. P. Putnam, 1942.

Itjen, Martin. *The Story of the Tour on the Skagway, Alaska Street Car*. N.p., 1934.

Jackson, Joseph Henry. *Bad Company*. Lincoln: University of Nebraska, 1949.

Johnson, Michael L. *Hunger for the Wild: America's Obsession with the Untamed West*. Lawrence, Kansas: University of Kansas, 2007.

Jones, R. D. *Correspondence of a Crook*. *Alaska-Yukon Magazine* (January 1907 and February 1908). Reprinted by Howard Clifford, Seattle: Sourdough, 1997.

Kittredge, William. *Owning it All*. St. Paul, Minnesota: Graywood Press, 1987.

Klapp, Orrin E. "The Folk Hero." *Journal of American Folklore* 62, no. 243 (January–March 1949): 17–25.

Lake, Stuart. *Wyatt Earp, Frontier Marshal*. Boston: Houghton Mifflin, 1931.

Lash, John. *The Hero: Manhood and Power*. London: Thames and Hudson, 1995.

Lusted, David. *The Western*. Harlow, England: Pearson Education, Ltd., 2003.

Masterson, W. B. "Wyatt Earp." *Human Life* (February 1907): 9.

Mathews, Mitford M. *Dictionary of Americanisms on Historical Principles*. Chicago: University of Chicago Press, 1951.

Mayberry, Genevieve. "The Hero of Skagway." *Alaska Sportsman* (August 1941): 18–19, 41–43.

McGrath, Roger D. *Gunfighters, Highwaymen and Vigilantes: Violence on the Frontier*. Berkeley, California: University of California Press, 1984.

McKanna, Clare V., Jr. *Homicide, Race, and Justice in the American West, 1880–1920*. Tucson: University of Arizona Press, 1997.

Miller, Max, and Fred Mazzulla. *Holladay Street*. New York, NY: Ballantine Books, 1962.

Miller, Mike. *Soapy, the Saga of Jefferson R. "Soapy" Smith of Skagway—Alaska's Most Notorious Outlaw and Con-Man*. Juneau: Alaskabooks, 1970.

Mighetto, Lisa, and Marcia Montgomery. *Hard Drive to the Klondike: Promoting Seattle During the Klondike Gold Rush*. Seattle: University of Washington Press, 2002.

Minter, Roy. *The White Pass, Gateway to the Klondike*. Fairbanks: University of Alaska Press, 1987.

Mitchell, Lee Clark. *Westerns: Making the Man in Fiction and Film*. Chicago: University of Chicago Press, 1996.

Murphy, Claire Rudolf, and Jane G. Haigh. *Gold Rush Women*. Anchorage, Seattle: Alaska Northwest Books, 1997.

———. *Children of the Gold Rush*. Portland: Alaska Northwest Books, 2001.

———. *Gold Rush Dogs*. Anchorage: Alaska Northwest Books, 2001.

National Park Service. *Jeff. Smiths Parlor Museum Historic Structure Report, Skagway and White Pass District National Historic Landmark, Klondike Gold Rush National Historical Park, Skagway, Alaska*. Anchorage: United States Department of Interior, 2011.

———. Klondike Gold Rush National Historical Park, "Jeff Smith's Parlor Building, Determination of Eligibility to the National Register." Draft manuscript on file, 2009.

Nolan, Frederick, ed. *The Billy the Kid Reader*. Norman: University of Oklahoma Press, 2007.

Norris, Frank. "Martin Itjen, The Star of the Skagway Streetcar." *Alaska Journal*, 16, 1986.

———. "Showing Off Alaska: The Northern Tourist Trade, 1878–1941." *Alaska History*, 2, no. 2 (Fall 1987): 1–2, 7.

Parkhill, Forbes. *Wildest of the West*. New York: Henry Holt, 1951.

Pullen, Harriet S. *Soapy Smith, Bandit of Skagway, How He Lived; How He Died*. Reprint, Seattle: Sourdough Press, 1973. First published by Skagway Tourist Agency, ca. 1929.

Robertson, Frank G., and Beth Kay Harris. *Soapy Smith, King of the Frontier Con Men*. New York: Hastings, 1962.

Rosa, Joseph M. *The Gunfighter: Man or Myth?* Norman: University of Oklahoma Press, 1969.

Rowling, J. K. *Harry Potter and the Order of the Phoenix*. New York: Arthur Levine, 2003.

Sandburg, Carl. *The American Songbag*. New York: Harcourt, Brace, 1927.

Settle, William A. *Jesse James Was His Name*. Lincoln: University of Nebraska Press, 1966.

Shea, Chris, and Fred Patten. *The "Soapy" Smith Tragedy*. Skagway, Alaska: *Daily Alaskan*, 1907. Reprint Seattle: Clifford Publishing, 1972.

Sinclair, James. *Mission Klondike*. Vancouver: Mitchell Press, 1978.

Slatta, Richard W. "Making and Unmaking Myths of the American Frontier." In *European Journal of American Culture* 29, no. 2 (2010): 84–85.

Slotkin, Richard. *Regeneration through Violence: The Mythology of the American Frontier*. New York: Harper-Collins, 1973.

———. *The Fatal Environment: The Myth of the Frontier in the Age of Industrialization*. Middleton, Conn.: Wesleyan University, 1985.

———. *Gunfighter Nation: The Myth of the Frontier in Twentieth Century America*. New York: Harper-Collins, 1992.

Smith, Edward H. *Confessions of a Confidence Man; a Handbook for Suckers*. New York: Scientific American Publishing, 1923.

Smith, Jeff. *Alias Soapy Smith: The Life and Death of a Scoundrel. The Biography of Jefferson Randolph Smith II.* Juneau: Klondike Research, 2009.

Spude, Catherine Holder. "Josiah M. 'Si' Tanner: Southeast Alaska's Favorite Lawman." *Quarterly of the National Association for Outlaw and Lawman History, Inc.* (January–March): 29–37.

———. "Con Man's Curse." *True West* (July 2007): 50–53.

———. "Christopher C. Shea, 'King of Skagway,' Progressive Era Mayor and Game Warden in Alaska." *Pacific Northwest Quarterly* 99, no. 1 (Fall-Winter 2008): 16–29.

———. "Saint J. D. Stewart Conned and Robbed." *Skaguay Alaskan* 31, no. 1908 (Summer 2008): 8, 24–25.

Spude, Robert L. S. *Skagway, District of Alaska, 1884–1912: Building the Gateway to the Klondike.* Fairbanks: University of Alaska Press, 1983.

Steckmesser, Kent Ladd. *The Western Hero in History and Legend.* Norman: University of Oklahoma Press, 1965.

———. "Lawmen and Outlaws." In *A Literary History of the American West,* edited by J. Golden Taylor et al. Fort Worth: Texas Christian University Press, 1987; 119, 130.

Steele, Samuel Benfield. *Forty Years in Canada: Reminiscences of the Great North-West with Some Account of His Service in South Africa.* New York: Dodd, Mead & Co., 1915.

Steffa, Don. "Soapy Smith: Bad Man and Bluffer." *Pacific Monthly* 20, no. 4 (October 1908).

Suydam, Harry. "The Reign of 'Soapy' Smith." *Frank Leslie's Popular Monthly* (January 1901).

Tangherlini, Timothy R. "'It Happened Not Too Far from Here . . . ': A Survey of Legend Theory and Characterization." *Western Folklore* 49:4 (October 1990): 371–90.

Tanner, Donald M. "Josias M. Tanner: Skagway's First Marshal of Law and Order." *The Skaguay Alaskan* (Summer 1995): 12.

Tatum, Stephen. *Inventing Billy the Kid: Visions of the Outlaw in America, 1881–1981.* Albuquerque: University of New Mexico, 1982.

Tefertiller, Casey. *Wyatt Earp, The Life Behind the Legend.* New York: John Wiley, 1997.

Thornton, Thomas F. *Ethnographic Overview and Assessment.* Klondike Gold Rush National Historical Park. Anchorage, Alaska: United States Department of Interior, 2004.

U.S. Department of Justice. "Jackson v. United States, Circuit Court of Appeals, Ninth Circuit, May 14, 1900, No. 570." In *The Federal Reporter: Cases Argued and Determined in the Circuit Courts of Appeals and Circuit and District Courts of the United States, July–September 1900.* St. Paul: West Publishing, 1900.

U.S. Department of Justice. U.S. Marshals Service. "History of District of
    Alaska." http://www.justice.gov/marshals/district/ak/general/history.
    htm

U.S. National Guard. *Report on Mobilization of the Organized Militia and
    National Guard of the United States, 1916.* Washington, D.C.: Government
    Printing Office, 1916.

Utley, Robert M. *Billy the Kid: A Short and Violent Life.* Lincoln: University of
    Nebraska Press, 1989.

Walden, Arthur T. A. *Dog Puncher on the Yukon.* Whitehorse, Yukon: Wolf
    Creek Books, 1928.

Warman, Cy. *Frontier Stories.* New York: Scribner and Sons, 1898.

———. *The Songs of Cy Warman.* Boston: Rand Avery, 1911.

Warmouth, Henry Clay. *The Twentieth Century Biographical Dictionary of Notable
    Americans:* Volume X, W. Boston: The Biographical Society, 1904. Data-
    base on-line through Ancestry.com, last accessed October 12, 2009.

Waters, Frank. *The Earp Brothers of Tombstone.* Lincoln: University of Nebraska
    Press, 1960.

Wector, Dixon. *The Hero in America: A Chronicle of Hero-Worship.* Ann Arbor:
    University of Michigan Press, 1963.

White, Richard. *'Its Your Misfortune and None of My Own': A New History of the
    American West.* Norman: University of Oklahoma Press, 1991.

Whiting, F. B., *Grit, Grief and Gold: A True Narrative of a Pathfinder in Alaska.*
    Seattle: Peacock Publishing, 1933.

"Will Irwin: 'The Greatest Reporter in the World.'" Printed pamphlet. (U.S.:
    Redpath). Electronic file available online at http://sdrc.lib.uiowa.edu/
    traveling-culture/chau1/pdf/irwinw/2/brochure.pdf (last accessed
    May 15, 2009).

Willoughby, Florence Barrett. *Alaskans All.* Boston: Houghton Mifflin, 1933.

Winslow, Kathryn. *The Big Pan-Out.* New York: Phoenix House, 1951.

Wright, Will. *Sixguns and Society: A Structural Study of the Western.* Berkeley:
    University of California Press, 1975.

Wyatt-Brown, Bertram. "Southern Violence." *American Historical Review* 74
    (1969): 906–25.

Interviews and Personal Communication

Gurcke, Karl, historian, Klondike Gold Rush National Historical Park, per-
    sonal communication to author, July 2009.

Hites, Steve to Catherine Holder Spude, e-mail dated April 24, 2009 and let-
    ter dated June 23, 2009, on file, in author's files, Santa Fe, New Mexico.

Rapuzzi, George to Robert L. Spude, interviews dated 1977–79.

Tanner, Lynn to Catherine Holder Spude, letter dated September 25, 2006.

Index

References to illustrations are in italic type.